Connecting Histories in Afghanistan

Connecting Histories in
AFGHANISTAN

*Market Relations and State Formation
on a Colonial Frontier*

Shah Mahmoud Hanifi

Stanford University Press
Stanford, California

Stanford University Press
Stanford, California

First published in paperback in 2011

Library of Congress Cataloging-in-Publication Data

Hanifi, Shah Mahmoud.
    Connecting histories in Afghanistan : market relations and state
formation on a colonial frontier / Shah Mahmoud Hanifi.
        pages cm
    Originally published online in 2008 by Columbia University Press.
    Includes bibliographical references and index.
    ISBN 978-0-8047-7411-6 (pbk. : alk. paper)
    1. Afghanistan—Commerce—History—19th century. 2. Afghanistan—
Politics and government—19th century. 3. Afghanistan—Commerce—
India—History—19th century. 4. India—Commerce—Afghanistan—
History—19th century. 5. Great Britain—Colonies—Asia—Commerce.
6. Great Britain—Colonies—Asia—Economic policy. I. Title.
HF3770.6.H36 2011
382.09581'054—dc22

                                                        2010043063

Printed in the United States of America on acid-free, archival-quality
paper. Typeset at Stanford University Press in 10/14 Minion.

De Afghanistan De Kochniano Depara
Baraye Atfal-e Afghanistan

Contents

Contents

List of Maps and Figures

Maps

Figures

(Sources and notes for the maps and figures appear on pages 239–42)

List of Tables

Acknowledgments

Because this work grew out of my research and time at the University of Michigan, I would like to restate my gratitude to the institution as a whole. The Department of History was my home base, and as such the object of my deepest gratitude. The departments of Anthropology and Near Eastern Studies also figured prominently in my years there, and to those units I convey my sincere appreciation for hosting and expanding my interests. At the University of Michigan, I received seemingly unlimited generosity from a number of faculty members, committees, and administrative personnel in and across those three departments and through the Center for Middle Eastern and North African Studies and the Center for South Asian Studies. I am particularly grateful to Professor Juan R. I. Cole for his sustained support, unceasing encouragement, and continually productive critique of my work. Also my thanks go to Professors Ronald G. Suny, Thomas R. Trautmann, Andrew Shryock, and Kathryn Babayan, and Professor Sir Christopher Bayly, who though not present in Michigan influenced my experiences in distant but important ways from St. Catharine's College at Cambridge University. Professors Shryock and Suny were very helpful and supportive over the long term and at critical junctures of research and writing. Professor Trautmann bestowed the gift of an editorial assistantship at the journal *Comparative Studies in Society and History* on me, and that experience is one I particularly cherish and continue to draw benefits from. My CSSH experience stands as a key symbol for all that I received at and from the University of Michigan.

I am also grateful to the organizations that funded the research on which this book depends. The list begins with a grant from the Horace H. Rackham Graduate School at the University of Michigan, which combined with funds provided by the American Institute of Iranian Studies to allow for a preliminary canvassing of research sites in India and Pakistan. Subsequent research in South Asia was made possible through grants from the Joint Committee on South Asia of the Social Science Research Council and the American Council of Learned Societies with funds provided by the Near and Middle East Research and Training Act, and the Council of American Overseas Research Centers in conjunction with the American Institute of Indian Studies and the American Institute of Pakistan Studies.

During the course of my research in South Asia I incurred a great many personal and institutional debts. My research was based at the Archives of the North-West Frontier Province in Peshawar, the Archives of the Punjab Province in Lahore, and the National Archives of India in New Delhi. My research encompassed other repositories including the Tribal Affairs Research Cell in Peshawar and the Area Study Centre for Central Asia Library at Peshawar University, the National Documentation Centre in Islamabad, the Library at the Centre of Advanced Study in History at Aligarh Muslim University, and the Khuda Bakhsh Oriental Public Library in Patna, although little of those materials has found its way into this book. I am pleased to renew my gratitude to the administrators, archivists, and staff at all these institutions. I would also like to thank the staffs at the Harlan Hatcher Graduate Library at the University of Michigan, at James Madison University's Carrier Library, and at the Alderman Library at the University of Virginia.

I am grateful to Dr. Michael Galgano in the History Department at James Madison University, who has consistently supported my efforts on this and many other projects, and to Dr. David Akin who more than any other taught me how to write. Kate Wahl at Stanford University Press deserves a special note of gratitude for taking interest in my work and for her helpful guidance throughout all stages of the print publication process.

My parents, Dr. M. Jamil and Marietta Hanifi, have shown me the grand complexity, the beautiful simplicity, and the general productivity of cross-cultural interaction that energizes this book in many ways. My father has shaped and challenged my thinking at every stage of my development and this book is fundamentally a product of his cultural and intellectual influence on me. I would rather be in no other physical place or socio-cultural position than "in my father's Way." My mother has taught me about dedication and perseverance and how to enjoy every moment even when the work-at-hand seems overwhelming. In doing so she has epitomized selflessness, generosity, and tolerance. To my wife Martie, son Qais Jabar, and daughter Ariana Aliya I cannot

Acknowledgments

say enough. You have contributed in tangible ways to this book through many dosages of help with images, citations, and a large number of other technical and labor-intensive issues, but your constant encouragement and support over the long term is what allows this book and me to be. Martie, the efforts and sacrifices you have made for me involve exponentially more than any single book. Together we have successfully navigated many challenging segments on the road of life and your superhuman commitment to me and my work has and will always energize and motivate me. Qais Jabar and Ariana Aliya, your names carry the burden of Braudel's longue duree, but this book has compromised many 'mere events' in your lives. Please know you are my world's most amazing treasures, that I cherish every single moment in your presence, and that when we are apart thoughts of you swell my mind and heart with incalculable joy and pride.

Preface: Querying the Kabul Hypothesis

————◆◆◆————

This book situates nineteenth-century Afghanistan in the context of British Indian colonialism. The general focus is commerce, mainly how local actors including Afghan nomads and Indian bankers responded to state policies regarding popular and lucrative commodities such as fruit and tea. Within those broad commercial concerns, specific attention is given to developments in and between the urban market settings of Kabul, Peshawar, and Qandahar. The colonial political emphasis on Kabul had significant commercial consequences for that city and its economic connections to the two cities it displaced to become the sole capital of the emerging state. The Kabul hypothesis therefore represents a colonial political strategy, and its effects on Kabul-Peshawar and Kabul-Qandahar economic relations are the subject of this book.

There are two basic conclusions to be drawn from the work as a whole. The first runs against standard interpretations of nineteenth-century Afghanistan. In most renditions of this period, Afghanistan remains immune from colonialism emanating from British India due to the outcomes of the two Anglo-Afghan wars of 1839–42 and 1878–80. The two conflicts are usually interpreted simply as either exceptional "failures" for the British imperial invaders or predictable "victories" for the local Afghan defenders. The basic point made in what follows is that despite the military results of the two wars, Afghanistan is in fact a colonial construct in political, economic, and intellectual terms, at least. However, it will also be made clear that Afghanistan's colonial moorings in British India by no means denied agency to local actors. A secondary conclusion derived from the facts of colonialism's determining influence on Afghanistan is that the development of a relatively strong state in the late nineteenth century signaled the beginning of intensifying market hardships for most Afghans.

Chronology Overview and Content Summary

At the state level, there are two principal groups of actors under consideration, namely, British colonial officials and representatives of the Afghan state. The relationship between those two political communities was conditioned by inequalities, ambiguities, and inconsistencies characterizing colonial encounters elsewhere in nineteenth-century India, and beyond. The political relationship between Afghan state officials and British colonial authorities in the 1800s evolved through a three-phase chronology of engagement, distancing, and re-engagement. The book is correspondingly organized on the basis of "experimental, interim, and routinization" phases that can be outlined as follows.

The experimental period begins in 1809 with the arrival of the first British colonial delegation at the Afghan court. It ends with the annihilation of the first British invasion force in 1842. The initial thirty-three years of British Indian contact with nascent Afghanistan involved a number of commercial experiments that in many ways culminated with the first Anglo-Afghan war. After a swift retribution campaign to account for the "Afghan disaster," the British generally kept political distance from Kabul for another thirty years or so until a second phase of more direct and re-intensified interaction began. The experimental period is richly documented by archival and published sources.

This interim period from the end of the first war in 1842 until the beginning of the second war in 1878 was an active one both locally and globally. This period of intense industrialization involved the large-scale development of railroads, telegraphy, and transoceanic steamship trade and travel that transformed an increasingly international and integrated world economy. Because there was not substantial or sustained contact between Durrani state and British colonial authorities during this interim phase, the period is weakly documented and as such not considered in this work. However, the transformations that occurred in terms of global commerce and the advancement of industrial technology reframed the context in which the second phase of active Anglo-Afghan relations occurred.

The second part of the book considers Abd al-Rahman's reign, for which there is a great deal of archival and published material available. In 1880 the British appointed Abd al-Rahman as the Amir of Kabul to facilitate their evacuation at the end of a second failed occupation, and he ruled until his death in 1901. During this twenty-one-year period, Afghanistan's relationship with British India was routinized in a number of ways. The Abd al-Rahman period is also significant for standardizing state-society relations in Afghanistan.

The periodization described earlier and detailed later in this work follows military and political calendars associated with the two Anglo-Afghan wars. In terms of content, however, each part of the book considers a different set of economic actors and sectors. After establishing Kabul's roles as a center of production and as a transition market, the first part of the book deals with the commercial contracts around which the British engaged local people to exploit the grounded and mobile resources previously identified. It also considers a larger grand plan for Kabul and its markets in relation to the global economy, and discusses the transformation of local commercial institutions and practices that occurred in the context of the first colonial occupation.

The second part of the book deals with Abd al-Rahman's reign and his relationship to the British by focusing on the cash subsidies he received, and how those resources were part of broader program of reconfiguring Afghanistan's relationship to colonial markets. Abd al-Rahman's agenda of fiscal reorientation toward India, and through it global capitalism, carried significant domestic consequences. In this crucial period, new routines in Afghanistan's dealings with the outer world were established, and new bureaucratic structures and state practices were institutionalized. During Abd al-Rahman's colonially configured reign, Afghanistan assumed its structural position on the periphery of modern global capitalism.

For chronological clarity, a list of Durrani rulers mentioned in this book appears below, although dates of reign for a given dynast can also be found in the text:

Ruler	Reign
Ahmad Shah	1747–72
Timur Shah	1773–93
Zaman Shah	1793–1800
Shah Shuja	1803–9 and 1839–42
Dost Muhammad	1826–38 and 1842–63
Sher Ali	1863–66 and 1869–78
Muhammad Afzal	1866–67
Muhammad Azam	1867–68
Muhammad Yaqub	1879
Abd al-Rahman	1880–1901
Habibullah	1901–19
Amanullah	1919–29

This print edition of *Connecting Histories in Afghanistan* published by Stanford University Press follows the electronic publication of the book by Columbia University Press through the American Historical Association's Gutenberg-e Program. A number of minor corrections and additions to the electronic text have been made for this print version, but an effort was made to keep the electronic and printed version of the text as parallel as possible. The Gutenberg-e version of *Connecting Histories* is a unique repository for images (http://www.gutenberg-e.org/hanifi/gallery.html), a number of which (the maps, documents and coins) have magnification features not possible to reproduce in print form.

Colonial Market Knowledge and Commercial Experimentation

Introduction: The Historical Location and Conceptual Framing of Afghanistan

Old Market Time and New State Space from the Silk Road to the Indian Ocean

The emergence of new states tends to transform old market relations. Modern states are fundamentally territorial entities, while markets are essentially time-bound to various daily, seasonal, and political calendars. But markets and states also overlap and share temporal and spatial interests in such things as cities. This generality is all to say that there is a range of possible relationships between markets and states in time and space that oscillate between complementary and oppositional polarities.

In the case of Afghanistan, we are dealing with very old markets and a very new state, and the Afghan state has not fared well in terms of market integration. The state structure that took shape in and around Qandahar under the direction of Ahmad Shah Abdali/Durrani in the mid-eighteenth century had deep roots in both Iran and India. Ahmad Shah was born in the Mughal district of Multan on the Indus river plain, but he gained political recognition to the west in the service of the Turco-Iranian ruler Nadir Shah Afshar. Ahmad Shah's use of Qandahar as the first capital of the Durrani Afghan state reflects the city's long-term function as transit market for the brisk overland trade between Mughal India and Safavid Iran that had deeper historic origins in exchanges between Mesopotamian and Indus valley civilizations.[1] These overland routes exposing two ancient worlds to one another were complemented by a series of aquatic linkages that integrated port city and hinterland markets across the Indian Ocean world encompassing South and Southeast Asia, the Persian Gulf,

MAP I.1. Interregional Satellite Map, 2008

Red Sea, and East Africa.[2] Qandahar can be seen as positioned amid a set of commercial routes and networks with a generally southerly orientation.

Ahmad Shah's son and successor Timur Shah transferred the Afghan capital from Qandahar to Kabul in 1775–76, and in 1809 Mountstuart Elphinstone made the first official colonial contact with Timur's son Shah Shuja at Peshawar, the Durrani winter capital city at that time.[3] Kabul and Peshawar fall within a set of ancient commercial routes known collectively as the Silk Road.[4] The Silk Road represents a more northerly commercial axis connecting the Chinese and Mediterranean worlds. Civilizations and emporia, and the routes within and between them, rose and fell across the Silk Road during its long history. These historic ebbs and flows occurred according to different rhythms in the north than among the port cities and empires associated with them to the south across the Indian Ocean. Kabul generally enters Silk Road discussions in the context of the Greco-Bactrian period lasting between roughly the sixth century BCE and the first century CE that was centered in Balkh but had a distinct presence in locations such as Begram in the Kabul valley. Peshawar is generally viewed as the center of the Silk Road culture area known as Gandhara. Gandhara has been variously and often quite liberally dated, but the culture seems to have flourished during roughly the first few centuries AD when Buddhism was patronized by a number of rulers and dynasties including the Kushan Emperor Kanishka in the second century. It is important to recognize the wide assortment of cultural exchange between Bactria and Gandhara spawned an array of smaller movements and developments in Afghanistan, and beyond. For example, Hadda near contemporary Jalalabad and Bamian in central Afghanistan were once thriving centers of Buddhist learning and innovation, sites of interreligious pilgrimages, and locations of cultural achievement.

MAP I. 2. Kabul, Peshawar, and Qandahar Satellite View, 2008

The colonial construction of Afghanistan involved some very aged market settings, and Timur Shah, not the British, transformed Kabul into a capital city of the Durrani polity. However, the colonial emphasis on Kabul as the sole political capital of an emerging Afghanistan had important consequences for Kabul as a commercial center and also for the city's market relations with Qandahar and Peshawar. Kabul's "rise" as a political capital entailed a reconfiguration of the city's role in domestic and transnational commercial circuits and networks. The body of this book considers transformations in a triangulated economic relationship between Kabul, Peshawar, and Qandahar that crossed two distinct political spaces to form an interactive consortium of colonial frontier markets.

Markets and Their Transformation: Mobility, Money, Machines, and Texts

Kabul, Peshawar, and Qandahar are ancient market settings between one and two thousand years of age. In a long-term historical perspective, Kabul, Peshawar, and Qandahar have combined in varying proportions exchange, finance, storage, and consumption activities. Despite these broad structural similarities, each market has been distinguished by special functions through historical eras. Over the long term, these three markets have interacted dynamically and together with the smaller markets between them and in their respective orbits this commercial zone has served to connect wider supra-regional economic networks in Central and South Asia.

In conceptual terms, markets are centers of production, consumption, exchange, and circulation where goods and services become commodities through coexistence and interaction that is either directly or ultimately mediated by standards of value measured in currency, either cash money as reflected in retail market prices or book monies of account as used in the fiscal registers of states and large merchant firms. The commodification process occurs through exchange and the medium of currency, and markets are places where cash money and other forms of moveable and fixed commercial capital accrue and are transformed. The exchange functions of markets attract the interest of commercial actors in other markets as well as political authorities, and Islamic states typically involve the institution of *muhtasib*, or (chief) market inspector. The activities and prosperity of any market or state is contingent on interaction with other markets and states. Markets are locations where movements of people and things intersect and where relationships between people and things are reproduced and transformed. In market settings, social groups can be identified through the commodities they engage and control. Market settings can be examined, therefore, with attention to the commodities being exchanged and the financial instruments involved in the transaction, the communities represented in the transaction, and the political context of the exchange. Market exchanges can be interrogated, then, with a few basic questions in mind. What was and who were involved in the exchange? How did the transaction happen in technical fiscal terms? What was the role of the state or other regulatory agency within the marketing activity, if any?

This book poses those basic questions to nineteenth-century Kabul, Peshawar, and Qandahar. Concerning commodity groups and trajectories of movement, the export trade in dried and fresh fruits and nuts from the Kabul and Qandahar districts to India was perhaps the most prominent and lucrative component of the economies of all three localities. Indian merchants financed this high-volume export of Afghan fruits and nuts, and Peshawar was an important base for the large numbers of bankers and financiers active in this trade. Peshawar's "natural" displacement as a staging area for wider distribution of fruits and nuts to South Asian markets where they were in high demand was dramatically transformed during the course of the nineteenth century as a result of political and economic developments associated with the the two Anglo-Afghan wars. Similar questions about other commodities generally moving to the south, such as timber, hemp, felt, horses, sheep and its derivate wool and woolens, hides, and meat, and opium will generate different answers about the role of state authorities and local actors. Flows of tea, sugar, textiles, industrial equipment, and its technical expertise in the opposite northern direction occurred across the same routes but had different commercial and political motivations, possibilities, and constraints for the actors. These commodity "counterflows" completed the commercial circuit and they entailed separate consequences for actors connected to the respective commodities or commodity groupings in each market on the return trajectory.[5] The body of this work seeks to answer a small set of basic questions about the material, social, and political dimensions of market exchanges and commodity movements in and between Kabul, Peshawar, and Qandahar during the 1800s.

In the course of striving for that basic goal, a number of other fundamental issues informing the political economy of this frontier zone will be considered. Labor processes are addressed from the perspectives of sedentary production

7

and mobile circulation and redistribution. Fruit and nut production involved relatively sedentary laborers and very mobile accountants and transporters. The producers themselves are viewed primarily through the products of their labor and the bankers and bureaucrats who financed, marketed, and taxed those commodities. The state-appointed accountants and scribes acted in conjunction with similar functionaries in the private sector/civil society to textually manage the fruit and nut trade. These state and private bookkeepers are treated as a laboring bureaucratic class in their own right. Bankers and financiers form another group of laborers. In the layers and interstices of the economy where money handlers and bookkeepers were jointly active, communities of Hindus, Sikhs, and Muslims of Indian origin collectively referred to as *Hindkis* were quite prominent. The Qizilbash community is the most prominent among the local Afghan actors involved in the textual and scriptural dimensions of state and private commercial activities. Wielding the power of literacy in these contexts helps distinguish the shia Qizilbash from the shia Hazara in Afghanistan, although one clear exception to that general rule is the high profile of Faiz Muhammad Katib, a Hazara scribe who authored the most important historical text produced in Afghanistan, the *Seraj al-Tawarikh*.[6]

Transportation is another form of labor receiving attention in this work. In various portions of what follows, individual tribal chiefs and through them nomadic communities who were contracted to transport popular consumer goods and war material are discussed. Colonial commercial contracts with two Afghan tribal entrepreneurs are treated in detail. Sayyid Muhin Shah, who adopted nomadic trade after difficulties in the sedentary world, is responsible for initially quantifying the profitability of trade through Kabul, Peshawar, Qandahar, and other markets for British colonial authorities. Sarwar Khan Lohani was the most important local figure in the overall organization of camel caravans for the first British occupation force. Carriage service was big business and a state concern. A long-established class of nomadic "tribal traders" was caught in a textual net comprised of passes, vouchers, and certificates associated with Abd al-Rahman's state monopolization of the fruit trade. These state texts and the new cadres of officials handling them were deployed to reroute the nomadic tribal carriers in a way that greatly intensified commercial traffic between Kabul and Peshawar at the expense of routes between other markets that were concomitantly deemed to be passages for smugglers.

The diverse communities of Indian merchants subsumed under the Hindki label (see later in this chapter and Chapter 1) did not act alone in Afghanistan.

Rather, they performed local roles for a number of extensive banking and commercial networks associated with resources concentrated in Hindustan and representatives spanning the old Silk Road and Indian Ocean circuits.[7] The high profile of Indian merchants in Afghanistan arose from their knowledge of and presence in the foreign markets where Afghan edibles were widely consumed. Furthermore, through global commercial networks, they had practically unlimited access to the ready cash in high demand by producers, merchants, and state authorities in Afghanistan. These diversified and widely dispersed Indian merchant family firms combined the abilities to identify receptive markets for multiple commodities, to provide large or small cash loans, and to transfer large sums of capital through paper notes known as *hundis* in India and *hawalas* in Afghanistan. The Hindkis in nineteenth-century Afghanistan are connected culturally and historically to communities of bankers, financiers, and large-scale traders associated with key Mughal markets in the seventeenth and eighteenth centuries, such as Multan and Shikarpur. Through the turbulent eighteenth century, the prominence of Multanis and Shikarpuris in state structures and political processes are expressions of continuity between Mughal and Durrani commercial regimes.

Cultural distinction did not impede the integration of Hindkis into Afghan society and state structures. It is thus unclear whether the Hindki community comprised a diaspora presence in Afghanistan, or if they should be considered a natural part of the economic landscape. From either perspective, Hindki communities should be viewed in light of their own social institutions and cultural practices in addition to those found in the "host" market settings. Features of local tribal cultures, such as *melmastia* and *nanawati* among Pashtuns, usually glossed as hospitality and asylum, respectively, are relevant for a holistic understanding of the local contexts in which Hindkis operated. A full sense of Hindki market positionings also requires attention to a more widely evident institution across the cultural communities forming Afghan society, *hamsaya*. Hamsaya is a Persian word, literally meaning shade-sharing, that has been interpreted to mean a neighborliness exhibited toward or an accepted-protected status for local economic and social minority populations, such as the small-scale Tajik tenant farming families found in localities where Pashtuns are the primary landowners and demographic majority. The Hindkis comprised one segment of large-scale merchant activity involving complex exchange networks and systems of communication that were centered in the markets of North India. North India's vast commercial resources and the social and economic structures that determined their movement and concentration in many ways dictated the terms of British colonial expansion in Hindustan and Afghanistan.[8]

The financial and marketing services provided by Hindki bankers and merchants in Afghanistan had another important dimension. The loans provided by these financiers to ordinary producers and the elite classes in Afghanistan came at interest rates that could quickly generate stultifying debt. The ability to provision large sums of cash on relatively short notice will be described in the context of the first British occupation of Kabul. The already profitable position enjoyed by the Hindki merchants in Afghanistan was considerably advanced as a result of the first Anglo-Afghan war. However, their collective position was dramatically eroded during Abd al-Rahman's reign. As part of a larger agenda of state monopolization of the export economy, Abd al-Rahman attempted to replace these private Indian entrepreneurs with a corps of Afghan state commercial agents. The Hindki financiers were able to "thin" the debt accrued in Afghanistan throughout their vast trans-Eurasian commercial networks. Abd al-Rahman's large-scale replacement of private Hindki financiers operating in Afghanistan with his own Afghan state officials and resources led to an increasing accumulation and concentration of national debt in Kabul. This policy also resulted in an elaboration of Kabul's commercial relationship with Peshawar that came under formal British East India Company rule with the colonial creation of the Punjab Province in 1849.

The routinization of political relations between British India and Abd al-Rahman beginning in 1880 revolved around the cash subsidies liberally dispensed by colonial authorities to the Afghan Amir. The subsidy funds were in many instances recycled back into British Indian and European hands through Abd al-Rahman's purchase of heavy industrial equipment and hire of technical expertise for his most consequential initiative, the *mashin khana,* a Persian compound literally translated as machine house, meaning in practice the Durrani state industrial workshops. In Western languages, Abd al-Rahman has been dubbed the "Iron Amir," by popular and professional historians alike, in large measure as a result of his industrial approach to the military that gave the state's troops tactical advantages, at least temporarily, in executing his notoriously brutal mechanisms of rule. Colonial funding and connections gave Abd al-Rahman these means and energy. Arguably the most consequential European import made possible by the subsidy was the industrial minting machinery that arrived in Kabul in 1890. Qandahar and its commercial relationship to

Kabul were particularly affected by the arrival of this new modern industrial technology.

Qandahar was the scene of a curious incident during the first British occupation fifty years earlier. In this episode, ordinary colonial foot soldiers nearly rebelled when faced with unfavorable terms for a currency exchange that was nearly forced on them by their military superiors. The revolt was averted, but its threat was predicated on the ready availability of currency conversion services in Qandahar's thriving public money market. In the original and now former capital of the Durrani polity the ubiquitous Hindkis with their liquid assets were also very well ensconced. The occupation troops knew from the market itself that the exchange-rate terms being imposed on them were inflated. Qandahar's commercial prosperity derived from its centrality along a primary Indo-Iranian trade route and its proximity to the larger Indian Ocean trading world through the ports of Sind. Its geographic location exposed the city to a wide array of currencies, and activity in Qandahar's mint was an important variable in helping the local money market players calibrate their daily exchange rates, whether or not the city was militarily occupied. The arrival of the European minting machinery in Kabul signaled the end for the prestigious mint in the first Durrani state capital where the politically sensitive craft was still practiced with hand tools.

A pair of new machine mints provided the Afghan state with an exponentially increased coin production capacity. Abd al-Rahman was personally struck by aspects of mercantilist economic philosophy where the measure of a state's wealth was specie (gold, or as in this case, silver bullion) that accrued through the state's close management of exports and heavy taxation of imports. In European history, mercantilist economic policies are associated with early modern absolutist states often legitimized by notions of divine right to rule, and Abd al-Rahman's policies and practices reflect these combined orientations. During his eleven-year residence in Samarqand (c. 1867–78), where he received a Russian pension, it is possible that Abd al-Rahman was exposed to the legacy of Russian imperial versions of mercantilism and absolutism, archetypically identified with Peter the Great (ruled c. 1682–1725).

It is clear that once the new mints were situated in Kabul Abd al-Rahman began an unrelenting quest to accumulate as much silver coinage, especially British Indian rupees, as possible. His goal was to melt down all foreign coins he could find and remint them with the new machines as state currency, thereby producing more Afghan money and wealth from his perspective. The problem here was that global economic processes had generally moved beyond mercantilist ideologies where mere physical money counted as the primary index of state power and status. The global economy was now running on paper money and telegraphic transfers, and while cash holdings still mattered, especially at the local level, the relative value of that cash was determined by inter-currency evaluations at the international exchange level. So as Abd al-Rahman committed to the machine minting of more and more state coins, the new Afghan money was increasingly losing its own value through inflation locally while being devalued in relation to other currencies circulating in the increasingly global capitalist economy.

The fuel for Abd al-Rahman's industrial ambition of mass-producing new state coinage came primarily from two sources. The first was his substantial British subsidy that amounted to approximately 15 percent more cash than estimates of internally generated state revenue. The subsidy generated a great deal of correspondence between colonial authorities and Abd al-Rahman who also used written orders and paper money instruments such as bills of exchange and letters of credit, that were much less transferable than the similar book money tools used by the private traders to disburse portions of the subsidy to his officials and appointees stationed in British India. Abd al-Rahman considered the political space of Afghanistan to be his own personal household that offered not constraints but possibilities for acquiring cold hard cash. Abd al-Rahman relied on a wide array of new state paperwork including forms, passes, certificates, and vouchers to obtain as much metallic money in circulation in Afghanistan as possible. The voluminous subsidy correspondence and a barrage of new government documents combined to fuel the industrial production of many commodities and coinage at the Afghan state workshops. From a vantage point informed by these two large bodies of written texts, at least, the Iron Amir appears as a paper prince.

Abd al-Rahman's reorganization and elaboration of the government bureaucracy in Kabul involved new colonial connections with Peshawar that had significant effects on Qandahar. Abd al-Rahman liberally deployed a new class of functionaries armed with textual command over new local breeds of state documentary weapons. State accountants and secretaries wielding various combinations of and competencies in numeric and written-word literacies were charged with ensuring the flow of silver to the mint in the state workshops. Kabul was saturated with state officials executing a personal hoarding scheme, but Qandahar also became a prime target of Abd al-Rahman's mulcting agenda.

Abd al-Rahman regularly dispatched his textual agents to Qandahar to announce and collect a large number of new taxes. Qandahar was especially prone to receive the silver currency Abd al-Rahman was most committed to recycling, British Indian rupees. Abd al-Rahman used new literary tools and paper weapons in Qandahar to help satisfy his dependency on and compulsive quest for cash coinage. No human subject was immune from this textual coercion, and the primary form of resistance to the arbitrary nature of these surgical strikes was to become an informer in the hopes that the state would protect its affiliates. This buffering tactic generally did not incur the intended result, in fact quite to the contrary, as one of the dangers of being a state paper handler for Abd al-Rahman was the probability of becoming an internal target of a state audit or investigation. In this atmosphere of cynicism and mistrust, the accused government functionary would have two choices. The ostracized bureaucrat now targeted could either rely on goodwill or secondary extortion to raise the requisite cash from kinsmen, friends, and neighbors, or try to instigate a separate case against an associate or superior to account for alleged misdeeds.

Revisions in the fiscal relationship between Kabul and Qandahar dramatically transformed state-society relations in both locations. In Qandahar, the state interventions generated new systems for the surveillance of commodity and human movements to, from, and within the city. The accountants, clerks, and messengers were active in public view, while an extensive network of spies and informants operated more covertly. However, both groups generated streams of correspondence that pooled together in the state bureaucracy Abd al-Rahman developed in Kabul around his person. The information received in the capital city generated subsequent outward flows of state texts and their literate handlers from Kabul to the remainder of the country. Kabul's increasing centrality in new circuits of information, textual flows, and commercial processes had different effects in Qandahar and British-controlled Peshawar. In Peshawar Afghan officials and state-appointed traders conducted business under the dual oversight of Abd al-Rahman and his British patrons who maintained a fiscal and symbolic posture of placation throughout the course of their relationship with the Kabul Amir.

A new class of state bureaucrats and writers emerged under Abd al-Rahman, and Afghanistan still suffers from the stain of their ink. Class formation entails the coagulation of previously separate social and productive units, usually in the context of institutional transformations associated with the emergence of new regimes of political economy. A new class of state bureaucrats was well en-

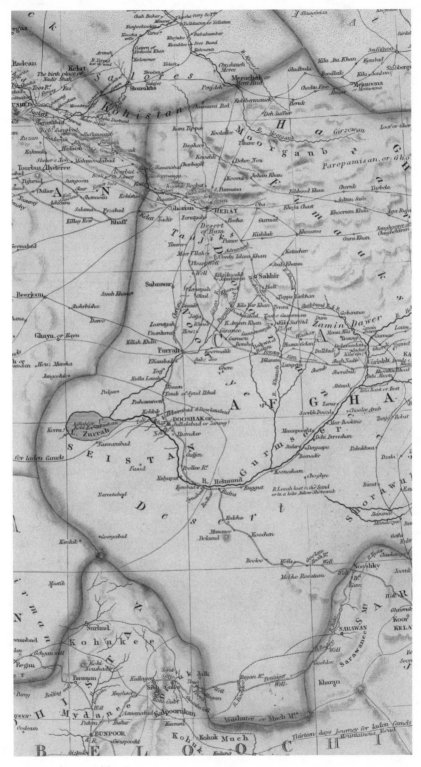

MAP I.3. Proto-Afghanistan, 1844

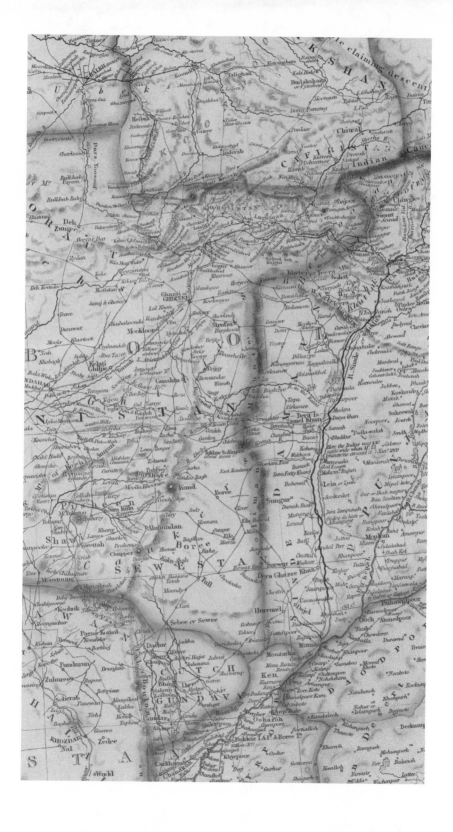

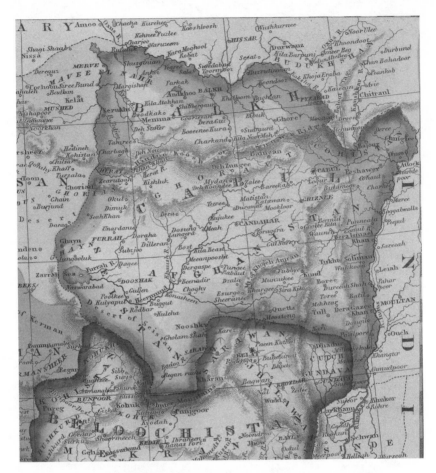

MAP I.4. Proto-Afghanistan, 1846

trenched in Afghanistan by the 1890s, and within this class the Qizilbash community in Kabul was very well represented. Roughly two generations earlier, in the 1830s, colonial authorities commented with great interest on the prominence of the Qizilbash of Kabul who were characterized as living in a distinct residential quarter, Chindawul, that utilized its own "separate police and courts of law and justice," and most important, as handling "all the local and foreign correspondence of Kabul so that their influence ramifies in every direction."[9] During the nineteenth century, the Qizilbash in Kabul elaborated and consolidated their high profile positions within a growing class of state writers, and as such they represent an increasingly important component of the state bureaucratic elite.

MAP 1.5. Proto-Afghanistan, 1856

The Colonial Archives and Their Discontents

The present consideration of commercial, human, and textual flows in the market zone bounded by Kabul, Peshawar, and Qandahar is made possible by a wide assortment of colonial archival documents. The analytical opportunities offered by this material carry the inherent danger of reproducing colonial epistemologies, identity categories, and interpretations of the material in question. The first challenge in using colonial material on Afghanistan is navigating through the uncertainty of what the term designates in time and space. A sampling of maps produced in the United States, Europe, and British India during the nineteenth century indicates that before the first Anglo-Afghan war, Afghanistan, if it was represented at all, was dwarfed in significance by Kabul and Qandahar. For example, Mountstuart Elphinstone's authoritative map emphasizes the "Kingdom of Caubul," as in the title of his book. It is important to note that the term Afghanistan appears occasionally in his text and faintly on the map produced by his delegation. But it is more important that for Elphinstone, like Babur before him, Afghanistan is a reference of secondary or even tertiary significance, particularly when considered in light of the overwhelming emphasis on Kabul.[10] The term Afghanistan received greater cartographic weight after the first Anglo-Afghan war, and in the 1850s and 1860s Afghanistan and Kabul are more evenly but still unequally weighted. In the 1870s and 1880s, Afghanistan is firmly on the map so to speak, but it is only in the 1890s that borders regularly appear. Maps are political and intellectual exercises, and Afghanistan's nineteenth-century cartographic lineage reads partially as follows. Afghanistan first emerges from within the Kabul radius, then competes with the city for primacy, and, finally, the term Afghanistan surmounts and subsumes Kabul.

The cartographic dynamic between Kabul and Afghanistan in the 1800s occurred as authorities in British India and England were taking the necessary intellectual and political steps to justify and formalize the central positioning of Kabul in the colonial design of Afghanistan. Market relations among Kabul, Peshawar, and Qandahar therefore evolved within the political and economic vision of a Kabul-centered Afghanistan. Over the course of the nineteenth century, there were hundreds if not thousands of competing views issued from various geographic, institutional, and strategic vantage points regarding how to construct and maintain the colonially constructed "compromise polity" of Afghanistan. One of the first obstacles to contend with in dealing with the colonial records for Afghanistan is the cacophony of claims and counterclaims about it. However, amplification of Kabul serves to sooth the archival dissonance about Afghanistan. In other words, the preoccupation with and presuppositions about Kabul are unifying elements in the colonial discourse about Afghanistan. The decision to compare and interrelate Kabul, Qandahar, and Peshawar was arrived at in order to engage and surmount the Kabul-centrism of colonial records about Afghanistan.

In many ways, imaginings about Kabul transcend the generally inconsistent and contradictory colonial records about what Afghanistan is, where it came from, what it is composed of, and ultimately what it can do for those acting in relation to it. Perhaps the most confusing dimension of the British colonial archive on Afghanistan has been reproduced by the vast majority of modern scholars. This is the polysemy and metonymy among the terms Afghan, Pashtun (and its primary variant Pakhtun, and permutations of vowels in both constructs), and Pathan. The labels carry multiple geographic, historiographic, and cultural characteristics that unite and distinguish them from one another, but yet it remains common practice to deploy them in unison, usually to make various points and positions appear larger or more important than they would otherwise be. The intermingling of the Afghan, Pashtun, and Pathan labels across various genres of literature including archival documents, academic literatures, foreign policy formulations, and popular writings about Afghanistan has generally been a casual and consistent practice. As such, the labels reflect cultural ambiguities and historical distortions that impede full and objective appraisals of the country and the social groups comprising it.

The details surrounding the three terms themselves, irrespective of cultural content, social referents, and political context are dense and can be distracting. However, given the salience of these complicated details for the historiography of Afghanistan and all that it entails culturally and historically, it is necessary to provide a basic sense of what unites and distinguishes these three words from one another. In general terms, the word Afghan comes into use through Persian texts beginning roughly one thousand years ago, circa 1000 CE, in geographical treatises and Ghaznavid historiography.[11] The Ghaznavids set into motion a millennium of migrations from the Hindu Kush mountains to the Hindustan plains that were motivated by commercial opportunities and state-building activities entailed in Islamization processes.

The term Afghan was used in Delhi Sultante (c. 1100–1300) historiography when both Afghans and Turks were primary actors as militarily potent slave troops who could and would also rule in the mold of other medieval Islamic *mamluk* populations.[12] The contentiousness involves the association between a community identified as Khalaj in the pre-Mughal period with the terms Ghalzai and Ghalji that appear in the Mughal period.[13] The Ghalzi became especially prominent in the eighteenth century when they instigated a revolt that ended the Safavid dynasty in Iran, after which they were disenfranchised from state rule in Iran by Nadir Shah Afshar and kept on the fringes of state power under the Durrani polity that arose in the wake of Nadir Shah's death.[14] Historical imprecisions and cultural ambiguities characterizing the categories Afghan and Ghalzi and the social relationships between those actors in practice were textually compounded during the construction of Pashtun genealogies that accompanied the writing of the Pashto language. What can be concluded here is Pashtun ethnogenesis occurring during the Mughal period after an Afghan identity congealed in Persian historiography and before the Pathan identity took root in English language texts.

The Mughal rulers of India were of Central Asian Turkish stock. They succeeded the Sur dynasty that claimed Afghan but not Pashtun origins and used Persian as the language of state.[15] Thus, the dynastic shift from the Suris to the Mughals did not involve a radical change in the language of the state apparatus but it did eliminate the prominence of those who used Afghan or "Pathan" identity as an idiom of their domination of northern India or Hindustan. From its inception, the Mughal state structure was dominated by Persian cultural features, including especially the use of the Persian language in governmental bureaucracies. There is no evidence of the production of Pashto language written texts in pre-Mughal India, although there have been claims about the textualization of Pashto in "Afghanistan" before the Mughal empire took shape.[16] It has been suggested that the first Pashto language texts, the Khair al-Bayan and the Makhzan-i Afghani, were written during the Mughal rule by non-Pashtun (probably Persian or Tajik) sufis, Bayazid Ansari, and Akhund Darweza, respectively.[17] The political context of these religious writings was the Roshaniyya insurrection. The Roshaniyya movement was a local response to the Mughal Emperor Akbar's policy of religious syncretism and the expansion of the Mughal empire westward across the Indus River into areas where the Pashto language was commonly spoken, a process that resulted in the Mughal incorporation of the Kabul province in 1585.[18]

Pashto was recognized as a language spoken by some Afghans in the pre- and early Mughal era, but the language was first indigenously textualized in the 1600s with the writings of Khushhal Khan Khattak.[19] During the seventeenth century, Pathan also appears in Persian language Mughal texts. From their base in Bengal in northeastern India in the mid-1700s, British officials encountered in speech and writing all three terms, Afghan, Pashtun, and Pathan. The Pathan label appeared in colonial records as early as 1784 when it was formally introduced in colonial discourse as having indigenous origins in the Ghaznavid and Ghorid period. The origin, referent, and historiographic reproduction of the Pathan term raise questions about distinctions between Persian speakers and Pashto-speaking Afghans, and about the nature and degree of connections between individuals and communities in Hindustan and claimed or purported "kinfolk" and a "homeland" outside of Hindustan, under the designates Khorasan, Roh, Kabul, Wilayat, and other labels.[20] From the late-eighteenth to the mid-twentieth century, colonial authorities increasingly favored the Pathan label that was transported via colonial documents "back" to the northwest frontier in the early 1800s as colonial authorities began to physically retrace the multiple hundreds of years of southeasterly migrations they were becoming aware of through Persian language texts and powerful theorizing about language and cultural origins throughout Eurasia such as that offered by Sir William Jones's ideas about Indo-European languages, their origin, and subsequent interaction.[21]

The preceding outline leaves a number of important specific issues regarding the Afghan-Pashtun-Pathan matrix unexplored. However, through all the intended and unintended distortion it appears reasonably clear that the British first encountered Pathan as the term to distinguish Afghans by the criterion of using Pashto in writing and/or speech in addition to or instead of Persian.[22] The referent was therefore imprecisely received and reified during retransmission of the term via colonial records closer to the relevant market settings where today it has morphed into a referent for Pashto speakers in Pakistan, an Urdu-speaking state environment. Afghan retained its territorial emphasis and became a weak national label in the context of the colonial construction of Afghanistan, a decidedly Persian language state environment. Pashtuns are recognized as speakers of Pashto in Afghanistan. The epistemological quandaries here involve the historical fact that in general the Durrani rulers of Afghanistan did not speak or use Pashto but portrayed themselves as Pashtuns.[23] The British colonial apparatus appeared comfortable with the inconsistencies of that portrayal because of its instrumental familiarity with the ambiguities of the Pathan term, and the connection of many Durranis to Pathan communities as pensioners throughout

North India, particularly Ludiana in the Punjab. Pashto, despite its prominence and centrality in these matters, remained weakly textualized and subordinated to Persian as the language of state in Mughal India and Afghanistan in the seventeenth and eighteenth centuries, and in nineteenth-century colonial India the roles of English and Hindustani gained increasing significance.[24]

To use British Indian records about Afghanistan effectively it is necessary to appreciate the variety of geographic, social, and political components, distinctions, and relations among the terms Afghan, Pashtun, and Pathan. It is important to reckon with the historicity and diversity subsumed within each of those three terms, and even basic historical and semantic dissection draws attention to rich bodies of cultural and historical data for future researchers. Here and in general terms it is therefore neither accurate nor productive to impose neat and clear divisions among Afghans, Pashtuns, and Pathans in Kabul, Peshawar, and Qandahar, at least because of the ongoing movement of representatives of these communities between the three market settings. Market constraints and opportunities motivate individuals to consciously self-identify, however loosely, with more than one category. In other words, market environments tend to favor complex and multiple identities.

The working solution for the terminological and conceptual quandaries involved in the Afghan-Pashtun-Pathan convolutions followed here is to contextualize use of each term by referencing relevant sources in the first instance and to provide necessary explanations or qualifications as required thereafter. Additional referential clarifications and general usage guidelines in this regard include: the term Pathan will not be used unless it is contained in quotation from original documents; Pashto speakers will be identified as Pashtuns; Afghan will designate a strong territorial and weak national referent (it also will be used in the Afghan society construct); the Afghan state will refer to the Durrani dynasts who ruled (Durrani is a major confederation of Pashtun tribes within which the Saddozai, Barakzai, Muhammadzai lineages produced the rulers), their non-Durrani confidantes, and the urban and urbanized "Kabuli" bureaucrats operating the state machinery; Durrani state and Afghan state will be used interchangeably; Durrani and Ghalzi Pashtun will be distinguished as functionally separate ethnicities based on their differential relationships to the Pashto language and the Afghan state. The distinctions and relationships between Pashtun tribal and ethnic identities, and between Pashtun tribalism and ethnicity, generally have been treated in piecemeal fashion and are yet to be fully dissected and analyzed.

Social identities emerge, merge, and diverge in markets settings. Market identities may belie an ulterior identity, and actors involved in multiple markets can manifest distinct identities in each public setting. The archival sources relating to Afghanistan generally do not address the fluidity, multiplicity, transformation, and strategic deployment of identity categories. The Afghan-Pashtun-Pathan identity quagmire arises partly from the tendency for colonial writers to uncritically integrate and recycle older voices that often remain anonymous. This tradition of repetition and redundancy is most evident in the gazetteer genre of colonial writings that are encyclopedic in scope and appear designed originally to administratively orientate bureaucrats who were new to their appointments in any given location. The emphasis on conformity within British colonial bureaucratic culture evident in the structure of gazetteer writings within and across administrative districts promoted a generalization of India that was defied by a subculture of colonial officials who diverged from standard interpretations and career paths. In the colonial archives relating to Afghanistan, Henry George Raverty is the most complicated and nonconformist voice.[25]

Colonial archival and published resources dealing with Afghanistan identify three major communities of market actors that will be considered in what follows. The first are state authorities, including both Afghan and British Indian officials. The European colonial personalities are generally easily identifiable. However, the social origins of the Indian officials involved in the colonial enterprise and portions of Afghan state officialdom are sometimes hard to identify with precision. In many instances, this is partly a result of Afghan-Pashtun-Pathan convolutions. The cultural, geographic, and historical variables uniting and distinguishing those three social categories have similarly complicating effects and nuanced influences on the two other major communities of market actors in Kabul, Peshawar, and Qandahar. The carriers and financiers of the trade between and beyond these markets are also treated with considerable imprecision and inconsistency in colonial records.

Until this point, the term Hindki has been a generic referent for a diverse community of bankers, merchants, and traders active in Afghanistan with social origins in and economic connections to various localities in India. Hindki is the term used in Afghanistan to refer to these Indian businessmen and their families.[26] Colonial archives have quite a bit to say about Indian commercial activities in Kabul, Peshawar, and Qandahar, but generally identify the actors only by names without much accompanying detail about the wide spectrum of their cultural identities and practices. The general background of these communities is as follows. Hindus of various castes and Muslims of various persuasions from Multan, Shikarpur, and other locations in North India rose to commercial prominence during the Mughal period when local and long-distance trade in South Asia and across the Indian Ocean expanded.[27] These bankers and financiers continued to prosper in the post-Mughal period, and it has been noted that Shikarpuris were prominent in the eighteenth-century Durrani empire.[28] The place of Hindkis in the nineteenth-century British Indian archives requires attention.

The Hindki community was vital to the long-term structure and short-term functioning of the political economy of this colonial frontier. They were primary money handlers and therefore actively involved in setting prices throughout the wider market, across retail, wholesale, and distribution sectors. The archival sources capture Hindki dealings with a large and complicated monetary vocabulary covering a wide variety of cash currencies including new and old local and foreign copper, silver, and gold coins of various denominations. Similarly, many of the large number of commodities the Hindkis and their associates handled were referred to by different words across the wide range of the commercial networks in question. Further terminological and translation issues arose and arise in the contexts of relating weights and measures of precious metals and less durable consumable commodities such as foods and textiles.

The Hindkis managed these various vocabulary sets as they handled items referred to by the words themselves. The high profile of Hindkis in these markets in many ways involved translation services between various cash money and commodity forms. The archival sources tend to separate the specific vocabularies of currencies and commodities in appendices and end tables, which in turn can lead investigators away from full comprehension of Hindki market activities. The Hindkis' translation between the languages of commodities and monies involved verbal, social, and textual practices. Hindki market prominence derived from their ability to combine oral competencies and written literacies in ways that would allow them to be comfortable, and profitably so, engaging British officers in English for large-scale movements of cash, and Pashto-speaking nomads in Pashto regarding the barter of nomadic products such as wool or hides for market-supplied metal products such as knives.

Hindkis moved large sums of cash and other forms of commercial capital using paper fiscal instruments identified by a number of English language constructs such as bills of exchange, letters of credit, and promissory notes. The variety of paper money forms, the endless number of specific uses for them, and the fact that they could be transferred and re-negotiated during their movement, all served to involve multiple parties playing well-defined roles in relation to that paper during the economic life course of a given bill, letter, or note. In any single market, there could be multiple local vocabularies designed to express particular economic relationships to paper money, or "flying money" as termed by the Chinese who invented it, during its passage through the given locale during potentially very wide-ranging and long-lived circulation. The preponderance of references in the archives to dehistoricized, generic, undifferentiated bills, letters, and notes masks much more complex sets of economic and social relations intersecting in colonial markets through these texts. The paper records themselves, that is, the hundis and hawalas and the assortment of merchant record books where they met their final demise and realization, do not appear in the colonial archives. This gap in the archival sources reflects the high levels of secrecy and trust characterizing Hindki market operations. Handlers of hundis and hawalas used largely unknown bookkeeping systems that may have been unique to particular merchant firms, families, or networks sometimes involving secret scripts similar to the colonial use of invisible ink that can be encountered in the archives.

The Hindkis' commanding presence in the markets of Kabul, Peshawar, and Qandahar arose from their collective capacity to determine relations between the monetized and textualized portions of the economy. Hindkis had access to information and knowledge about states and societies well beyond the local market triad under consideration. The tools and strength behind the Hindki commercial success in Afghanistan depended upon at least two long-term strategic relationships that were mediated, incompletely and inconsistently, by colonial and Afghan state authorities. These two connections were interrelated, because it was through their contractual engagement of nomadic transport services that the Hindkis maintained regular commercial and financial ties to their market bases in North India. Because the relationship to the nomads was contractual, it might be argued the primary constitutive bond for the Hindkis was to the markets of India, and through them to far more distant markets. In this sense Hindkis perhaps best represent Afghanistan's relationship to an increasingly global economy, and as such there is clearly a need for much more research in this area than the limited view provided in this book. The commercial relationships between the Hindkis stationed in the colonial frontier markets, and between them and their network affiliates in and beyond North India, were physically articulated in two ways: first through the commodities, that is the commercial goods, cash currencies, and paper money forms collectively helping to form large and diverse commercial capital portfolios, and, second, through the transportation services provided by a separate and similarly socially and economically diverse class of nomadic tribal carriers.

These nomadic "tribal traders" were the everyday conductors of the commercial relationships among Kabul, Peshawar, and Qandahar. They did so on behalf of Hindki and other commercially active communities including themselves, foreign merchants such as Armenians and Iranians, as well as local Afghan traders that included, perhaps most significantly, Durrani state officials. These three major markets and their interrelationships subsumed smaller markets in localities such as Ghazni and Jalalabad. As a totality, this economic zone in the east of the country connected Afghanistan to India, and India's commercial tentacles connected Afghanistan to the world. The archives allow an appreciation for the roles played by a ubiquitous but historically opaque group of contract carriers known varyingly as *kochis*, *Lohanis*, and *pawendas*. Sources addressing these "trading tribes" are vexing for their contradictions and what they do not address regarding perhaps the most elementary and therefore perhaps seemingly superfluous commercial actors insofar as market connections are concerned.

The archives indicate the trading tribes are performing the same basic commercial function of transporting commodities between markets. The archives also indicate, however implicitly, significant cultural, geographic, and historical distinctions among the kochis, Lohanis, and pawendas. In general, in both local and Western languages, the label "kochi" is the most generic and most used designate for the trading tribes. A basic distinction within the kochis and other trading tribes is between localized pastoralism involving the breeding and exchange of animal products such as hides, dairy products such as ghi and wool in smaller markets, and long-distance commercial migrations wherein carriage and transportation services were important components of economic life.[29] This book is primarily concerned with the latter long-distance commercial migrations.

Kochis have a wide territorial distribution, but they are particularly associated with the routes between the Kabul and Peshawar valleys, regions, and markets. Kochis are Pashto speakers, but the word itself is a local Persian word for nomad. The use of a Persian language label for this Pashto-speaking community is an important instance of the Afghan state's use of Persian-language texts in dealings with commercially active nomadic communities. Abd al-Rahman utilized an innovative set of texts to reorganize the kochi carriage services around his subsidy-based relationship with the British and state monopolization of commodity exports from Afghanistan. The resulting intensification of economic relations between Kabul and Peshawar was colonially inspired and the new dyadic link was achieved through the textual and territorial reconfiguration of kochi commercial activities and movements in relation to each and between both markets.

Of the three communities of trading tribes, the Lohanis are the first to firmly enter the historical record in the late fifteenth and early sixteenth century. They are widely noticed during the Lodi and Suri periods, the two short-lived dynasties usually referred to as the last of the Afghan principalities in North India, who competed with and then were displaced by the Mughals as they became established as the ruling dynasts in Delhi-centered Hindustan. Genealogies of Pashtuns that were textualized most often in Persian during the contentious "identity-politics" of the seventeenth century when the speaking or writing of Pashto in addition to Persian (or Marathi, Hindustani, etc.) carried increasing social and political significance. In some of these genealogies, Lohanis are represented as structurally complementary kindred to the Lodis and Suris, and all three stand in structural opposition to Ghalzis who in turn appear opposed in relation to Durranis, thus reflecting the structural tensions and dynamics at work in this "segmentary society."[30] When the colonial gaze turned toward the trans-Indus territories in the 1820s and especially the 1830s, British authorities took close note of migrating and settled communities of Lohanis in, around, and through the Gomal Pass and the market of Dera Ismail Khan. This official notice resulted in formal contractual arrangements with the Lohani chieftain Sarwar Khan for a wide range of carriage services in logistical support of the Army of the Indus and the first colonial occupation of Kabul.

The considerable historical depth of the Lohanis and their relatively well-defined territoriality reflect long-term interaction with state structures. Lohani relationships with the Mughal and British Indian states involved military and commercial arrangements and possibly administrative functions. Lohanis are a recognized tribal segment and as such the word is capitalized according to English usage here. The colonial records tell quite a different story for the kochis and pawendas who appear more as commercial classes, thus the lowercasing of those words in English. These two groups have a more shallow history, at least in textual terms, coming into clear view only through the early ethnographic accounts of colonial authorities.

The colonial archives for Afghanistan situate the pawenda community in commercial orbit around the Qandahar entrepot. They are responsible for connecting the Qandahar markets to Quetta and from there to the Indus, Indian, and Indian Ocean markets. Colonial authorities offered various tracings of the word pawenda through both Persian and Pashto terminology without any clear pattern. Connections to political authorities and centers are important variables in the activities and identities of the trading tribes and their subgroupings, and compared to kochis and Lohanis, pawendas appear less subject to state intervention in commercial, military, and administrative arenas and more associated with the Pashto language and territories where Pashto-speakers preponderate. Among the pawendas, Ghalzi Pashtuns are by far the most prominent and significant grouping.[31]

Colonial records make a clear association between kochis and the markets of Kabul and Peshawar while distinguishing that constellation from the pairing of pawendas with Qandahar. Lohanis are generally written out of the markets of Peshawar and Qandahar by colonial authorities, but the Lohanis become central for the original colonial commercial plan to link Kabul to the Indus River that contextualized the first Anglo-Afghan war in the terms of global colonial economic strategy. That first plan, tied as it was to the Army of the Indus, worked out poorly for the British. After the second Anglo-Afghan war, the policies enacted by Abd al-Rahman reveal his dependence on British capital, commodities, and expertise, and his desire to keep those resources and connections within his own personal purview, out of social sight. Through his policies, kochis became the key carriers along the increasingly important Khaibar Pass route between Kabul-Peshawar.

The archival treatment of these three communities of nomadic tribal traders reveals nineteenth-century British Indian colonialism to have focused on Kabul and intensified the market connections between Kabul and Peshawar, at the expense of Qandahar. Colonial officials first worked with and through the Lohanis and then the kochis to physically integrate markets across state boundaries and allow both state powers to profit from and keep track of the new terms of trade between Afghanistan and the world. This increasing commercial proximity and integration between Kabul and Peshawar had the unintended consequence of amplifying the economic distance and political tension between Kabul and Qandahar. One important result is that the pawendas and

Qandahar were marginalized, economically and politically, by these Kabul-centered colonial processes. The combined histories of the kochis, Lohanis, and pawendas illuminate the market complications of state building activities on both sides of this colonial frontier.

Afghanistan, Colonialism, and Global Capitalism

The history of Afghanistan over the long term is in many ways a geographical tale, whereas colonialism, with its subtleties and punctuations, is the master narrative of the country's recent past. The history of colonialism is intimately linked to capitalism, and India was arguably the world's most important colony. This book can be read as a study in the local geography of capitalist expansion and as an examination of the colonial inability to integrate Afghanistan. Market relations between Kabul, Peshawar, and Qandahar have been framed by interconnected workings of colonialism and capitalism. The preceding discussion of the archival sources discussed areas in which social and economic identity categories were treated ambiguously and contradictorily. Colonial records reveal dynamism and evolution regarding the categories of Afghanistan, Afghan, Pashtun, Pathan, Hindki, kochi, Lohani, and pawenda. It is clear that colonial authorities and texts are responding to some degree of variation and strategic choice exhibited by local actors themselves in relation to these identity categories verbally and in the texts they produced. Any conclusions drawn about cultural authenticity or purity in these matters should be treated with the utmost caution if not outright skepticism. However, it should be clearly recognized that flexible identities and identity boundaries not only facilitate market transactions but also serve to open the whole system up, culturally, economically, and politically. So, at first glance, the archives' infinite and haphazard variation and apparent confusion turn out in fact to be both the adhesive and the lubricant of the local system.

The Hindkis and trading tribes under any moniker represented indigenous capitalism for colonial authorities whose engagement of those groups dramatically transformed the political economy of this frontier region. The course of that colonial engagement finished with what is generally referred to as modern Afghanistan, with Kabul as its capital. Culturally, historically, and politically Pashtuns are perceived to be at the core of that fundamentally colonial construction. This framing raises questions about the commercial and cultural interactions between Pashtuns and Hindkis, and the relationships of both communities to cities and states. Afghanistan is a colonially constructed and disaggregated unit of political economy that simply cannot be understood through Kabul or Pashtuns alone. A far more developed understanding of the relationships between Pashtuns and Kabul, and between other communities and markets throughout the country, is necessary before knowledge about Afghanistan can transcend its colonial moorings. The point of emphasis now is that colonialism and capitalism conspire to operate at multiple levels, so that a full treatment of market relations must include attention to geographic, historical, cultural, and political variables and contexts. Kabul does not have the singular ability to absorb and resolve its periodic but increasingly intense saturations with colonial politics and intensive capitalism. Kabul's fate has been and will remain tied to the economic and political destinies of proximate markets and more distant urban centers.

Views of Afghanistan through the history of capitalism throw a number of relevant comparative issues into greater relief. Fernand Braudel, the principal conceptual and historical stratigrapher of capitalism, uses enticing imagery to show that market life stands apart but throws out feeders that are grabbed by the tentacles of true capitalist activity occurring at a layer above the market. Below the affairs of the market, and sustaining them, is a deeper layer of human activity involving basic material existence and subsistence. The attraction of Braudel's three layers is that they correspond to three layers of time, something along the lines of geographical time applying to material life, market activity establishing a kind of medium-term stable structure, with events relegated to quick surface time, as foam is to waves and waves are to currents. Braudel raises the crucial issue of historical conjuncture, when the old gives way to the new over a span of generations. In a number of ways, Braudel will be looming throughout this analysis, as will Immanuel Wallerstein, who uses a global division of labor approach to capitalism, so to speak. This model has cores, peripheries, semiperipheries, and an external zone, and this geographic division is inspired in part by Braudel. Eric Wolf places human labor migration in the global historical terminology of capitalism, and Sidney Mintz considers the possibility of one commodity providing a certain sweet key to capitalism's expansion.[32] Each of these authors helps to identify and conceptualize global historical structures of capitalism informing this analysis.

When the sinews of global capitalism reach their local destinations, often through various forms of coercion, the resulting cultural adaptations and transformations can be quite unexpected and profound. It is never the case that a single hegemonic entity called capitalism enters new settings that simply succumb in mimetic fashion to the new order that is thus reproduced neatly and cleanly over these remote environments. Local cultures on the margins of capitalism do not merely imitate metropolitanism; instead, they bring their own ingredients and senses of distinction to the encounter. Marshall Sahlins drew attention to the cultural frontiers of capitalism where patterns of local consumption do not predictably digest the new global commodities, and that perspective provides an important analytical compass for this work.[33] The small movements along the path of capitalism's cultural history made here are facilitated by a few insightful guides who provide different types of vehicles to traverse Afghanistan's unique and diverse colonial terrain.

David Akin and Joel Robbins deploy an "enlarged spheres of exchange" model that treats state money use as a key index of both the transformation and resilience of indigenous economies.[34] The enlarged spheres framework supports the present inquiries into the social dimensions and structural modalities contextualizing the introductions of and accommodations to new forms of state money. Jack Goody identifies the cultural and historical connections between literacy and the state via scribal classes and practices that reveal important bureaucratic similarities across what can otherwise appear as widely disparate cultural and political zones. Goody's comparison of literate social groups and his integration of issues related to bookkeeping, literacy, and state bureaucracy set the textual parameters of this investigation.[35] Arjun Appadurai's proposal of a commodity ecumene that unites producers and consumers through a combination of ordinary or customary movements and unusual diversionary paths resonates strongly here.[36] The commodity trajectory aspect of this paradigm combines biographies of people and things, and this work is similarly trying to capture synergies between materiality and sociality. Perhaps the most relevant aspect of Appadurai's perspective is the distinction he finds between the forms of knowledge held by producers and consumers in relation to the commodities that unite and distinguish them, and the important role intermediate merchant communities play in bridging, or not bridging, those gaps in commodity knowledge across the various trajectories of the ecumene.

The global cultural and structural histories of capitalism eventually merge into the history of colonialism. From the perspective of British colonialism in India the works of Christopher Bayly have provided a rich canvas that best lays out the "sociocommercial" background and landscape of this study. Bayly demonstrates the significance of and connections between medium-sized market settings through merchant network analysis that attends to nomadic transport and the textual practices of large merchant firms that fed into British Indian imperial policy and political practice. Bernard Cohn has provided this study with its concern for the intellectual dimensions of British colonialism.[37] None of these authors offers the single key to the only analytical lock on Afghanistan, but as a whole they provide some good questions about Afghanistan for students of colonialism and capitalism. As such, this work is essentially explorative in nature, although some revision and reorientation are also intended. With capitalism and colonialism as organizing agents, useful subsidiary questions are raised about the relationship between Afghanistan's atypical colonial target status and its ill-positioning on a hypermarginalized periphery of capitalism. The master framers can only help us see the terms of the relationship between capitalism and colonialism, on the one hand, and our three markets, on the other. They do so by identifying themes such as human migration, commodity circulation, forms of currency (and contours of intra- and inter-currency exchange), urban-rural interaction, commercial routes, textual practices, and debt (its creation and circulation) that can trump or circumvent the archival market nomenclature quagmires previously outlined. At the very least, archival sources reveal precious material for comparative questions and theorizing organized for the broader challenge of fully comprehending the emergence of the modern world system.

No such summits will be reached here. The goals of this book are drastically more limited. They have to do primarily with routing. The story might be reduced to the Khaibar Pass between Kabul and Peshawar becoming a colonial toll road, with subplots revolving around what happens to other markets such as Qandahar in that context. A kaleidoscopic view of capitalism and colonialism focusing on Kabul conveys the imagery of periodic overdoses of capital resulting in unforeseen results. In a less dramatic way, these infusions of colonial capital transformed the market mix among Kabul, Peshawar, and Qandahar. What seems clear within the confines of this book is that Kabul is not well disposed to being a center of capital accumulation. Kabul, Peshawar, and Qandahar share market profiles that do not suggest any one of them will fare well as a political capital of any substantial magnitude. Each of these cities is reputed for its hawalas and hundis, not its harems or hammams. In the historical long view, only in combination with either or both of the others does any one of these cities assume global political significance. It might therefore be that in the local historical view the three markets become nearly interchangeable on the political hierarchy. At the minimum for Kabul, Peshawar, and Qandahar, the function of each market derives from its relationship to the other two, and as such, the activities and destinies of these markets are increasingly contingent on their interrelations and respective connections to exterior influences. A variety of relations between these markets become tangible through colonial archival sources that illuminate interactions between three groups of actors in and in between each setting. These interactive communities of commercial classes are state authorities (Durrani Afghan and British Indian), bankers and merchants (primarily Hindkis), and nomadic tribal traders (primarily kochis, Lohanis, and pawendas). At a basic level, this history is just a glance at the longstanding tension between markets and states.

With the historical background, geographic context, thematic orientation, and descriptions of the actors and sources in hand, a brief narrative guide to how these variables intersect in what follows is in order.

Part I deals with the experimental period of Anglo-Afghan relations between 1809 and 1842. Chapter 1 describes the production, financing, and consumption of the fruits and nuts exported from Kabul and eastern Afghanistan to India.

Chapter 2 examines how the British assessed the value of this lucrative trade using nomadic commercial experiments that validated the project of opening up the Indus River to international commerce. It also considers the role of nomadic carriage in the Indus Army's occupation of Kabul.

Chapter 3 deals with fiscal issues associated with the first Anglo-Afghan war including the challenges surrounding the introduction of new currencies, the desperate overborrowing by the occupation army before its demise using paper money instruments, and the effect of the British reorganization of the Durrani state revenue bureaucracy on the financing and functioning of the export fruit trade.

Part II deals with the reign of Abd al-Rahman, whom the British appointed as the Amir of Kabul in 1880 to facilitate an evacuation that would avert another disastrous conclusion to the second Anglo-Afghan war. Kabul-centrism characterized British Indian policy and practice leading up to the first Anglo-Afghan war, and Abd al-Rahman intensified the colonial commercial emphasis on Kabul after the second war. This part of the book considers the consequences of concentrating colonial capital in Kabul for the markets of Qandahar and Peshawar.

Chapter 4 discusses the British subsidy that structured Abd al-Rahman's relationship with colonial authorities and how its handling and management reconfigured market relations between Kabul and Peshawar, capital of the British Indian North-West Frontier Province since 1849. The Durrani state industrial workshop complex is the institutional focus of this chapter. The demarcation of Afghanistan's boundaries occurred in exchange for increases in Abd al-Rahman's stipend, and he ultimately became dependent on colonial capital emanating from Peshawar. Those resources gave Abd al-Rahman the strategic upper hand, allowing him to consolidate his autocracy around a new class of state officials. These new bureaucrats and the texts they wielded were enabled by colonial capital and facilitated Abd al-Rahman's further concentration of capital in Kabul.

Chapter 5 considers two areas of impact made by these further Kabul-centric developments. The first area affected by these new state policies was the Qandahar marketplace, which experienced the systematic textual and physical siphoning of its commercial resources. A second area of consequence was upon the nomadic commercial carriers who were textually conscripted by a maze of new state papers to execute a coordinated plan by Abd al-Rahman and British Indian authorities to route commerce between Kabul and Peshawar through the Khaibar Pass.

Chapter 6 offers a brief case study of the Peshawar-based Sethi merchant family in Abd al-Rahman's Afghanistan. The Sethis were commercially favored by Abd al-Rahman, and they provided commercial intelligence to the colonial authorities. In this sense, the Sethis were getting the best from both sides out of a bad commercial situation between Afghanistan and India. The vastly more common counterexample to the exceptionally favorable experience of the Sethis is the commercial evasion and flight from Afghanistan. This chapter also examines the widespread evasive action taken by merchants when confronted by the new policies and practices occurring in these old markets. The case study on the ordinary side of the commercial equation are a consortium of North Indian tea traders who avoided the required and highly surveilled and taxed Khaibar route by tapping into the Indian Ocean's seaborne routing circuit and engaging new technologies such as telegraphic money transfer services to circumvent Abd al-Rahman and his commercially poisonous state paper.

CHAPTER 1

Financing the Kabul Produce

The Primary Commodities and
Their Main Trajectories

Babur spent the years between 1504 and 1520 living in and campaigning around Kabul before proceeding to India and founding the Mughal empire. Babur's reputation was established during the years he was based in Kabul, and the city's reputation grew as a result of his time there. Babur's love for Kabul was expressed in a number of ways including his burial in a garden complex of his own construction overlooking the city.[1] Furthermore, Babur was a voracious consumer of wine, and his passion for Kabul can be explained by the abundance and quality of grapes grown in the city's vicinity. Babur opines "Kabul wine is intoxicating" then offers readers this couplet:

Only the drinker knows the pleasure of wine.
What enjoyment can the sober have?[2]

Wine drinking seems to have favorably colored Babur's view of Kabul, and his description of the city is often couched in that context. For example, the Bala Hissar fortress complex is a very prominent feature of Kabul, and Babur invoked the consumption of wine to describe this structure. Having described the northern side of the citadel as being well ventilated, he then quotes an earlier description of the Bala Hissar written by a Mullah Muhammad Talib Muammai:

Drink wine in Kabul citadel, send round the cup again and again,
for there is both mountain and water, both city and countryside.[3]

This wording alludes to Kabul as a fertile and productive setting. Babur clearly articulates such a view by deploying imagery of his own to describe the mountain slopes surrounding the Kabul valley as irrigated orchards. He mentions an area at the end of one irrigation canal known as Gulkana, "a secluded, cozy spot ... (where) much debauchery is indulged in" and offers this parody of Hafiz he heard there:

> How happy that time when, unbridled and unconstrained,
> We spend a few days in Gulkana with persons of ill repute.[4]

Written nearly five hundred years ago, Babur's description of Kabul and its dependencies is peppered with references to heavy wine-drinking bouts set in lush and bountiful venues. The grapes used to make wine receive a good deal of attention in the Kabul section of Babur's memoirs. About Laghman, an important region to the east and north of Kabul, readers are told:

> It also has grapes and the vines all grow over trees. (Here) Dara-i-Nur wine is famous. There are two sorts, *arratashi* and *sawhantashi*. The arratashi is yellowish, while the sawhantashi is a beautiful bright red color. The arratashi is more enjoyable, although neither is equal to its reputation.[5]

In addition to grapes, Babur mentions an array of fruits grown around Kabul. Among these are pomegranates, apricots, apples, quinces, pears, peaches, plums, and jujube.[6] For example, while referring to the dependencies of Kabul, Babur states:

> Most of these villages are located on the slopes of the mountain. There are many grapes in the orchards. There is also an abundance of all sorts of fruit. Among these villages there are none like Istalif and Istarghij.[7]

In his *Atlas of the Mughal Empire,* Irfan Habib (1986) confirms Babur's portrait of Kabul as a fruit-filled region. Habib plots the production sites of apples, apricots, citron, grapes, melons, oranges, and pomegranates in his mapping of the natural resources of the Kabul *suba* or provincial administrative division during the Mughal period.[8] In addition to those fruits, Habib mentions the local production of other commodities including barley, iron, lapiz lazuli, madder, rice, salt, silver, sugarcane, and wheat.[9] However, fruit was clearly the most abundant category of agricultural produce in and around Kabul, and Babur definitely carried his taste for it to North India.

The Mughal nobility descended from Babur (ruled c. 1526–30) inherited his love for Central Asian fruit. India was accustomed to receiving dried fruits and nuts from Kabul and Central Asia. Muzaffar Alam argues that Mughal rulers after Babur exhibited a heightened concern for the security of interregional traders and the routes they plied through Kabul and Qandahar.[10] Alam contends this was especially so in the seventeenth century when Mughal state policy of securing a steady trade with their Central Asian homeland resulted in an expanded presence in India of fresh fruits imported from Kabul, Balkh, Samarqand, and beyond. Jahangir (ruled 1605–26) is said to have enjoyed imported fresh apples, grapes, and melons, and boasted that his father Akbar (ruled 1556–1605) also loved such fruit.[11]

It is important to appreciate that dried and fresh fruits imported from Kabul and greater Central Asia were broadly consumed in Delhi and greater South Asia during the Mughal period. Certain fresh fruits may have been generally restricted to the elites and nobles, but other fresh and most dried fruits and nuts appear as both appealing and accessible to the popular classes of Indian consumers. Bernier, who wrote about his travels in Hindustan during the midseventeenth century, supports the claim of widespread consumption of Central Asian fruit in India. He describes the popularity and abundance of imported dried and fresh fruits in Hindustan generally and Delhi specifically. Regarding the former, he indicates:

> Hindustan consumes an immense quantity of fresh fruit from Samarkand, Balc, Bocara, and Persia; such as melons, apples, pears and grapes, eaten at Delhi and purchased at very high price nearly the whole winter; and likewise dried fruit such as almonds, pistachio and various other small nuts, plums, apricots, and raisins, which may be procured the whole year round.[12]

And concerning the presence and visibility of Central Asian fruits in Delhi, Bernier wrote:

> . . . a fruit market (in Delhi) makes some show. It contains many shops which are well supplied with dry fruit from Persia, Balk, Bokara, and Samarkande; such as almonds, pistachios, and walnuts, raisins, prunes, and apricots; and in winter with excellent fresh grapes, black and white, brought from the same countries, wrapped in cotton; pears and apples of three or four sorts, and those admirable melons which last the whole winter. These (fresh) fruits are however very dear . . . (b)ut nothing is considered so great a treat.[13]

It is also important to consider the local consumption of fruit grown in Kabul and greater Central Asia. Early colonial sources provide abundant information in this regard. The first substantive published account of economic and social life in and around Kabul comes from the British mission of 1808 to the Durrani monarch Shuja. This diplomatic and research collective was led by Mountstuart Elphinstone. James Strachey served in the important post of

Secretary for this Anglo-Indian delegation, and he was responsible for relating information about the prices of commodities to Elphinstone.[14] The published text resulting from the Elphinstone-Strachey labor consortium indicates a profuse supply of fruit for local residents. Therein we find the following quote that comes from a discussion of the foods of the "common people" in Kabul:

> Provisions are cheap and people derive a great luxury from the prodigious abundance of fruit. At Caubul grapes are dear when they sell for more than a farthing a pound; pomegranates are little more than a halfpenny a pound; apples sell at two hundred pounds for a rupee (two shillings and four pence); two sorts of apricots are equally cheap; and the dearer sorts are less than a halfpenny a pound; peaches are dearer but quinces and plums are as cheap; and melons are cheaper; grapes often bear scarce at any price, and the coarse sort, which is exported with so much care to India, is sometimes given to cattle. Nuts of all kinds are very cheap; and walnuts, with which the hills north of Caubul are covered, sell at two thousand for a rupee. The price of vegetables is also extremely low . . .[15]

According to this first British account, the prices of fruit and nuts harvested locally appear quite accessible for everyday consumers in pre-colonial Kabul. Next in the line of colonial officers deputed to Kabul was Alexander Burnes. Whereas Elphinstone's extensive delegation did not proceed beyond Peshawar, and it is unclear precisely how that mission collected and recorded information, Burnes passed through and stayed in Kabul a number of times, with much smaller entourages, and his published accounts reflect his own rendition of firsthand experience. Burnes describes public culture and social life as centered in fruit tree-laden gardens in and around Kabul. Images of flowers, birds, and poetry characterize his accounting of Kabul's garden culture.[16] In marked contrast, Burnes's description of grapes is less lofty, more mundane, and results in the impression of widespread local use, perhaps even dependence, on this single fruit group.

> Cabool is particularly celebrated for its fruit, which is exported in great abundance to India. Its vines are so plentiful, that the grapes are given, for three months of the year, to cattle. There are ten different kinds of these: the best grow on frame-works; for those which are allowed to creep on the ground are inferior. They are pruned in the beginning of May. The wine of Cabool has a flavour not unlike Madeira; and it cannot be doubted, that a very superior description might be produced in this country with a little care. The people of Cabool convert grape into more uses than in most other countries. They use its juice in roasting meat; and, during meals, have grape powder as a pickle. This is procured by pounding the grapes before they get

ripe, after drying them. It looks like Cayenne pepper, and has a pleasant acid taste. They also dry many of them as raisins, and use much grape syrup. A pound of grapes sells for half a penny.[17]

Burnes's appreciation for the role of grapes in the local diet of Kabul arose from his contacts with and experiences among ordinary Afghans. But Burnes also had a number of important interactions with elites generally and the Durrani ruler in Kabul, Dost Muhammad (ruled 1826–38 and 1842–63) specifically, before the first British occupation of the city. In the following passage, Burnes provides a window into the personal political histories and communal social life surrounding the production and consumption of wine in Kabul:

> (T)he present chief of Cabool, with the best intentions, has put a finishing blow to the Armenian colony, by a strict prohibition of wine and spirits. . . . After a life by no means temperate, this chief has renounced wine, and, under the severest penalties, commands that his subjects should be equally abstemious. The Armenians and Jews of Cabool have, therefore, fled to other lands, as they had no means of support but in distilling spirits and wine. There are but three Jewish families left in Cabool, the wreck of a hundred which it could last year boast. If Dost Mohammad Khan can succeed in suppressing drunkenness by the sacrifice of a few foreign inhabitants, he is not to be blamed; since forty bottles of wine or ten of brandy might be purchased from them for a single rupee . . . we shall not criticize his motive, nor comment with severity on the inconsistency of a reformed drunkard. Cabool seems to have been always famed for its revels.[18]

Writing about his journey through eastern Afghanistan in 1836, G. T. Vigne also comments on the plentiful supply of grapes in the region. Vigne's narrative addresses the intricate preparation and packaging of certain grapes for export to India, and implicitly advocates their further distribution to Europe:

> I have no where seen such an abundance of fruit. Of grapes there are four or five different kinds; but I think that the *husseini*, a long grape which is sent to India in cotton, in flat, circular boxes is the only one that will bear competition with those of the south of Europe.[19]

The colonial imagination conceived the export of Afghan fruit to be a profitable enterprise, and such a commercial conception of the area involved much more than a single type of grape grown in Kabul. For example, Henry Bellew outlined a wide array of fruits harvested in Qandahar. Bellew noted at least four types of apples, ten types of apricots, two types of figs, ten types of muskmelon, eight types of mulberries, two types of peaches, three types of plums,

FIG. 1.1. Grape Drying Hut in Vineyard, 2004

FIG. 1.2. Peshawar Market, 1930s

six types of pomegranates, three types of quinces, six types of watermelons, in addition to nineteen types of grapes produced in that locality alone.[20]

As colonial knowledge about Kabul developed the British began to recognize the large amount of capital linked to fruit production in addition to the service of that commodity group as a medium of exchange in its own right. Compared to Burnes, Charles Masson had a greater amount of firsthand interaction with people in and around Kabul. Masson commented on the revenue generated by fruit trees in the royal gardens and other orchards that, either through outright confiscation or a form of sale, became a given ruler's personal and therefore the Durrani state's property.[21] He also described an incident at Honai, on the road linking Bamian and Kabul, where armed men demanded a monetary duty that was ultimately satisfied by a payment in grapes.[22] In his published account, Masson equates the fruit market of Kabul with the Shikarpuri quarter and claims that brokers controlled all commercial traffic passing through the city.[23]

Durrani State Mints and Hindki Money Handlers

Fernand Braudel invokes a useful turn of phrase to convey the disorientation experienced by a local French community when first exposed to the growing global forces of money and credit during the medieval period. In typically erudite fashion he says:

> This uneasiness was the beginning of the awareness of a new language. For money is a language . . . it calls for and makes possible dialogues and conversations; it exists as a function of these conversations.[24]

If money is a language, there have been many tongues spoken in Kabul, Peshawar, and Qandahar, and communities between the three cities, arguably throughout recorded history. More intriguing than the historical depth of money use in this region is the multiplicity of currencies circulating in the area at any one time. Most significant for our purposes is Braudel's attention to three different "dialects of money." These are metallic money or what we have termed state currency, paper bank notes including bills of exchange that Braudel argues to be the most important of all instruments of credit, and scriptural money that was strictly a textual or book money used for account-keeping purposes.[25] The thrust of this chapter deals with the interaction between metallic state currencies and a derivative fiscal instrument, namely credit, which is a paper product, during Anglo-Durrani state formation.[26]

State coinage, or metallic money, precedes paper credit in conceptual terms, so it will be considered first. The Mughal period is a reasonable point of departure in this regard. Irfan Habib locates two silver rupee mints in both Kabul and Multan, one in each city built in 1595 by Akbar (ruled 1556–1605), and another set dating to the reign of Aurangzeb/Alamgir (ruled 1658–1707).[27] During the Mughal period, Kabul served as a frontier provincial capital inside the Hindu Kush range. It was an important supply center and staging area for Mughal forays to the north. Multan's location just east of the Indus River, between the Punjab in the north and Sind to the south, gave the city a distinct commercial appeal and vibrancy. For example, Multan was a primary if not the principal wholesale market for horses imported into India through Kabul and Qandahar.[28] Merchants from Multan were active in Iran, Central Asia, and Russia between 1600 and 1900.[29]

Control over Multan's marketing and minting functions were important variables in the rapid expansion and contraction of the early Durrani empire.[30] Ahmad Shah (ruled 1747–72), the ephemeral empire's founder, was born in Multan in 1722. The breadth of his suzerainty accounts for the large number of mints which at one time or another operated under Ahmad Shah's controlling authority, and this helps explain the wide variety of coins struck in his name. During Ahmad Shah's reign, copper, gold, and silver coins were issued from a number of cities, including Qandahar, Kabul, Peshawar, Attock, Dera Ghazi Khan, the Derajat (Dera Ismail Khan and Dera Fateh Khan), Multan, Bhakkar, Thatta, Sind, Kashmir, Lahore, Aonla (Anwala), Bareli, Farrukhabad, Muradabad, and Najibabad.[31] When the British first reconnoitered Multan between 1835 and 1837, the town was estimated to have eighty thousand residents, making it the third largest city in Sikh territory behind Lahore and Amritsar.[32] At that time, the annual farm of Multan's mint sold for *nanak shah* or Sikh Rupees 22,563.[33]

In addition to the mint, the early British commercial surveillance reports make it clear that Multan's credit and money exchange markets were also very active in the period leading up to the first Anglo-Afghan war. Colonial authorities registered local rates on bills of exchange, or *hundi chalan*, in the city through a listing of transaction amounts in eight currencies at many different time intervals for bills circulating between Multan and five other cities.[34] In the early colonial documents about Multan there is a good deal of attention devoted to the transit taxes paid by camel and pony commercial caravans moving from Bukhara to Multan.[35] Multan was further characterized as an important site of production in its own right. In Multan, imported Central Asian silk was refined into clothing for the Amritsar market, and indigo was harvested and packaged for export to Central Asia. The only form of local commercial insurance covered the silk, in finished piece good form, moving from Multan to Amritsar.[36] These sources indicate that trade between Bukhara and Multan was routed through Kabul and dominated by Shikarpuri Hindus and Lohani Afghans.

For the Mughals and early Durranis Multan was important as a mint city, as a hub of the interregional trade networks linking Central and South Asia, and as a production center in its own right. Dale (1994) has proffered a good deal of evidence about Multanis in Central Asia, Iran, and Russia during roughly the same period. But during the nineteenth century, there is little indication of a Multani presence in eastern Afghanistan. There is, however, a wide and relatively thick array of information about Shikarpuris in Kabul, Qandahar, and territories between those points during the 1800s. The early British commercial intelligence about Shikarpur indicated that the city held about thirty thousand people, was only recently founded, and did not seem to have an active state mint.[37] Shikarpur was not noted for any significant local production or marketing of local or imported commodities. The city was known almost strictly as a money market and banking center, and its reputation was garnered by those claiming or being ascribed the Shikarpuri identity who resided far from the city itself.[38] Individuals identified as Shikarpuris were found in approximately forty major markets between Astrakhan and Calcutta.[39] Lal hints at that fact by noting Khattri Hindus from Shikarpur were spread out all over Central Asia and that in the city itself:

> ... you will see all the shop keepers writing hoondees, or bills of exchange, which you can take in the name of agents at Bombay, Sindh, the Punjab, Khorasan, Afghanistan, part of Persia and Russia.[40]

Burnes is more explicit in his caricature of a widely dispersed but well integrated Shikarpuri commercial network by noting that while in Kabul he:

> ... made the acquaintance of many of the Hindoo or Shikarpooree merchants. The whole trade of Central Asia is in the hands of these people, who have houses of agency from Astracan to Meshid to Calcutta. They are a plodding race, who take no share in any other matters than their own, and secure protection from the Government by lending it money. They never bring their families from their country, which is Upper Sinde, and are constantly passing to and from it; which keeps up a national spirit among them. In Cabool, there are eight great houses of agency belonging to these people, who are quite separate from the other Hindoo inhabitants. Of them there are about 300 hundred families. I met one of these Shikarpooree merchants on

the island of Kisham in the Gulf of Persia. With such an extensive agency distributed in the parts of Asia which we were now about to traverse, it was not, as may be supposed, a very difficult task to adjust our money matters, and arrange for receiving a supply of that necessary article, even at the distance we should shortly find ourselves from India. . . . I had a letter of credit in my possession for the sum of five thousand rupees, payable from the public treasuries of Lodiana or Delhi; and the Cabool merchants did not hesitate to accept it.[41]

Here, Burnes contradicts himself by first equating the Hindus in Kabul with Shikarpuris then claiming the Shikarpuris were a separate community from the other Hindus in the city. Elsewhere, Burnes notes the residents of Shikarpur city itself to be about 50 percent Baba Nanak Sikhs and 10 percent Muslim, most of the latter group being identified as Afghans who received land grants from the early Durranis.[42] This leaves a Hindu resident population of approximately 40 percent, but their importance was proportionately much greater because members of this community comprised most of the Shikarpuris found so widely outside the city. Among these Shikarpuri Hindu businessmen spread throughout Asia Burnes noted three different "tribes," the "Bunya, Lohana, and Bhattea."[43]

Khattris are conspicuously absent from Burnes's list of Hindu communities in Shikarpur. Burnes would therefore not count Khattris among the numbers of commercially active Shikarpuris residing outside the city. But Burnes's elision in this regard is destabilized by a number of other sources. Nearly contemporaneous with Burnes's account of Shikarpur, Lal indicated that Hindu Khattris from Shikarpur were highly visible if not dominant in Multan's trade with Bukhara. Alam notes an "extraordinary strong Khatri participation" in the trade between Central and South Asia during the Mughal period, and Dale counts Khattri Hindus among the three main groups of diaspora Multanis in Iran, Turan, and Russia during the same period.[44] A Khattri Hindu from Shikarpur, Lala Jeth Mall, served as Shuja's finance minister in 1832 during the former sovereign's failed attempt to reclaim his throne.[45]

It is important to emphasize the variety of groups subsumed within the Shikarpuri or Multani label. Shikarpur and Multan and arguably all markets contain representatives of communities carrying multiple layers of identity, some of which overlap with those of other local groups and as a result serve integrating purposes, and others of which serve to differentiate the many social sectors calling the same location home. For representatives of those communities residing or traveling outside of the home locality, any particular aspect of their identity package could become the distinguishing feature for that person or group, and furthermore different people from within the host setting could refer to the same "guests" in different ways based on those features. Thus an Indian, who might be a Khattri Hindu from Shikarpur or Multan, could be reasonably identified in historical sources in Central Asia by any one of five valid designations. It is also important to note that significant pieces of these identity puzzles are missing. This results from so little being known about how people labeled Multanis, Lohanis, or Shikarpuris identified themselves differently in different contexts, as all people do, and what social and economic calculations laid behind the invocation of any one of many possible, and all equally valid on some level, self-referents. The fluidity and simultaneity of social categories, the interactive and relational nature of social action, and the situational ways identities are constructed and practiced are necessary considerations when trying to historically unpack the identity layers of a diaspora group.[46]

This is especially true for the Lohanis, who are regularly and all-too-unproblematically conflated with Afghans, Pashtuns, and Pawendas.[47] Over time, through space, across cultures, and in texts, heterogeneity and movement stand out as defining features of the Lohanis. To accept the social and historical diversity and fluidity of the Lohanis sensitizes one to the same basic but unspoken variety subsumed in each of the three other terms. Treating the four labels as static surrogates for one another compounds the original obfuscation and avoidance of the assorted and imprecise nature of each category. Anthropologists have shown that for nomadic, pastoral, and tribal societies economic adaptation and cultural accommodation explain the fundamental diversity and resilience of these populations. For example, there has been a healthy discussion of the wealthier and poorer segments of pastoral communities, the multiple possibilities for those at each pole of the economic spectrum inside and outside the original group, and the role of commercialization and access to markets in creating and responding to those disparities.[48] The Lohanis were known for long-distance commercial migrations, so any sedentarization among these nomadic trader-carriers implies significant social change and economic disparities that are generally downplayed in diaspora studies of this fundamentally heterogeneous group.

Recognizing but undervaluing pre-existing social diversity and ongoing social change are features of studies of diaspora merchant communities.[49] The trade diaspora approach tends to emphasize the cultural homogeneity of both guest and host communities. One response to the trade diaspora paradigm has been to focus analytical attention on the circulation of resources through merchant networks connecting the dispersed communities and the home setting or network center of the group. Claude Markovits is the proponent of this "merchant network with a center" alternative to the trade diaspora analytical scheme. In this model, circulation of resources to and from the center and through the network is primary. In his words:

> ... a network generally consists of a centre, a locality or a cluster of localities where capital is raised and where capitalists have their main place of residence, and of dispersed colonies of merchants and commercial employees which keep close links with the network centre. Between the network centre, on the one hand, and the dispersed colonies on the other hand, goods, but also men (and sometimes women), credit and information circulate. While goods may circulate widely outside the network (otherwise there would not be any exchange), men, credit, and information circulate almost exclusively within it. Most crucial is probably the circulation of information.[50]

In this view, circulation of resources, movement of people, and economic adaptation are key, whereas proponents of trade diasporas tend to focus on long-term stability, cultural unity, and generally do not problematize social reproduction of the communities. In Afghanistan during the nineteenth century, the experience of Indian bankers, including the Shikarpuris, was quite varied. During the early part of the century, they were favored by the state, while later in the century representatives of the Shikarpuri banking community in Kabul, Qandahar, and eastern Afghanistan were relocating and reallocating their resources as a result of unfavorable state policies and practices. In a dramatic change of circumstances, the Shikarpuris were largely dispersed from the Durrani polity Markovits credits with ushering their commercial network to interregional prominence in the first instance.[51]

The sheer range of Shikarpuri and other Indian bankers' experiences in nineteenth-century Afghanistan attenuates the applicability of the static trade diaspora framework to this context. But unfortunately the kind of data Markovits musters in support of the merchant network with a center model is not available for the Afghan context. For example, there is little precise data about the circulation of resources between Shikarpur and localities in Afghanistan during the nineteenth century. More important, Markovits refers to *panchayats* as the institutional loci for communication within each Shikarpuri community located away from the center, between those dispersed communities, and between each of those communities of Shikarpuris and their network center in Shikarpur.[52] The information about panchayats in Afghanistan does not conform to, and in substantive ways contradicts, this model. A panchayat institution first appears in Kabul during Abd al-Rahman's reign. However, this was not an exclusively Shikarpuri or even Indian institution. The Durrani panchayat was an instrument of state control over merchant communities, and as such served a very different purpose than suggested by Markovits.[53]

The present concern is not with Indian or Shikarpuri bankers per se, but, rather, with the interaction between those diverse communities, other local social groups and state authorities in nineteenth-century Afghanistan. Although they are nominally identified, there is little direct reference to the activities of Shikarpuri bankers in Durrani state finances specifically until the early 1880s when they appear in the context of Abd al-Rahman's redistributions of his prized British subsidy. In these records, the group reasonably understood as "Shikarpuri bankers" was never identified by that construct, but, rather, interchangeably, as "Peshawar bankers," "merchants of Shikarpur," and "Hindu bankers at Kabul."[54] All descriptions are valid, including the "Shikarpuri bankers" compound favored by modern scholars. It is important to appreciate that other sets of documents dealing with the nineteenth-century Afghan economy reference Peshawris, Hindus, and Indians in a variety of other contexts in which it might be appropriate to infer the presence of Shikarpuri bankers. Deductive reasoning is essential given the available data, but analysts should pay greater heed to the variety of local categories in addition to the labels that appear in and can be inferred from historical documents and contemporary literature. Not simply mentioning but incorporating the specificity of local conditions, including local terms of reference, however complicating and analytically tedious they are, would shore up future studies of Indian and Shikarpuri merchants in Central Asia and elsewhere. In this regard, the most common term applied by locals to Shikarpuris and other Hindus and Indians in Kabul, Qandahar, and eastern Afghanistan is Hindki, which does not appear as a designation for Indian communities outside of these areas. The following are two excerpts from nineteenth-century colonial sources about the identity and activity of Hindkis and related groups in Afghanistan:

> The Hindkees ... are all of Indian descent ... their language is a kind of Hindostaunee, resembling the dialect of the Punjab ... the Hindoos ought perhaps to be enumerated with this class. They are found over the whole kingdom of Caubul (they are indeed, to be found as far west as Astrachan, and they are numerous in Arabia; while on the east they extend as far as Pekin). In towns they are in considerable numbers as brokers, merchants, bankers, goldsmiths, sellers of grain, &c. There

is scarce a village in the country without a family or two who exercise the above trades, and act as accountants, moneychangers, &c. . . . They are encouraged in Bokaura and other towns in Tartary. They are all, or almost all, of the military class of Kshetree, but it must not be supposed that they are all, therefore, soldiers. On the contrary, the idea of a Hindoo soldier would be thought ludicrous in Caubul. . . . They are often employed about the courts in offices connected with money or accounts; the duty of steward and treasurer about every great man, is exercised by either a Hindoo or a Persian. There have even been Hindoo governors of provinces, and at this moment the great government of Peshawar has been put into the hand of a person of that religion. . . . I have mentioned the degree of toleration which the Hindoos meet with, and have only to add, that many of them are in very good circumstances, and that they possess the best houses in every town, if we except the palaces of the nobility.[55]

[Hindki is the] name given to the Hindus who live in Afghanistan. They are Hindus of the Khatri class, and are to be found all over Afghanistan even amongst the wildest tribes. They are wholly occupied in trade, and form and important and numerous portion of the population of all the cities and towns, and are also to be found in the majority of large villages. This enterprising people transact much of the banking business of the country, and by these means they prove useful to the Afghans, who, indeed, could not get on without them. . . . They number about 300,000 souls. . . . The important post of Accountant-General at Kabul is held by a Hindu, Niranjan Das.[56]

Hindki applies to the Shikarpuri bankers in nineteenth-century Afghanistan because the word targets a larger community of Hindus and other Indians in the country. In other words, Hindki as used locally referenced Hindus in the first instance, but it served as a metonym for all Indians in Afghanistan. The term is said to apply to Khattri Hindus specifically, which is an important point in support of the Hindki category encompassing the Shikarpuris, if one accepts that most Shikarpuris outside of Shikarpur were Khattris. It is possible that Hindki developed as a local appellation or compound of Hindu and Khattri.[57] Gankovsky and other Russian and Soviet scholars are unequivocal in situating Shikarpuris in the early Durrani polity. Gankovsky claims that during the reigns of Ahmad Shah and Timur Shah Durrani (1747–93 combined) Shikarpuris were most noticeable among the Indian merchants and bankers who financed military campaigns, supplied armies in the field, redistributed booty, conveyed luxury goods to the court, loaned money to khans, served as revenue farmers (especially in the eastern provinces), and as a result controlled government income and the circulation of money throughout the kingdom.[58]

However defined, Hindkis were not and could not be replicates of other communities of Shikarpuris dispersed throughout Eurasia because of the conditions unique to Afghanistan that created a culturally distinct set of guest-host relations. For an important example, in Afghanistan the institution of hamsaya or clientage creates bonds between prosperous members of any community, such as local khans and castle-holders (*qaladars*), and various categories of dependents, some of who are culturally distant such as Indians. Hamsaya relationships between patrons and clients were and remain malleable but strong in Afghan society. Concerning hamsaya relations between Afghans and Hindus, particularly between Durrani elites and Shikapuri bankers in the nineteenth century, the concept of clientage must be seen as dynamic, contradictory, and applying well to both sides of the social and economic equation. Despite the aforementioned quote from Elphinstone about the prevalence and importance of Hindkis in Afghanistan, and the possibilities of great power they enjoyed, he elsewhere treats the hamsaya relationship between Durranis and Hindus as decidedly lopsided in favor of the former. Elphinstone considered the hamsayas as non-Afghans attached to every Afghan tribe. According to him every adult male Afghan had the duty to protect hamsayas under threat of dishonor, the defense of honor being a core cultural value among Afghans:

> As used in this place (hamsaya) has exactly the force of our word denizen ... it is a point of honor for every man to protect his Humsauyehs ... one of the few quarrels I have heard of among the Dooraunees, originated in an injury offered to a Humsauyeh. A Hindoo Humsauyeh of one Noorzye chief, had gone to the village of another; while, on his return, he was seized by a third, on pretence of owing this chief money. The two other chiefs joined, and attacked the one who had seized the Humsauyeh. Blood was shed, and it required the interposition of the Naib of Candahar to compose the quarrel.[59]

Scholars need to exert greater effort to integrate the cultural values and social institutions of host societies into their analyses of the Indian mercantile diaspora. Interaction between the South Asian guests residing abroad and their host communities was structured by the economic institutions, social traits, and cultural values evident in the Indian communities and among the other residents of the setting in question. Analysts of the Indian guests involved in these guest-host relations have given attention to elements such as the family firm, literacy, and trust, but the host communities have been painted with much broader and far less-nuanced analytical strokes.[60] If a balanced analysis of the history and structure of relations between Afghans and Indians in and between Kabul, Peshawar, and Qandahar is to be produced, detailed consideration of a variety of local values and practices, including but not limited to those surrounding honor and hamsaya associations, would be required.

To appreciate the role of Hindki bankers as handlers of money, credit, and debt in and around Kabul, Peshawar, Qandahar, and other relevant markets, it has been necessary to first identify that social group with and against a number of terms, including Khattri, Shikarpuri, and Multani. This exercise has drawn attention to the importance of local conditions and context against the over-emphasis on diaspora groups in their own right when attempting to historically identify and socially situate such communities. In the Afghan context Indians appear very much woven into the local social fabric. Indians performed important functions in multiple sectors of the economy, they were designated by a distinct local term, they appear as prominent components in important social institutions, and active in political processes at the tribal and state levels. At the popular, society-wide level, Indians engaged Afghans and vice versa in normal, everyday, routinized, and mundane manners. Of course, this does not mean an existence free of complications, challenges, and difficulties. The point to be made is that there was a broad and rather "natural" presence of Indians in the area we now call Afghanistan; in fact this was so much so that it appeared somewhat "unnatural" when Abd al-Rahman drove them out of the country.

In nineteenth-century Afghanistan, Hindkis constituted between approximately 6 percent and 12 percent of the total population, and within that group Khattri Shikarpuris appear prominently. According to Burnes, the three hundred Shikarpuri families in Kabul alone were organized into eight family firms in the 1830s.[61] Shikarpur was the network center of the widely dispersed but well-integrated Shikarpuri financial communities found throughout Eurasia. The city of Shikarpur played a significant role during the experimental period of Anglo-Durrani relations. The British strategy to open up the Indus River to navigation by flat-bottomed commercial steamships was the lynchpin of the first phase of colonial strategy toward the territories lying north and west of the great river. The Army of the Indus was formed to secure Kabul as a staging ground for traders active in Central Asia who were targeted for rerouting on entry and while in India as a part of the Indus commercial navigation plan. In Kabul, the British expected commercial caravans to be directed to Mithenkote, which was projected to be the main entrepôt along the Indus, but Shikarpur's traditional role as a banking center was also slated to be augmented by a colonially planned market.

CHAPTER 2

Contracting Nomadic Carriage
for an Aquatic Agenda

Sayyid Muhin Shah and the Validation
of Market Profitability

Sayyid Muhin Shah became a nomadic trader in response to unfavorable political conditions in his home village near Qandahar. He met Arthur Conolly in Herat and the two traveled to Delhi where Muhin Shah impressed the Governor General and Viceroy of India, and other high-ranking colonial officials. Muhin Shah was immediately contracted to perform a series of commercial experiments for the British that validated the profitability of exporting Indian and European goods to Afghanistan and Central Asia.[1]

Muhin Shah came from a family of sayyids, or descendants of the Prophet Muhammad, who resided in Peshin, a village about twenty miles north of Quetta on the road to Qandahar. The sayyids' social status carried economic and political benefits. In nineteenth-century Afghanistan and elsewhere in the Muslim world, sayyids, saints, and sufis received monetary offerings from ordinary people and political elites in return for a variety of blessings, consultations, and ritual performances. For example, during his aborted attempt to reclaim the Durrani throne in 1833, Shuja borrowed Rs. 2,000 from a merchant in Sind to use as monetary "blessings" to the Peshin sayyids as he advanced to Qandahar through their village.[2] More important than this single episode is the fact that their sayyid status gave them access to an active and expanding interregional network of Muslim merchants. The Peshin sayyids used their piety, capital, and network connections to become significant actors in the horse and slave trades through Qandahar and Quetta and prominent landholders in Peshin, as the following quotes reveal:

The Syads of Peshin and other small traders carry on the traffic in human beings in Western Afghanistan, and some 400 or 500 are annually disposed of in Kandahar alone. . . . There are a good many African slaves in Qandahar; most of these I find, are brought by pilgrims from Muscat, through Persia and Herat or Seistan, while some . . . are smuggled up with 'kafilas' (caravans) from Bombay. The principal dealer on the Persian line is a Syad (Mir Ali Syad) who has an agent at Herat, while Najak Shah, one of the Peshin Syads, used to be notorious on the Bombay route . . .[3]

The Syads of Peshin, Kakars, Bakhtiars, and Bilochis generally are the tribes chiefly engaged in the horse trade, which usually flourishes for six months of the year, but is stagnant for the hot months and during winter, when the roads are partially closed by snow; about 2,000 or 3,000 are said to pass through Qandahar annually. The chief breeding districts drawn on by these traders are Sarakhs, in Iraq (sic), Maemana in Turkistan, Nur and Kala Nao in Hazara; Daria Gaz and Kalat-i Nadar in Mashad; Gulza and Firozkoh in the Herat district. . . . Animals of much higher blood are to be found in these places; but they are seldom purchased by traders, as there is great chance of such horses being picked out by the Durani Sirdars in transit, at their own valuation, and all together the profit on blood horses is not so great as that on the cheaper breeds.[4]

The sayyids' mercantile precociousness in the horse and slave trades was accompanied by large-scale landholdings in Peshin. However, at the beginning of the nineteenth century, Durrani sardars or petty nobility in and around Qandahar were becoming increasingly prominent. Their rise in economic and political stature resulted from extensive state patronage repeatedly dispensed toward them by various kinsmen who needed to reaffirm and buttress political alliances among tribal constituencies as they replaced each other as dynasts in Kabul.[5] Muhin Shah was an elder in a family of Peshin sayyids whose lands were confiscated by the ever more active and aggressive Durrani nobility concentrated around Qandahar. Muhin Shah joined the ranks of the Afghan nomadic traders in response to adverse local political and economic circumstances that resulted in disenfranchisement from his landed capital.[6] His transition to nomadism was advantaged by being able to tap into the extensive trading networks and circuits populated by other sayyids from Peshin.[7]

In September 1830, Muhin Shah came to Herat to recover a debt the capital from which he reinvested for thirty "tolerably good" horses destined for sale in the Indian markets.[8] While in Herat, he met Arthur Conolly, who was *en route* to becoming the first Englishman to document overland travel from England to India through Russia, Persia, and Afghanistan. Conolly lacked ready cash and was in debt, and Muhin Shah rescued him from a situation of financial insolvency. Through a bill of exchange transaction based on interaction between gold and silver currencies, Muhin Shah acquired a bale of Kashmiri shawls that he promptly sold to pay off Conolly's debt. Muhin Shah assumed the liability of standing as security for the *farengi* or Christian foreigner, which speaks to his interest in escorting the woebegone European to Delhi. Pecuniary compensation surely motivated Muhin Shah because he mentioned with satisfaction to Conolly that about twenty years previously Elphinstone had given his nephew a "handful of money for answering a few questions."[9] It will be shown later in this chapter that Muhin Shah's hopes regarding monetary compensation from colonial authorities were amply fulfilled.

There were approximately fifty quality horses among the four hundred carried by Muhin Shah and the dozen or so other traders, who were mostly Peshin sayyids, in their *qafila* or caravan when it left Herat.[10] Conolly's inquiry about how profits could be made on this generally pathetic lot of animals elicited two responses. First, the Peshin sayyids said in Bombay they dealt with merchants from Basra who could pass their average horses, worth between Rs. 400 and Rs. 500, on to British buyers as Arab-bred for between Rs. 1,200 and Rs. 1,500 per animal.[11] The Afghan nomads' trade in horses from Iran and Central Asia to India during the fall was not the most profitable part of their business enterprise. The Peshin traders said the majority of their profits came from the second or spring leg of their annual interregional trading cycle when they transported and sold Indian and English goods in Afghanistan, Iran, and Central Asia.[12] Conolly claims to have seen a partial accounting of commercial transactions made by Muhin Shah in 1828. That year in Bombay the Peshin sayyid invested Rs. 7,000, mostly toward English piece-cloths, which he transported by boat to Sind and from there overland to Kabul and Bukhara. Conolly claims Muhin Shah made a profit of 110 percent on the goods he sold in Kabul, and between 150 percent and 200 percent profit on the remaining portion he disposed of in Bukhara.[13]

Conolly depended on the services of an Indian sayyid named Karamat Ali to get him from St. Petersburg to Herat.[14] Karamat Ali had been living in Iran for many years and maintained cordial relationships with a number of British officials in that country. Conolly and Karamat Ali were essentially stranded in Herat when Sayyid Muhin Shah came to their rescue. While traveling through Afghanistan to India, Muhin Shah bore all forms of financial and physical responsibility for his two adopted companions and literally delivered them as human cargo to Delhi in mid-January 1831. Conolly's gratitude toward Muhin Shah is amply expressed at the end of his travelogue narrative:

> The reader will have formed some idea of the care, and of the difficulty, with which Syud Muheen Shah conveyed us (Conolly and Karamat Ali) from Heraut to Dehlee, but I could not in words express the kindness and delicacy of this man's conduct towards us during the whole of the journey. Wherever he met friends, they laboured to convince him that I was an imposter, and he was exposed to extreme vexation and danger on my account; yet he never relaxed his endeavours to promote my safety and comfort, he paid all of our expenses, and avoided alluding to my debt to him. I have to express my gratitude to many different Englishmen in different parts of India, who have made a point of showing attention to this friend, and I am happy in the assurance that he is every way satisfied with the result of his generous conduct towards a stranger in distress.[15]

Conolly alludes to the fact that almost immediately on their arrival in Delhi a significant relationship began to form between the Peshin sayyid and British officials. Muhin Shah entered colonial bureaucratic discourse at a fortuitous time. Eleven months before Muhin Shah deposited Conolly and Karamat Ali in Delhi the Secret Committee of the British East India Company's Court of Directors issued an important directive. The Secret Committee budgeted Rs. 50,000 for the transmission of a consignment of "European and Indian goods to a principal city between Persia and the Indus to promote commerce and try the markets" of Central Asia.[16] The anti-Russian British policy toward Afghanistan is articulated in the following passage that helped to inaugurate the so-called "Great Game" of Anglo-Russian colonial intrigue and competition over Persia and Afghanistan. In order to thwart recent Russian "advances" in Central Asia, the British resolved to:

> . . . use the Indus route to undermine Russian commercial enterprises in Central Asia by transporting cheaper and higher quality British goods to Cabul so as to secure a large portion of the Central Asian trade. The object being to introduce English goods not Englishmen into Central Asia.[17]

There was a near temporal coincidence between the Secret Committee's declaration of a commerce-based colonial strategy for Central Asia which led to the solicitation of certain forms of market intelligence to achieve their anti-Russian commercial goals, and Muhin Shah's entry into the colonial field of vision. In the end, between 1831 and 1835 Muhin Shah performed a series of four commercial experiments for the British that validated the profitability of sending Indian and European goods to Afghanistan and Central Asia via two different sets of routes. The Company's patronage of Muhin Shah's commercial activities generated the trade statistics used to justify the British invasion of Afghanistan in 1839. Muhin Shah provided British officials with the prerequisite data necessary to launch the great colonial project of transforming the Indus River into a commercial thoroughfare for flat-bottomed steamships docking at the inland riverine port of Mithenkote.[18]

The Army of the Indus was a manifestation of the colonial imagination then dominated by the Indus commercial navigation project. The first Anglo-Afghan war was about issues much larger than Shuja and his Durrani dynastic privilege. The British reinvigoration of the Durrani monarchy was a lower-level concern in a hierarchy of considerations dominated by interregional and global commercial aspirations and considerations. An anti-Russian political posture in South Asia, Eurasia, and globally, also weighed more heavily in the British colonial mind-set regarding Kabul and Afghanistan than Shuja's political career. The first colonial revamping of the Durrani monarchy was a less significant issue in the British Imperial worldview than the strong cultural emphasis on science, in this case the technological abilities to manipulate the general course, seasonal flow, and depth of the Indus in order to accommodate commercial steamers.

Sayyid Muhin Shah's British-sponsored commercial experiments between South and Central Asia covered a pair of latitudinal trajectories of trade through Afghanistan, one through Qandahar and another through Peshawar. The southernmost of the two east-west route series linked Qandahar with Mashhad and Herat to the northwest, and Quetta, Karachi, Shikarpur, and Bombay to the southeast. The northerly route sequence linked Peshawar and Kabul with Mazar-e Sharif (Balkh), and Bukhara to the northwest, and Lahore, Amritsar, Delhi, and Calcutta to the southeast. Nomadic traders such as Muhin Shah could and did use both trajectories during the two seasonal movements comprising a full year's migration cycle, but strutting north or south between the two constellations of route segments during one migratory period was less common. The British intended to alter the trajectory of the southern east-west route sequence by diverting a greater portion of the trade north from Qandahar to Kabul. The north-south route between Qandahar and Kabul was considered viable by the British despite that road's reputation as notoriously treacherous for non-Ghalzi Pashtun nomadic traders.[19]

TABLE 2.1

*Summary of Sayyid Muhin Shah's First British-Sponsored
Commercial Experiment in Central Asia, 1831–32*

Articles	Invoice price at Bombay	Sold at Qandahar	Sold at Kabul	Sold at Bukhara
Light blue broadcloth	Rs. 2.8 per yard	Rs. 5.13		
Small flowered chintz	Rs. 5 per piece of 25 yards	Rs. 17.8	Rs. 15.13	Rs. 16.4
Striped chintz	Rs. 9.6 per piece of 25 yards	Rs. 22.5	Rs. 23.5	Rs. 22.12
Large printed chintz	Rs. 16 per piece of 25 yards	Rs. 30.4	Rs. 31.1	
Cambric	Rs. 12 per piece of 12 yards	Rs. 20		
Plain muslin	Rs. 10 per piece of 22 yards	Rs. 21.1	Rs. 21.1	
Flowered muslin	Rs. 5 per piece of 10 yards	Rs. 10.15	Rs. 9.2	
Long cloth	Rs. 12.6 per piece of 35 yards	Rs. 39.1	Rs. 29.3	
Aloran (?) bolstered to be shawl stuff	Rs. 1.12 per yard	Rs. 2.7	Rs. 3.2	
Satin	Rs. 18 per piece of 22 yards	Rs. 35	Rs. 35.7	
Muslin "a" (illegible)	Rs. 4.8 per piece of 10 yards	Rs. 9.2	Rs. 9.15	
Muslin "b" (illegible)	Rs. 5 per piece of 20 yards	Rs. 8.5	Rs. 10.13	

Sources: "Commercial and Political Resources of Central Asia," NAI, Foreign S.C., November 25, 1831, Proceeding Nos. 7–12. See also NAI, Foreign P.C., September 5, 1836, Proceeding Nos. 9–19, cited as both "Trevelyan's Note on Commerce of Afghanistan" and "Trevelyan's Note on Trade of Cabul."

The Peshin sayyid's first British-sponsored trading excursion from South to Central Asia, summarized in Table 2.1, was initiated approximately eight months after he deposited Conolly and Sayyid Karamat Ali in Delhi. During the interim period, Muhin Shah communicated with and made a favorable impression on a number of high-ranking colonial officials, including the Assistant Commissioner of Delhi, C. E. Trevelyan, and the Governor General of India, William Bentinck.[20] For his "pecuniary assistance and protection" of Conolly the British Indian Government offered Sayyid Muhin Shah an official reward of Company Rs. 20,000, of which only Rs. 12,000 was accepted and "faithfully repaid."[21] The reward was actually an interest-free British loan advanced without any form of security deposit that was designed to "further Muhin Shah's commercial activities and to allow him to benefit from increased commercial capital" in keeping with the Secret Committee's directive.[22]

Muhin Shah invested his initial dose of British speculation capital in a variety of textiles that he purchased in Calcutta. These were popular consumption materials, not luxury items. It is unclear whether the Peshin sayyid traveled overland or by ship to Bombay from where he accompanied the goods by sea to Karachi or one of the smaller ports in Sind, then overland to Bela, Kelat, Qandahar, Kabul, and Bukhara. He sold the British Indian textiles in Kabul and Bukhara. The following is a narration of the first commercial experiment concluded between Sayyid Muhin Shah and the British:

> The Syud carried an investment of broad cloths, chintz, cambrics, long cloths, satins, etc. from Bombay via Bayla and Kelat to Candahar and Cabul where, though he had to pay duties, etc. amounting to 12 per cent, he disposed of his goods some at 200 per cent and the greater part at 100 per cent above his price at Bombay. . . . The successful speculation of Syud Muhim Shah, the companion of Lt. Conolly's journey, gives ground for believing that English manufactures when brought into competition with Russian should in a few years completely drive the latter from the markets not only of Afghanistan, but all of Central Asia.[23]

Despite incomplete documentation, the Peshin sayyid's first trial carriage of British Indian goods from South to Central Asia was received as a resounding success. He was rewarded for his honesty in executing the first experiment by another loan of the same amount and on the same terms. Muhin Shah repeated the same cycle with the same commodities during the following year, the only difference being his catering to shifting consumer demands by bringing a greater volume of chintz with large flowery patterns for disposal in Kabul on the second journey.[24] The first two joint ventures between Muhin Shah and the British validated the profitability of routing goods to Kabul and Bukhara through Qandahar, the key market node in the southern series trade route segments traversing Afghanistan. The use of water transport from Bombay in the initial pair of Muhin Shah's company-contrived commercial experiments reflects the burgeoning colonial emphasis on the Indus navigation project.

The British underwrote and oversaw at least two additional commercial experiments conducted by the Peshin sayyid to whom Connolly owed his life. The third and fourth commercial experiments regarding the export of British Indian commodities to Central Asia were entirely overland affairs, and they were more thoroughly documented than the first pair of partially aquatic ventures in 1831 and 1832. The second pair of official British experiments in Central

Asia and evaluations of those markets via the services of a contracted Afghan nomad occurred in 1834 and 1835. These two commercial experiments validated the profitability of the northern route sequence through Peshawar to Kabul and Bukhara. The results of Muhin Shah's third and fourth experiments were fully implicated in the colonial attempt to develop the Mithenkote market as the lynchpin of the Indus navigation project (see later in this chapter).

A conspicuously unfavorable opinion of Muhin Shah and his activities accounts for the repetition of the transactions executed along the northern strictly overland route from Calcutta to Bukhara. Claude Wade, the influential British Political Agent in Ludiana, cast the solitary dissenting voice on the Peshin sayyid's ability to "ascertain whether British goods can compete with Russian goods in markets of Bukhara by way of India."[25] His reasons were twofold. First, Wade felt there was a methodological shortcoming in the experiment because Sayyid Muhin Shah did not accompany the goods for the duration of their marketing life. Muhin Shah did not escort the British Indian commodities from Kabul to Bukhara and Wade felt that the decision not to see the experiment fully through to its proper conclusion:

> . . . redounded neither to his zeal nor his discretion (and that) the object of the Government's experiment has been defeated by his employment (and that) no fair conclusion can be drawn by an experiment so conducted.[26]

Wade also accused the Peshin sayyid of a form of abuse of privilege. The Ludiana Agent objected that the first northern experiment was concluded in Bukhara without Muhin Shah's supervision. Wade was offended that after abrogating his duties to fully execute the British commercial experiment Muhin Shah asked him for a recommendation for a proposed sale of horses to Ranjit Singh.[27] Wade's appeal to ultra-orthodox commercial methodology adhered among colonial policy makers who satisfied his stated concerns by advancing another Rs. 12,000 to Muhin Shah with instructions to improve his written accounting of the colonially contrived transactions.[28] Wade eventually came to believe the sayyid's claim that the reason for his subcontracting the Kabul to Bukhara portion of the 1834 experiment was illness that forced him to retire to his home village of Peshin.[29] There is no data indicating variation in the commodities, routes, or prices between the third and fourth ventures, so it is reasonable to assume they were exactly repeated. The apprehension expressed by Wade about the third speculation helps to explain the far more thorough documentation of Muhin Shah's fourth and final British commercial experi-

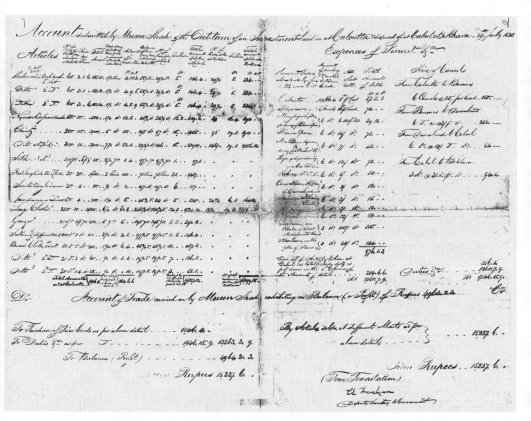

FIG. 2.1. Full Accounting of Sayyid Muhin Shah's Fourth British-Sponsored Commercial Experiment in Central Asia, 1835

ment, summarized in Table 2.2 (Figure 2.1 provides a full accounting of this experiment).

With all expenses in this accounting (items I–IV) being Rs. 13,263, and the proceeds from sales (items V and VI) totaling Rs. 18,227, the final joint commercial venture between Muhin Shah and the British yielded Rs. 4,964, or approximately 37.42 percent profit.[30] In order to establish the feasibility and profitability of exporting British Indian commodities, particularly textiles, to Central Asia and thus undermine the Russian presence in that region, colonial officials depended on communication and commercial interaction with Muhin Shah. Muhin Shah appears as a rather typical Afghan nomadic trader whose fortuitous encounter with Conolly resulted in extended and extensive British patronage of his commercial activity. The Peshin sayyid surely benefited from

TABLE 2.2

Summary of Sayyid Muhin Shah's Fourth British-Sponsored
Commercial Experiment in Central Asia, 1835

I. Rs. 11,416 toward Muhin Shah's purchase of cloth piece goods at Calcutta[a]
II. Rs. 976.1 toward 13 transit tolls and related extractions[b]
III. Rs. 586.8 toward the hire of camels[c]
IV. Rs. 284.6 toward a 2.5 percent exaction on all goods at Kabul[d]
V. Rs. 9,827.12 derived from the sale of goods in Kabul[e]
VI. Rs. 8,399.15 derived from the sale of goods in Bukhara

Source: "Results of Muhim Shah's Commercial Speculation," NAI, Foreign P.C., August 17, 1835, Proceeding Nos. 70–73.

[a]Ibid. The items and quantities were: "60 pieces of shubnum (or book muslin) of the first sort, 60 pieces of shubnum of the second sort, 60 pieces of shubnum of the third sort, 50 pieces of nynisook (or Jaconet) muslin, 200 pieces of chintz, 300 pieces of striped chintz, 100 yards of silk net, 80 pieces of red English town cloth, 20 pieces of imitation jamawar, 50 pieces of jamdanee (or lenoo), 250 pieces of long cloth, 200 yards of gauze, 100 yards of satin of different sorts, 50 yards of broadcloth of the first sort, 20 yards of broadcloth of the second sort, 20 yards of broadcloth of the third sort."

[b]Ibid. The points and/or persons collecting transit tolls were, from east to west, "Calcutta, Bikaner, Moughgurh, etc. (dependency of Bhawulpore), Bhawulpore, Multan (a dependency of the Sikh territory), Leya (a dependency of Multan), Kehree (a dependency of Multan), Omer Khan (Afghan of Darabund), Sarwar Khan (Afghan of {Tuck}??), Jagree (??), Babian (an *ellaka* of Dost Muhammad Khan), Khullum (in the *zilla* of Kundoos)." I have rendered these persons and places as close as possible to how they appear in the source cited, and indicated any ambiguities with question marks. More will be said about Sarwar Khan and Omar Khan in the next section. Tuck as rendered in the original is today's Tank; Babian, Bamian; Jaghree, Jaghori.

[c]Ibid. Six camels were hired for the Calcutta to Benaras, Benaras to Darraband, and Darraband to Kabul stages of the journey, and three camels were needed for the final segment between Kabul and Bukhara.

[d]Ibid. This exaction represents the *chihil yak* or one-in-forty exaction claimed by Muslim rulers. The Islamicate chihil yak shown here differs from the exactions claimed by Sarwar and Omar Khan in Tank and Darraband, respectively (see earlier). Sarwar Khan charged Rs. 3 and Omar Khan Rs. 2 on each of the six camels employed by Muhin Shah that traversed their territories.

[e]Ibid. Of the sixteen cloth groups, five were disposed of in equal amounts in Kabul and Bukhara, eleven were not. See Yapp (1980), ch. 6 for more on the Indus River in colonial Kabul-Afghanistan policy considerations.

the repeated infusions of colonial capital into his resource base. For our purposes, it is more significant that Muhin Shah provided the British with vital commercial information that was deployed as the empirical foundation and economic rationale of a much larger colonial program, namely, the Indus navigation project.

Kabul, the Indus River, and Global Trade

During the experimental period of Anglo-Afghan relations under consideration here, British officials most commonly used the term "Lohani" in reference to Afghan nomad traders. Lohanis were the central figures in the Indus navigation project and the Mithenkote market scheme underpinning it. Communication between the British and the Lohanis about the proposed Mithenkote market was multifaceted. This section deals with the British advertisement of their Indus-based commercial agenda among the Lohanis through intermediaries stationed in Kabul.[31]

Muhin Shah's British-sponsored commercial experiments and the Mithenkote scheme were key elements of the colonial project to "open up" the Indus River for commercial navigation. During the nineteenth century, the British used epistemological and genealogical connections to ancient Greece to construct their political lineage. The British regularly claimed direct political descent from Alexander the Great and the democratic traditions of ancient Greece. Officials and intellectuals in England and the colonies practiced this Greek-centered political history narration. For example, in India colonial officials regularly invoked Alexander as one who appreciated the potential of the mighty Indus. The affiliation felt by British officials in India to Alexander was reflected in the following comment on the Indus navigation project: "to establish a direct intercourse between the Indus and Babylonia and Egypt was Alexander's project, and in a later age the plan was revived by some English speculators."[32]

During his early missions (1830 and 1831), Alexander Burnes gathered the scientific, social, and commercial data used by colonial policy makers to inaugurate the Indus project. Burnes's later appointments and roles in Kabul (1836 and 1839) represent the British attempt to foster the political conditions in Afghanistan deemed necessary for the riverine commercial navigation scheme to succeed.[33] There was a vigorous internal debate among colonial authorities about the most suitable location to develop a large inland port capable of handling the anticipated exponential increase in commercial activity on and around the Indus. Although Burnes favored Dera Ghazi Khan and Macnaghten preferred Dera Ismail Khan, Mithenkote was the site ultimately chosen for the establishment of a major inland port on the Indus.[34] The Mithenkote market scheme was the cornerstone of the Indus navigation project, and the Lohanis' attendance was essential for Mithenkote to succeed. Referring to the Lohanis as the "chief carriers of the trade" between Bukhara, Kabul, and India, British officials claimed that:

> ... [b]y establishing a market at Mithenkote for products of India (the Lohanis) will get a reduced price and suffer less inconvenience, delay and trouble arising from being away from their own frontier. Also (British Indian) merchants will have facility for bartering their merchandise for the Bokhara and Cabul markets, which will extend and develop commercial resources of Hindustan with those countries making a mutual interest and dependency not hitherto exerted.[35]

One of the ways that the British advertised their Indus commerce agenda was to write directly to Dost Muhammad and other Durrani political elites in Kabul. In 1835, Macnaghten, then the Secretary to the Governor General of India, wrote directly to Dost Muhammad Khan, Nawab Jabar Khan, and other influential people in Kabul.[36] Macnaghten posited a commercial affinity between the British and the Afghans and expressed a desire that the Durrani government use its resources and influence to direct merchants from Kabul and Qandahar to the Indus:

> It is the sincere desire of my nation to cultivate a close friendship with the Afghans, and this is one of the principal objects I had in view in the formation of the late arrangements for re-opening the navigation of the Indus. The Afghans, like ourselves, are a people fond of commercial pursuits, and it is hoped that our mutual intercourse will now become much closer than it ever has before. A direct and easy communication with the merchant vessels of England has been opened by the channel of the Indus and there is nothing to prevent the merchants of Kandahar and Cabul from bringing the wares of their own country and the more distant marts of Bukhara and Central Asia to the Indus, and receiving in return chintzes, metals, and other manufactured goods of England.[37]

The British believed exerting leverage in Kabul was the best way to direct the Lohanis to Mithenkote. In addition to state-to-state or official "diplomatic" correspondence, the British relied heavily on their Newswriter in Kabul to circulate information about the Indus navigation project among the Lohanis and other interregional traders using channels of popular communication. Sayyid Karamat Ali, who traveled with Conolly and Muhin Shah from Herat to Delhi, occupied the important post of British Newswriter in Kabul from 1831 to 1834. Karamat Ali's service to the British in Kabul involved both the collection and dissemination of information on a wide variety of subjects. Regarding Mithenkote, the Hindustani sayyid, was instructed:

> . . . to tell all the merchants in his quarter of the establishment of a mart at Mithenkote and the advantage of their finding a market at that place for the fruits of Cabul (and to) inform all the merchants of those countries that whatever quantity of fruits they may bring to the aforementioned mart, they will find purchase for it among the merchants of Hindustan and other parts who will probably supply them with any kinds of goods they may require. By this means they will be saved the trouble and inconvenience to which they are exposed to on a long journey through the Punjab to Hindustan.[38]

Karamat Ali's colonial employment was based on his literacy, and his textual skills were marketable and apparently in demand. Karamat Ali was dismissed from his position as the British Newswriter in Kabul partly for hiring out his scribal services to Nawab Jabar Khan who was the brother of the Amir of Kabul, Dost Muhammad (ruled 1826–36 and 1842–63).[39] Another reason for Karamat Ali's dismissal from Kabul was his alleged failure to adequately disseminate Mithenkote market propaganda to the Lohanis.[40] Mithenkote lay in allied Sikh territory, and the colonial effort to transform the site into a high-volume inland commercial port resulted partly from a British desire to displace Shikarpur as a commercial and banking center. Shikarpur was then under the political purview of the Sind Amirs who were generally not cooperating with the increasing colonial inundation of the Indus.[41]

British policy makers conceived Mithenkote as the midway market between South and Central Asia, and as mutually accessible for traders from each region. Rather than a single substantially longer annual commercial migration eastward as far as Calcutta, the Lohanis were imagined as being able to run multiple shorter trading circuits to the banks of the Indus during one year. The goal was a constant rather than seasonal exchange of Afghan fruit and other commodities from inside and beyond the Hindu Kush at Mithenkote. Similarly, the British conjured North Indian products as continually flowing overland westward to the collection point of Ludiana, then down the Sutlej river south to Mithenkote, from where the Lohanis would incessantly transport and market the goods in Afghanistan and Central Asia. European and other commodities, such as Chinese tea and Caribbean sugar, were envisioned as being shipped from Bombay up the Indus to the proposed entrepot for transnational and global traders at Mithenkote.

In 1835, Charles Masson assumed the duties, although not the title, of British Newswriter in Kabul from Sayyid Karamat Ali.[42] Masson was instructed to contact Mullah Badr al-Din to begin the process of routing the Lohanis to Mithenkote from Kabul. With a portfolio valued between 10 and 20 lakhs of rupees, Mullah Badr al-Din was considered the "richest" merchant in Kabul, was honorifically referred to as *baba* or father by Dost Muhammad, and figured prominently in the trade between Russia and Bukhara.[43] Mullah Badr al-Din's son Khair al-Din also enjoyed a glowing mercantile reputation in Central Asia. Mullah Khair al-Din was among the most prominent and prosperous merchants of Bukhara, and considered the "greatest" merchant in Kabul.[44] Khair al-Din held the farm to the transit duties of Kabul, and this was perhaps the most attractive element of his resource base from the British perspective.[45] Between at least August 1834 and April 1836, Muhin Shah, Karamat Ali, and Masson facilitated communication between Mullah Khair al-Din and a number of colonial authorities including the British Indian Governor General and Wade. This correspondence, portions of which are reproduced below, involved an exchange of gifts and panegyric letters peppered with reference to Mithenkote and "free trade" rhetoric.[46] It was reported that with his immense wealth Mullah Khair al-Din:

> ... wishes to establish a factory in British territory ... (and) will lend any sum of money which may be required by the English who may visit Cabul or Bokhara ... (and) also offered to supply (the British Newswriter in Kabul) or any person recommended by him any sum of rupees that may be wanted ... (and) all that he wants from them is protection.[47]

Wade responded to these overtures by encouraging the Mithenkote initiative:

> A project for opening the navigation of the Indus and Sutlej has lately been formed and an extensive mart is to be established at Mithenkote. Lieutenant Mackeson an officer on the part of the British Government has been appointed to protect and superintend the interests of merchants and afford them every facility in trading with that place. Agreeably to my invitation the Lohanee merchants have resorted to that mart and began to barter their goods with the merchants of Hindustan. Every kind of merchandize the produce of China and Europe will be had there. I would therefore suggest that you should inform your agents as well as other merchants in your quarter to conduct their sales and purchases hereafter at Mithenkote by which means they will avoid the inconvenience and trouble to which they are now liable in trading by the Punjab to Hindustan.[48]

To which Khair al-Din replied:

> Information shall be given by me to all the merchants of these countries, and I will endeavor to induce them to resort to Mithenkot as a general entrepot of commerce. Verily! You have formed a scheme no less beneficial to the people at large than to the mercantile community.[49]

Masson clearly articulated the tactical importance of harnessing the Lohanis to the Mithenkote market scheme, and how Kabul would benefit from such a relationship. He recognized the interrelationships between the Lohanis, Mithenkote, and Kabul, and communicated information about each element in a series of reports and letters constituting a significant elaboration and justification of the British commerce-based strategy toward Russia in Afghanistan and Central Asia. Over roughly the previous decade before becoming a *bona fide* British Agent, Masson was not in colonial service, but he spent considerable amounts of time in and around Kabul where he cultivated local relationships and became a repository of knowledge and information in his own right. He argued for the necessity of prompt and strong British advocacy of the Mithenkote market among the Lohanis by referencing the Russian sponsorship of a competing commercial fair at Nangkishlak on the northern banks of the Oxus river in Turkistan.[50] When considering ways to contact the Lohanis and attach them to the Mithenkote market, Masson specifically referenced Muhin Shah's successful commercial speculations in Central Asia and the sayyid's roots in the strategic Peshin valley:

> ... [t]hat the Lohanis be used to introduce British goods into Kabul, no one is better placed to facilitate this than Syad Mohin Sha because he is a Syad from Peshin through which the route from Mithenkote to Qandahar goes. He is well disposed and anxious to serve the Government and his pervious commercial loans were successful experiments in introducing British goods into Central Asia.[51]

Masson indicated the Lohanis traveled *en masse* for self-protection and that they did not pool their capital or engage in collective commercial action.[52] He characterized Lohani trading activity as measured and frugal and involving regular but small transactions determined by the conservative disposition of individual carriers. According to Masson, the Lohanis were prone to:

> ... entrust small investments to individuals among them ... no other traders can afford to bring or carry merchandize at so cheap a rate, and they have therefore no competitors in the markets they frequent able to undersell them ... their caution and perhaps apathy cause them to form their investments in such goods as they know will sell, and by no means of such as may sell, seeming to prefer a certain but small profit to a large but doubtful one.[53]

Despite their conservative fiscal practices, Masson believed that at least some Lohanis would recognize the profitability of handling "such articles as it might be desirous (for the British) to introduce into the markets of Kabul."[54] Arguing the Lohanis already monopolized the trade in specifically Indian commodities such as "spices, indigo, muslins, fine sugar, drugs, etc.,"[55] Masson articulated an agenda of attaching them to Mithenkote and the Indus scheme for the purpose of conveying more profitable British manufactures to Central Asia. The commodities produced in Europe specifically targeted for Lohani transport from Mithenkote to Kabul and Bukhara included:

Chintzes, fine calicos, muslins, shawls etc. of British manufacture, broad cloth, vel-
vet, paper, cuttery, China ware, gold and silver lace, gold thread, buttons, needles,
sewing silks and cotton thread, iron bars, copper, tin, brass, quicksilver, iron and steel
wire, looking glasses and a multitude of various little articles conducive to comfort
and convenience.[56]

The British were confident in the ability of European commodities to pen-
etrate and restructure the appetites of Central Asian consumers. Masson proffered a list of Russian goods found in the bazaars of Kabul which he dissected
item-by-item in order to demonstrate the superiority of comparable English
commodities on each count.[57] His attention to paper is typical:

> It is singular that not a sheet of English manufactured writing paper can be found in
> the bazaar of Kabul while Russian foolscap, of coarse inferior quality abounds, and it
> is generally employed in the public departments.[58]

Masson expressed a clear belief in Kabul's subsidiary benefit from the Mithenkote plan:

> The opening of the navigation of the Indus, and the establishment of British facto-
> ries at Mithenkot cannot fail to have salutary effect in increasing the extent and fa-
> cility of commercial transactions between India and Kabul and of inducing a much
> larger consumption of British manufactured goods both in Kabul and Turkistan.[59]

Kabul occupied a central place in the British strategy toward Central Asia.
The city was important as a site to exchange information with the Lohani nomadic traders about the burgeoning inland river port-market at Mithenkote.
To disseminate Mithenkote market propaganda among the Lohanis colonial
officials exploited their communicative links with local merchants including
Mullah Khair al-Din and other British Agents and Newswriters stationed in
Kabul such as Karamat Ali and Masson. Masson's reports specifically addressed
the interrelationship between the Lohanis and Mithenkote and the amenability
of Kabul and other Central Asian markets to select British Indian and European commodities over Russian ones. Collectively, his official correspondence
reaffirms and highlights the British need to deal directly with Afghan nomad
traders to attain their political and commercial goals in Afghanistan and Central Asia. When the British decided to invade and occupy Kabul to actualize
the Mithenkote and Indus plans, they communicated directly and extensively
with two Lohani nomad chiefs about an array of subjects. The most significant
realm of interaction between the Lohani chiefs and colonial officials concerned
the provision of carriage services for the Army of Indus.

Sarwar Khan Lohani, a Tribal Khan
in Colonial Service

There was extensive communication and interaction between the British and Lohani chiefs before and during the first Anglo-Afghan war. British agents and officials contacted a number of Lohani chiefs to convey information about the proposed Mithenkote market. However, the colonial riverine port scheme, like the greater Indus navigation project, never came to fruition because of the resounding British defeat during the first Afghan war. The markets and masses in Kabul and Bukhara did not experience the lopsided commercial competition between English and Russian goods the colonial imagination envisioned to result from the inland Indus port. Although British agents and officers and the Lohani chiefs communicated extensively about Mithenkote, the market never developed. Colonial authorities disseminated false or misleading information about the market on a number of occasions. For example, during his 1834 communication with Mullah Khair al-Din about Mithenkote, Wade claimed the Lohanis accepted his invitation to attend the new Indus market.[60] However, this claim is contradicted in a letter written to Wade in 1838 by Omar Khan, "a principal Lohani chief":

> A few years ago you informed me as well as other merchants that you would establish an entrepot at Mithenkot and open the navigation between that place and Bombay which the people anxiously expected, but as nothing has hitherto come to pass they appear to be disheartened.[61]

Wade later compromised the veracity of his earlier statement about the Lohanis' attendance of the Mithenkote market. In his own words penned in 1838:

> ... finding no adequate efforts made by our merchants to meet their wishes the Lohanis remain disappointed in the realization of the benefits which have been held out to them and are likely to remain so until the merchants of Bombay can be induced to consign cargoes of goods suited to the wants of these people. There are many motives of self interest which operate to deter the great merchants of India and partly those of Shikarpur from using any effectual exertions to exempt the Lohanis from the necessity of visiting their own marts.[62]

In the British view, the reluctance of Indian merchants to meet Afghan nomads on the Indus was the main impediment to the development of Mithenkote. A Lohani chief expressed interest in the Mithenkote project, but ordinary Indian merchants did not. Omar Khan Lohani was the brother of Sarwar Khan

Lohani who was identified by Elphinstone and Masson as a prominent tribal chief in the daman plains of the Sulaiman mountains in the area of Dera Ismail Khan on the west bank of the Indus.[63] Various forms of leadership existed among the tribes of this area. For example, Elphinstone noted a number of expressions of the single institution of *chelwashtee* or the temporary magistracy granted to an individual by the *maliks* or heads of families in each *khel* or lineage among the "pastoral merchant carriers" of the daman.[64] Elphinstone also discussed how external political involvement led to the emergence of a chief among the daman tribes who was so strong as to warrant the military despot label. He narrated how Sarwar Khan Lohani combined local cultural institutions and Durrani political patronage to reclaim, consolidate, and expand the authority and resources purportedly usurped from his father by a constellation of competing local elites.[65]

Roughly twenty years later, when Masson arrived on the scene, Sarwar Khan had developed the trappings of a local potentate.[66] Sarwar Khan was then publicly voicing the superiority of settled agricultural pursuits over nomadic commercial endeavors. His fortress was under constant expansion and upgrade, and there were over two hundred women in his harem. He taxed travelers and local producers, dammed and diverted the Gomal River to irrigate his lands, held a public court where he received political agents and diplomatic guests, and constructed a cannon foundry and other industrial workshops. Sarwar Khan and his elder sons maintained gardens where wine was drunk, poetry read, and music played.[67] Sarwar Khan Lohani was a nomadic tribal chief whose prosperity and influence were very well recognized by colonial authorities.

In 1832, Burnes met Omar Khan and Sarwar Khan Lohani in Bukhara. Burnes referred to the brothers as "two of the principal men among the Lohanees engaged in carrying on the trade from India to Cabul and Turkistan."[68] The Lohani brothers are also referenced in the final accounting of Muhin Shah's company-sponsored commercial speculations in Central Asia. These records show Omar Khan in Darraband collecting Rs. 2 and Sarwar Khan in Tank receiving Rs. 3 on each of the six camels employed by the Peshin sayyid to execute the British commercial experiment between Calcutta and Bukhara.[69] In Darraband, Muhin Shah either exchanged or rehired camels.[70] The area under the control of the Lohani brothers was a market for transport animals, and a general supply center for interregional commercial caravans. Mohan Lal reported that on being funneled out of the Gomal Pass to the daman, Lohani caravans arrived in Majingorah, a place:

... ruled by Sarwar Khan Lohani, to whom two rupees and eight annas are paid on each of the loads and sometimes he extorts large sums of money from the merchants. In Majingorah they buy provisions and passing through Zarkani they come to Daraband where their family remains under the protection of Omar Khan until they return.[71]

While stationed in Kabul from September 1836 to October 1838 Burnes actively promoted the Mithenkote market, and secured the services of the Lohani brothers to transport commodities to the inland Indus port.[72] As the Lohanis' annual commercial migration to Hindustan commenced in October 1837, Burnes drew very favorable attention to Sarwar Khan and Omar Khan in a letter to the Governor General of India.[73] Sarwar Khan had just come from Bukhara to Kabul and was preparing for the move to India where he intended to seek out the Governor General. While drawing attention to Russian commercial initiatives in Central Asia, Burnes notified his superiors that:

> ... [a]fter the anxiety displayed by the Russians to show every attention to the Afghan merchants visiting their fairs, I have felt myself more than solicitous to exhibit to these men the equal interest the British Government takes in their welfare. ... I avail myself of the opportunity to introduce to your notice, Sarwar Khan and his brother Omar Khan, two of the principal men among the Lohanees engaged in carrying on the trade from India to Cabul and Turkistan. Sarwar Khan is the individual who acted so very friendly a part when I visited Bokhara in 1832, from where he has just come and where he still enjoys much of the confidence of the Kosh Begee or first minister of the King. ... Sarwar Khan is a man well acquainted with all mercantile affairs here and in Toorkistan, and if His Lordship wishes a *viva voce* of them and other subjects, I am certain Sarwar Khan's intelligence will enable him to give satisfactory information.[74]

The collusion of interests between Burnes and the Lohani brothers was extensive and multifaceted. In the spring of 1838 Burnes arranged for Sarwar Khan and Omar Khan to deliver three hundred sheep and eleven rams to Mithenkote for shipment to the Governor of Bombay.[75] In order to secure their passage through Sikh-controlled territory, Burnes provided the Lohani chiefs with his own personal passport and a letter from the Governor of Multan, within whose jurisdiction Mithenkote lay. When Sarwar Khan and Omar Khan reached Dera Ghazi Khan, then also under Sikh control, the animals were taxed, which the Lohanis perceived to be an illegal and unjustified act. The Lohanis wrote to Burnes about the incident:

Jawahar Mull, the ruler of that place, behaved very ill towards us. We showed him your passport and a letter to Sarwar Mull . . . but he paid no attention to their contents nor believed that the sheep were sent for the Governor of Bombay. He made us to pay him Rs. 427 as a tax on the sheep which was very shameful.[76]

It is unclear how this issue was resolved, but the British attachment to Lohani carriers became even more evident during the occupation of eastern and southern Afghanistan. The Army of the Indus relied heavily on the transportation services provided by the Lohanis, and the dependence of colonial forces upon Sarwar Khan is particularly noticeable during the buildup to and the early stages of the invasion. To prepare for the invasion and during their occupation of Kabul, Qandahar, and parts of eastern and southern Afghanistan, the British depended on Burnes's ability to communicate with and secure the services of Omar Khan and Sarwar Khan.[77] At the end of September 1838, Burnes was reassigned from Kabul to a special mission to Kelat.[78] Before proceeding to Kelat, Burnes was directed to Shikarpur, where he was:

> . . . authorized to draw bills totaling 19 lakhs of rupees . . . (and) arrange for supplies in advance of the army in conjunction with communication officers and to use his abilities to secure provisions from certain chiefs and the Lohanees.[79]

Relations between the British and the territory being transformed into Afghanistan were taking a critical turn. In November 1838, a force that would later come to be known as the Army of the Indus was gathering at Ferozpore in the Punjab. At this time, roughly a year after Burnes first brought the utility, if not indispensability, of the Lohanis to his superiors' attention, Sarwar Khan and Omar Khan received a letter directly from the Governor General of India. The Governor General wrote to announce the invasion and solicit the Lohani chiefs' assistance regarding transportation and supply services for the colonial army:

> At this time it is not concealed that an Army composed of British troops and those of Shah Shooja ool-Mulk is about to enter Afghanistan by the route of Shikarpore to place Shooja on the throne of his ancestors.
>
> Having the greatest desire that no injury should befall men so respectable as you and your brother I thought it right to let you know this that injury may not accrue you.
>
> I have deputed Captain Burnes to Shikarpore to make arrangements in carriage and provisions for the army and as that officer tells me you are the well wishers of this Government and have it in your power to give assistance at this time, I request

you to attend to the wishes of that officer, and it will hereafter give me great pleasure to reward those who perform good service.

The going and coming I am sorry to report is now shut up between Cabol and India, but by the blessings of providence, enemies will soon be dispersed and the roads of commerce become passable. This will give me the highest pleasure, as I have no wish nearer my heart than the encouragement of trade, and the protection of enterprising merchants like you and your tribe.[80]

Faithful to Burnes's expectations and the Governor General's invitation, Sarwar Khan arrived in Shikarpur to market his carriage services to the British. In May 1839, the British Political Agent in Shikarpur, W. J. Eastwick, reported having made a cash advance of Rs. 1,06,063 to Sarwar Khan. This payment covered the hire of 3,098 camels and security men for the animals and the baggage they carried.[81] In this transaction, Sarwar Khan was contracted to carry supplies from Shikarpur to the Army of the Indus that was then camped near Qandahar. The vast preponderance, nearly 98 percent, of the money received by Sarwar Khan on this occasion went toward the employment of camels and their human supervisors.[82] Colonial officials valued the combination of informality and constancy of their loyal Lohani, who in this instance arrived in Shikarpur without an "official account of the terms of the agreement" that brought him there. For receipt on departure from Shikarpur on May 9, 1839, Sarwar Khan provided the following text:

> I Moolah Surwar Khan Loohanee give this written receipt to the British Government that the amount of one lac six thousand sixty three rupees, fifteen annas, eight pies, have been received by me from Captain W. J. Eastwick official Political Agent on account of the hire of 3098 camels which are now proceeding to Khorasan.[83]

The 2 percent not mentioned in this quotation involved the compensation that Sarwar Khan successfully petitioned for regarding a number of camels that were stolen from his camps in Shikarpur and Khairpur. The colonial account of how the Lohani chief responded to one of the thefts produces and reflects the reputation bestowed upon him by the majority of his British patrons and interlocutors. Eastwick differentiated Sarwar Khan's noble actions in response to the theft from the baser instincts of the seven hundred security personnel he employed and whom he had "difficulty managing":

> The Afghans were greatly excited at this (robbery) and (I) could scarcely prevent their committing an outrage in retaliation for the plundering ... [but] Sarwar Khan behaved with temper and moderation, pursued the robbers, recaptured his camels

and brought back four prisoners, one of whom was a thief of some celebrity he delivered over to the Diwan of Shikarpore to be hung at the city gates, which was carried out the next morning. The three others, seeing the fate of their comrade, delivered valuable information on the haunts, names, and tribes of those engaged in the outrages.[84]

Sarwar Khan does not appear to have been threatened or disrupted by the events and processes defining the first Anglo-Afghan war. Quite to the contrary, he seems to have behaved with comfort and ease as a result of the formation of the colonial army. The business dimensions and profit potential of state-sponsored war were familiar and perhaps appealing to Sarwar Khan. Even when the states controlling the trade routes he traversed were not at war, certain route segments were particularly treacherous for trade caravans. As a result, Lohani commercial migrations typically involved both the display and use of force against other tribal populations at certain points and in certain areas. Masson's foundational description of the Lohanis highlights their use of weapons and need to fight their way through certain areas.[85] The region of commercial depredations (e.g., banditry, plundering of caravans) referenced by Masson falls within a larger area of eastern and southeastern Afghanistan, roughly between Kabul, Jalalabad, and Qandahar, known as Ghalzi country. This mountainous zone, particularly the passes leading from it to the Indus plains, were noted by the Lohanis as requiring either forced-passage or prominent displays of force.[86] During the Army of the Indus's very first march from Qandahar to Kabul through Ghalzi country, the British Envoy and Minister to Shuja's court, Macnaghten, reported the following to the Governor General:

> We were detained by some time in expectation of the arrival of Lohanee merchants, but they refused to go beyond Qandahar on the plea that their families were in the hands of the Ghiljies. The grain brought by them was therefore left at Candahar.[87]

Ghalzi country and Ghalzi chiefs impeded the movement of the well-armed Lohanis, the Army of the Indus, and Shuja to Kabul. British officials indicated that the ability of the Lohanis to transport thirty thousand maunds of grain from Dera Ismail Khan to Kabul depended on whether the Ghalzis decided to support Shuja.[88] And although the Ghalzis generally did not support Shuja or his colonial patrons during the first British invasion and occupation, it was reported that Sarwar Khan successfully traversed the Ghalzi impasse between Qandahar and Kabul. Sarwar Khan's "high standing, sense and enterprise" be-

FIG. 2.2. Afghan Nomads and Commerce, 1978

came a model for the British as they sought to contract other Lohanis to convey personnel and supplies through Ghalzi country to Kabul.[89]

In addition to Ghalzi country, Sikh territory also presented challenges for Sarwar Khan and his efforts to assist the British in their invasion and occupation of Afghanistan. The critical distinction between Sikh and Ghalzi territory is that the former was represented by one clear ruler, Maharaja Ranjit Singh, who was explicitly allied to the British and Shuja through the Tripartite Treaty of 1838. The Ghalzi did not have a single identifiable agreed-on political representative, and apparently none of the multiple Ghalzi chiefs committed to supporting either Shuja or the British. The Sikhs did not provide men, arms, or money to the cause of restoring Shuja. The expected role of the Sikhs during the first Anglo-Afghan war was to provide uninterrupted passage through their territory for the British and the Lohanis as they proceeded toward Qandahar and Kabul.[90]

Sikh officials appointed by Ranjit Singh who were stationed in districts relatively far from Lahore were not always or even consistently cooperative with the Lohanis in their role as colonial baggage-handlers. For example, in July 1840

Sarwar Khan wrote to Macnaghten in lengthy detail about fifty camels that a Sikh official detained at Ataree.[91] The incident originated in February when Sarwar left his home in the daman with twelve hundred camels destined for Ludiana to transport Shuja's family and much of his entourage and material possessions to Kabul. During a river crossing between Multan and Ludiana a Sikh official named Diwan Missur demanded unexpected and steep taxes on the Lohani camels that Sarwar Khan could or would not pay. As a result, fifty camels were left as security and the first leg of the journey was extended by twenty-three days. The detention was costly in tactical terms, as by the time Sarwar Khan arrived in Ludiana Shuja's family announced it had become too hot for them to travel from Ludiana to Kabul.[92] Sarwar Khan's letter to Macnaghten about these circumstances concludes with an informative statement of account. The Lohani chief claimed the following expenses in connection with his British-contracted transportation of Shuja's family:

Rs. 340 paid to ferry men at Kheree, Mooltan, and Ataree for crossing the camels;
Rs. 30 for hire of messengers from Doman to Loodianah and from Mooltan to Loodianah;
Rs. 1024 paid to Jemadars appointed on each 100 camels @ Rs. 20 per month;
(sub) total: Rs. 1394.[93]

Sarwar Khan then adds, almost as a footnote:

The hire of 1,200 camels for four months and 8 days at 20 rupees amounts to Rupees. 1,02,400, in all Rs. 1,03,794.0.0. Of this we have received Rupees. 30,000 and the balance Rupees 73,794 is due to us.[94]

These are consequential sums that reflect the breadth and depth of British attachment to Sarwar Khan Lohani during the first Anglo-Afghan war. Perhaps because he played such a crucial and prominent role in the prosecution of the war, Sarwar Khan was subject to criticism by English officers stationed in Afghanistan. The few colonial officials who voiced disapproval of Sarwar Khan may not have known or appreciated the extent of the British dependence on this mobile but also locally grounded and influential Lohani chief. William Hough, a major in the Bengal Native Infantry who served in Afghanistan, cast aspersions on Sarwar Khan's loyalty and service to the British during the first Anglo-Afghan war. Hough was a lesser player in the conflict but his words form an interesting counternarrative to the official discursive posture of the colonial regime toward one of its most important local collaborators. Hough introduces Sarwar Khan in conspicuously unfavorable terms as follows:

The convoy experienced much opposition in the Bolan and Kojuk Passes from predatory hordes, who plundered and wounded many people belonging to it. The people attached to the convoy were all armed, and Surwar Khan, their leader, is a most determined man. He said that if he was refused grain at any place, or was plundered near any village, he invariably attacked the place . . . putting all he caught to the sword, he then destroyed the village, &c. Captain O(utram) says, "had the chief himself remained faithful, of which there is some reason to doubt." The conduct of Surwar Khan was of a very doubtful character.[95]

Hough's comments about Sarwar Khan originate in the summer of 1839 when Shuja and the Army of the Indus were moving from Qandahar to Kabul. They arose in a context that was unfavorable to the British, namely, the failed transport of twenty thousand maunds of grain from Qandahar to the Ghazni vicinity where Shuja was bunkered. Hough stated that near Quetta on the road from Shikarpur to Qandahar the caravan commanded by Sarwar Khan was boarded by emissaries of Dost Muhammad, the Durrani ruler whom the colonial army intended to replace with Shuja.[96] Hough's accusation is that illicit communication resulted in Sarwar Khan nearly handing over the British supply caravan to Dost Muhammad's forces.[97] This assertion destabilizes understandings of Sarwar Khan's uncompromising loyalty to the British. Hough quotes a circular order from the Commissariat Department of the invasion force to support his position that the Lohani caravan did not proceed from Qandahar because Sarwar Khan was trying to sell the camels he rented in Shikarpur to British officers in Qandahar.[98]

However valid his interpretation of the events may have been, Hough's evaluation of Sarwar Khan was atypical. The vast preponderance of colonial officials involved in the first Anglo-Afghan war habitually lauded Sarwar Khan. Data from a later period supports the favorable majority opinion of the influential Lohani chief formed during the first war, and indicates the relationship between Sarwar Khan and colonial authorities may have been more extensive than indicated in contemporaneous documents. In November 1893 Sarwar Khan's son Mushka Khan petitioned the British Indian Government for Rs. 1,00,000 with interest.[99] Mushka Khan claimed his father delivered six thousand camels of wheat and one lakh of rupees to Macnaghten while colonial forces were besieged in Kabul during the winter of 1840–41. In return, Sarwar Khan was given two hundis that served as money orders, one for Rs. 85,000 payable at the Ludiana treasury, and another for Rs. 15,000 payable from the Peshawar treasury.[100]

Mushka Khan said that on his father's death the orders were not cashed for fear of the whole amount being confiscated by Sher Ali (ruled 1863–66 and 1869–78), who was then the Durrani dynast in Kabul.[101] Mushka Khan detailed how Sher Ali initially conspired and negotiated with him to hand over the valuable paper notes, but then threatened him to do so. He indicated that Sher Ali ultimately tried unsuccessfully to forge and cash the hundi money orders.[102] Mushka Khan narrated his imprisonment in Turkistan and the confiscation of his property at the beginning of Abd al-Rahman's reign in the early 1880s. He claimed to have escaped confinement and fled to Russian Central Asia during a jailhouse revolt prompted by a more widespread rebellion against Abd al-Rahman.[103] After chasing down outstanding debts due to his late father from other Afghan traders in Central Asia, Mushka Khan traveled to Quetta to plead his case to Major James Browne. According to "Russian spies and others who had recently" come from that city, Browne was the British officer best suited to hear the case.[104] Despite appeals to the great service his father provided the British during the first war, and the assistance that Mushka Khan claims to have rendered during the second war, his petition does not appear to have been successful.[105]

CHAPTER 3

Fiscal Instability and
State Revenue Reformulation
during the First British Occupation

Occupational Hazards of Cash and Credit
in Kabul and Qandahar

We can now deal with the interaction between British occupation officials and local Indian bankers or Hindkis in Qandahar and Kabul. The relationship between colonial authorities and Indian bankers concerned both the cash and credit realms of economic exchange. The cash-based interaction unfolded primarily in Qandahar where the British encountered unexpected difficulties from their own troops when trying to institute a currency exchange-rate change. This money matter was more of a short-term concern than the credit-based exchanges between the British occupation authorities and Indian bankers in Kabul. The British occupation came to an end in the capital city they helped define as such. At its very end, the occupation force was by default led by a colonial officer who, during the most dire of straits, negotiated the receipt of large sums of cash from bankers in Kabul. These transactions posed a very real threat to the fiscal solvency of the British East India Company because of the way the Afghan occupation ended and the volume of merchant capital that was lost as a result. The demise of the Indus Army posed a long-term financial challenge for the British in India.

Two general principles regarding interregional currency flows through Afghanistan during the nineteenth century are evident. The first rule is that gold currencies moved through Afghanistan in a southeasterly direction from Russia to India rather than being consumed in the country. The companion notion concerns the British Indian rupee, a silver-based currency, which found a greatly expanded range of use to the northwest of Delhi as a result of Durrani state minting practices in Kabul. Before discussing the Qandahar exchange-rate change, it is important to emphasize that the movement and interaction of currencies were themselves sources of state revenue. Burnes's reformation of the Kabul customs house or chabutara during the first occupation reflects the British intent to capitalize on the movement of currency through the city.[1]

Burnes's reforms of the customs house in Kabul were consistent with the basic colonial plan for the country's economy, namely, to increase revenue, streamline its collection, loosen local restraints on the flow of merchant capital, and revise the accounting practices associated with state resources. Burnes intended to centralize the collection of transit duties or *rahdari* on the movement of foreign goods through the country at the Kabul customs house. Consequently, his reforms reflect a severe diminution in the collection of various forms of road tolls and transit duties by local notables such as khans, foujdars, and qaladars outside of Kabul.[2] Burnes was confident about the profit his reforms would reap on the movement of silver-based money, but he was especially optimistic about the profits derived from the passage of gold currencies found in Iran, Central Asia, Russia, and China, such as generic bullion, *yamous*, *ducats*, and *tillas*, through Kabul *en route* to the cash siphon that was India. Burnes declared his reforms yielded a 400 percent increase in the state revenue derived from the movement of money through Kabul. He claimed Rs. 30,000 would be generated from this revised source, whereas the previous fiscal year only Rs. 6,000 was received.[3]

The British were well aware of the revenue possibilities from taxing the movement of money through Kabul. Colonial officials were also very cognizant of how in Afghanistan, particularly the eastern portion of the country, Shikarpuri and other Indian bankers profited from transactions involving more than one form of currency, whether the exchange involved bills of exchange and a state money, or two metallic currencies. Elphinstone's foundational economic dictums about Afghanistan gained wide circulation and credence during more than two decades between their appearance in print and the first British invasion of the country. Occupation authorities surely heeded his opinion regarding the Hindkis of the country:

> They derive their profits from lending money, which they do at an enormous interest, by negotiating bills of exchange, and by transactions connected with the fluctuations of the exchange in the place where they reside. They also mix trade and agency

with their banking business. Another source of profit arises from advancing money to government for bills on the revenue of provinces, and this hazardous speculation is recommended by a premium, always large, and increasing with the risk of non-payment. Some of the bankers are very rich, but there are numberless little shops set up with very small capitals, which practice the same trade as the great ones, among the poor people of their particular neighborhood.[4]

During October and November 1840, roughly a year before the occupation's demise, the British Political Agent in Qandahar, Henry Rawlinson, exchanged letters with his superior Macnaghten in Kabul about plans to institute an exchange-rate change between a local currency, the Qandahar rupee, and the Company rupee.[5] Rawlinson's attempt to fashion a greater role for Company rupees in Qandahar was motivated by the success of similar efforts in Kabul. The British officers recognized the important role of the colonial army in spreading Company coin throughout occupied territory. Correspondence between Rawlinson and Macnaghten was concerned with precisely when and how to implement the local exchange-rate change. Their discussions highlight the complex relationships between the metallic currencies circulating in a given locality, and the money-market rates on hundis or bills of exchange involving at least one of the currencies affected by the proposed rate change.[6] With Elphinstone's coded warning about the profits turned by Hindki bankers on exchange-rate transactions and Macnaghten's direct advice, Rawlinson certainly knew about some of the obstacles and potential dangers to the enactment of a new exchange-rate scheme, but he could not prepare for all of the possible complications. The interaction between coinage and paper credit can easily become confusing for participants and distant analysts alike, especially during conversion sequences occurring like this one when monetary values fluctuate rapidly, and no less an authority than Braudel refers to this interplay as "not only complicated but diabolical."[7]

Rawlinson wanted to devalue the local Qandahar rupee by approximately 11 percent in relation to the British Indian or Company rupee. Instead of the current Qandahar Rs. 133 1/3 for every Company Rs. 100, he wanted to make the exchange rate Qandahar Rs. 150 for every Company Rs. 100.[8] Rawlinson did at least two things in an effort to secure the greatest possible advantage for the Company during the transition to the new rate. Before announcing the change he quietly collected as much Company currency as possible while concurrently dispensing with the Qandahar rupees held in the Indus Army treasury.[9] The Company agenda was to pay the occupation troops in its own rupees, and by taking such steps Rawlinson was trying to avoid having to enter Qandahar's hundi money market for Company rupees, which would have been both an ironic and expensive undertaking. As soon as the rate-change plan was announced or even rumored to occur, Rawlinson expected the local Hindki bankers, moneychangers, and currency dealers to elevate the bill of exchange rate from the current 4 percent to at least 10 percent, and maybe even 12 percent.[10] He was trying to avoid such potentially heavy losses by having Company rupees and not the Qandahar variety on hand. Rawlinson's surreptitious gathering of Company rupees from the local economy was successful in the sense that he achieved that end without his scheme becoming known by the local Hindki community, but it was apparently incomplete in terms of having acquired the necessary amount.

Rawlinson was also successful in purging his treasury of Qandahar rupees, but this achievement was simultaneously viewed as a potentially worrisome point. Rawlinson knew that if he was forced to enter the hundi-based money market for Company rupees, the 150:100 rate would apply to his disadvantage in the first instance. Compounding that problem was his knowledge of local banking practices which required one-third of the total value of such a transaction in Qandahar rupees as up-front security, and he now lacked that form of money. However, it was the unexpected that proved most troublesome for Rawlinson. Although he had been able to keep news of the exchange-rate change from the local Hindki banking community and dispense of Qandahar rupees, Rawlinson could not suppress information about his actions on those fronts from his own troops who cried foul. The Company troops in Qandahar held mainly Qandahar rupees, and they demanded to exchange them at the Company treasury at nothing less than the prevailing 133 1/3 to 100 rate. Now foreseeing an unexpected run on the Company's money in an amount he had not yet fully acquired, Rawlinson decided to delay instituting the new exchange rate.[11]

As a result, for a short time the troops had the opportunity to dispose of some of their Qandahar currency on the open market or exchange it at the 133 1/3 to 100 rate. During this transition period of a few weeks during October and November 1840 it is unclear whether local Hindki bankers learned of the impending exchange-rate change. When the new rate was finally made official on December first, Rawlinson found himself in possession of nearly a lakh of this local money or Qandahar Rs. 1,00,000, a currency form and volume he had recently taken steps to purge from the occupation army's treasury. To dispose of this unexpected batch of devalued rupees returned by his troops, Rawlinson paid the "camel contract," or the local official in charge of providing camels used to supply and transport the occupation army.[12]

Rawlinson's dilemma lay in his inability to avoid engaging Qandahar's hundi-based money market. As just noted, the everyday terms of credit provided by local Hindki bankers to the occupation army in Qandahar was 4 percent per month. This is twice the sum cited by Yang as an average amount of monthly interest charged on hundis in colonial Patna.[13] Hundis or bills of exchange were the defining fiscal instrument of the Qandahar money market, and their issuance structured the circulation of cash currencies and credit and debt relations in the locality. Bills of exchange served similar purposes in other locations throughout South and Central Asia.

According to Braudel, bills of exchange had a dual nature.[14] First was their official role as a form of long-distance payment necessary in large-scale trade. More significant for our purposes is Braudel's distillation of a second function for bills of exchange, namely, a debt-servicing aspect. According to Braudel, a bill of exchange could also serve as "a concealed instrument of credit at interest, an opportunity for some to lend and make their money earn profits, and for others to obtain the advances necessary to any trade."[15] In nineteenth-century Afghanistan, many of those who borrowed or sought cash advances through the hundi-based money market had exhausted familial and kin-based economic support and were not fiscally solvent. For many of the economically vulnerable who sought cash from Hindki bankers, the infusion of capital they received contributed only to short-term fiscal buoyancy, say for a season or a year, after which time they would again engage the hundi-based money market for more credit and greater debt. Individual producers, smaller merchants, larger traders, local notables, and government officials throughout nineteenth-century Afghanistan were in many ways dependent on the cash advances, credit provisioning, and debt-maintenance services provided by Hindki bankers.

Before their invasion and occupation of Kabul, Qandahar, and eastern Afghanistan the British relied on bankers throughout North India who served the expanding and maturing colonial state in substantial ways including as revenue farmers and as financiers of war. Indian bankers invested heavily in the British colonial project in all its forms, including the invasion of Afghanistan. Revenue documents from the occupation period reveal a reluctant and fragile dependence of British officials on Indian bankers. We have just seen how British occupation officers stationed in Qandahar tried in vain to evade the controlling influence exercised by Hindki bankers over the availability and interaction of different currency forms in the city. In Kabul, the most senior British authorities were similarly unable to avoid engaging local bankers, but in the capital city colonial officers sought large-scale cash advances, realized through hundis, in an unsuccessful effort to save the occupation. Given the outcome of the occupation, the final British hundi transactions in Kabul jeopardized the survival of the colonial state India.

War and political flux usually entail significant effects on inter-currency relations that can in turn complicate hundi transactions. In occupied proto-Afghanistan the pace of currency transformations was rapid and fluctuations in bilateral currency exchange rates such as in Qandahar occurred elsewhere in the country. Each local exchange-rate change was a sensitive political topic and had ramifications in distant markets. For example, in Herat during the fall of 1840 Major D'Arcy Todd used invisible ink to explain and justify his withdrawal of Rs. 31,200 cash from the Company treasury.[16] Todd also issued six hundis from Herat in October of that year. These bills were payable on the Bombay, Qandahar, and Ludiana treasuries, and totaled Company Rs. 68,503. However, Todd failed to indicate the exact terms of the transactions on the bills themselves, which prompted the Indian Government to write to his superior Macnaghten in Kabul who was the British official in charge of the colonial occupation. As a result, in December 1840 Macnaghten issued a circular to all colonial officers in Afghanistan concerning their issuance of hundis. Macnaghten instructed that henceforth all bills should include the rate of exchange at which the transaction occurred, and the amount of local rupees or other currency received in lieu of every 100 Company rupees.[17]

A year later, during the late fall of 1841, the situation had declined considerably for the British and their occupation of Kabul. Burnes was killed on 2 November as was Macnaghten on 23 December. Major Eldred Pottinger, elderly, wounded, and apparently still in his capacity as British Political Agent at Charikar, assumed charge of negotiations with local leaders in eastern Afghanistan for a British retreat from Kabul to Peshawar. Pottinger, by default, had become responsible for the fate of approximately 16,500 people including European and Indian officers and troops, family members of European officers, and many categories of Indian laborers and camp followers forming the Army of the Indus. When he assumed the mantle of leadership Pottinger might well have held the legitimate view that he and a great many others were about to face their own mortality on the ill-fated retreat from Kabul in January 1842. However desperate he might rightly have been, his financial conduct at this time compromised the buoyancy of a number of banking firms in North India whose resources were thoroughly implicated in the fiscal infrastructure of the British East India Company.

Under siege in the British cantonment in Kabul and understandably frantic, at the very end of 1841 Pottinger issued bills of exchange payable at multiple British treasuries throughout North India for more than 13 lakhs, or over one million three hundred thousand Company rupees.[18] Pottinger was clearly hoping to purchase safe passage through hostile tribal territories primarily inhabited by eastern Ghalzi Pashtuns. In return for the hefty sums of cash advanced to him, Pottinger issued hundis on the Ludiana treasury for Rs. 105,000 to Rorsukh Rae, Rs. 30,000 to Dodum Rae, and Rs. 30,000 to Basha Mall. A number of other treasuries in India were affected by Pottinger's desperation hundis, but no information about recipients is given. These include bills of exchange payable at British treasuries in Ferozpore for Rs. 238,400, in Delhi for Rs. 390,000, in Agra for Rs. 200,000, and Cawnpore for Rs. 20,000.[19]

The India banking firms whose representatives in Kabul advanced the cash to Pottinger represent a substantial and perhaps controlling interest in the Company's finances in Hindustan. In the cities named earlier and elsewhere these banking firms regularly supplied the British treasuries with cash. The firms recognized the impending doom of the occupation and as a result began to restrict the flow of cash to British treasuries in North India. Their rationale in doing so was to guard against the expected losses of their capital in Kabul as a result of the British failure there. The British government also recognized the gravity of the situation in Kabul and therefore instructed their own treasury officials in Ferozpore and Ludiana to "delay without refusing remittance" on bills drawn on those treasuries.[20] In response, a number of North Indian banking firms reneged outright on cashing hundis issued to the British government and its officials. The affairs in Kabul were transforming cooperative relations between North Indian bankers and colonial authorities into exchanges based on negative reciprocity. The anticipated and real losses of transnational merchant capital in Kabul as a result of the British occupation's collapse threatened to force the closure of a number of North Indian banking firms, which in turn seriously destabilized the fiscal integrity of the British government in India.

Government Account Book Fluidity

Before the first Anglo-Afghan war of 1839–42, colonial officials accrued basic information about the fruit produced and consumed in the area between Qandahar and Kabul. The invasion and occupation were motivated by a number of economic considerations, foremost among them being the transformation of the Indus River into a thoroughfare for commercial steamships. The British then perceived Kabul as a staging area for Central Asian traders doing business in India. Colonial policy makers envisioned the city as a node from which to direct commercial caravans carrying fruit and other commodities from the Hindu Kush mountains and southward to the planned market at Mithenkote along the Indus. At the same time the British imagined Kabul as a center of consumption in its own right, and as a site from which to launch the distribution of Indian and European goods into the markets of Bukhara and greater Central Asia. The significantly increased role for Kabul in the Indus-based commercial scheme required a pliant political edifice. The colonial Army of the Indus ultimately restored a Durrani monarch deposed thirty years earlier, and who had since been residing in British India as a colonial state pensioner.

The British occupation of Kabul began in September 1839, but it was not until the fall harvest of 1841 that the colonial authorities assumed full control of the kingdom's account books from their Durrani puppet Shuja. For the first two years of the occupation the British paid for Shuja's artillery, musketry, and foot soldiers who were responsible for maintaining a "superior protection of the merchant and the cultivator" when compared to the previous regime of Dost Muhammad in Kabul.[21] Crediting these improved conditions, the British Envoy and Minister to Shuja's court, William Macnaghten, noted an increase of Rs. 2,25,051 over the Rs. 9,00,000 collected in taxes by Dost Muhammad the year before the occupation. However, Shuja continued appealing to his colonial patrons for more and more material support and in May of 1841 asked for Rs. 50,000 monthly to pay for his civil administration, court, and family.[22] This request turned out to be the last straw, so to speak, which severed Shuja's financial umbilical cord to the British. This petition was received as presumptuous and piqued the ire of the Governor General of India who commented that Shuja appeared uninterested in using his own resources to govern. The Governor General's conviction resulted in Macnaghten assuming full fiscal responsibility for the colonially contrived polity.

Macnaghten deputed R. S. Trevor to revise the Kabul account books and thus transform the revenue scheme of the fledgling Anglo-Durrani state. Trevor removed fiscal authority from Mullah Shakur who served as Shuja's main confidante while pensioning in Ludiana. Until his dispatch from office in Kabul, Mullah Shakur was for all practical purposes Shuja's untitled finance minister, and in that capacity made a series of substantive changes to the land revenue and customs collected in and around the city during the occupation.[23] For translation, explanation, and interpretation of the Kabul account books, and general information about the fiscal machinery of the Durrani state, Trevor relied quite heavily and almost exclusively on Mirza Abd al-Raziq.[24] Abd al-Raziq was the main repository of knowledge about the financial infrastructure of the Kabul kingdom and the primary element of bureaucratic continuity between the revenue regimes of Mullah Shakur and Trevor during the British occupation.

The British occupation ended with the besieged Army of the Indus attempting to retreat from Kabul in January 1842. The resulting massacre and hostage taking led to the formation of an army of retribution. During the fall of 1842 this force destroyed important parts of the commercial infrastructure in Kabul such as the Mughal era covered bazaar known as the *chahar chattah*, and fruit-producing villages surrounding the city such as Istalif.[25] The occupation's end left the British attempt to transform Kabul's role in regional and interregional marketing networks incomplete, and the vengeful retaliation for the loss of the Army of the Indus dealt a severe blow to the local economy. However, records from the occupation, particularly the documents resulting from Trevor's revision of the Kabul account books, reveal much about the financial infrastructure of the Durrani state and how the British planned to transform Kabul into a colonial capital.[26]

An increasing prominence and reliance on revenue farmers was the most noticeable theme in a wide range of alterations made by Trevor at all levels of the economy and in all territories subject to the Kabul-centered Durrani state. In terms of fruit production and marketing, which traversed and integrated many economic sectors and social groups throughout eastern Afghanistan, the British agenda was favorably designed for the community of brokers who financed and organized the export trade in that commodity. The colonial revisions of the Kabul account books created the opportunity for commercial brokers to become state-contracted revenue farmers with much greater levels of interest and influence in the fruit-laden valleys and villages surrounding Kabul.

The fiscal restructuring of Afghanistan, though never fully realized because of the occupation's demise, was a complicated undertaking in textual terms. The Kabul account books were difficult to fully decipher in the first instance, and to restructure them in accordance with the British budget, mercantile philosophy, and political ideology was a challenging task. At the outset of his assignment, Trevor questioned the accuracy of the Durrani state revenue records and commented with a mixture of curiosity and remorse on the textual practices constituting their maintenance. Trevor qualified his own interpretation and manipulation of the state's fiscal registers by claiming the "system of public accounts" facilitated the Afghan propensity to practice fraud and graft.[27]

Trevor noted a number of problematic distinctions within the Kabul account books. He presented these curiosities as evidence predisposing his revisionist task to failure, and almost pleaded for the numbers he proposed and the reasoning used to arrive at them "be considered merely as the nearest approach to the truth within my reach on a subject where much uncertainty is in my opinion quite unavoidable."[28] The first and most consequential ambiguity in the Kabul account books was between the two main forms of the Durrani state's revenue, namely, money and agricultural produce. Trevor qualified his understanding of the distinction between cash and kind in the following way:

> It must be observed however that the statement of the revenue in money though usual and in some respects convenient is in reality a fiction, the greatest portion of it being claimable and actually paid in kind. . . . In the Registers kept at Cabul the rule is to set down in kind whatever part of the revenue is derived from the various sorts of corn, rice, cotton, pulse and seeds yielding oil which are usually cultivated and to enter in money the dues from all other produce as fruit, melon beds, straw, clover, lucerne, sheep, etc. But even these registers give but an imperfect notion of the real state of things, there being several whole districts and parts of others in which the revenue whether of grain or money cannot possibly be levied but by taking in payment cloathes, stock furniture, cattle, or whatever else the armed force sent once a year to collect in can come by. Also when the revenue of a district is farmed, it is usual for government to bargain with the contractor for payment in cash or produce as may be convenient without reference to its exact rights, and leaving him to make the necessary arrangements with the cultivator.[29]

In this testimonial about the Kabul revenue scheme, it is important to note that fruit was a commodity group clearly associated with a monetary value and that revenue farmers could bargain for combinations of cash and kind to pay for their government contracts. Trevor also noted farmers collected revenue at the time of harvesting the principal crops of each district.[30] Brokers were already active in converting commodities into currency at harvest time,[31] and the British planned to increase the role of revenue farming in the Durrani state's fiscal structure (see later in this chapter). For the fruit-producing regions surrounding Kabul in particular the colonial fiscal regime facilitated the direct entry of commercial brokers into state revenue-farming roles. This move was designed to give brokers a greater interest in governing Afghanistan and their merchant capital wider circulation in the frontier economy between Central and South Asia and from there into the burgeoning global economy.

Trevor also noted an unclear distinction between land revenue on the one hand, and customs and petty taxes on the other. In his discussion of the "professed separation" between those two forms of state revenue he outlined five instances where the customs and petty taxes of a district bled into the land revenue.[32] Trevor was particularly perplexed at the entry of debits and credits in the Kabul fiscal registers. Any tax abolished in a district was not completely so, it seemed, because instead of disappearing from the books they were maintained textually as debits and credits of equal amounts. This allowed the amount credited to be easily resuscitated in another form as a debit when it came to the district-wide tallying of many and various kinds of revenue claims and exemptions.[33] Even when landed property was confiscated by the state and became *khalisa* or crown lands, the tax formerly associated with the property remained in the given district's account as a debit. Furthermore, there were multiple types of crown lands and different relationships between the government and cultivators and others involved in the production process (such as those furnishing seed, implements, or animal labor) in each type, all of which appeared hard for Trevor to sift through and comprehend let alone reform. For most "rules" in the Kabul accounts there appeared to be many and different kinds of exceptions. Trevor noted that "the general effect is not a little puzzling," and he attached "great importance (to the) simplification of the system of public accounts."[34]

From the perspectives of his superiors, the arbitrary and fluid nature of the Kabul account books presented an opportunity for Trevor to favorably reconfigure the resource base of the Durrani polity. Trevor reported the results of his efforts to Macnaghten who received instructions directly from the Governor General of India. In the cover letter of his tabular report to Macnaghten Trevor referenced Burnes's concomitant reorganization of the Kabul customs house that was an important institution known locally as the chabutara.[35] Burnes claimed his reforms would increase the customs house revenue by Rs. 8,400. However, Mirza Abd al-Raziq and other central state officers told Trevor the net gain arrived at by Burnes was both inflated and a premature evaluation. Trevor opined to Macnaghten that the effectiveness of the customs house or any other account reforms could not be known until medium-range and long-term financial cycles had run their course. Trevor's uncertainty about all the

Kabul-based revenue statistics reflected a set of methodological reservations about Durrani state bookkeeping practices.

Burnes posted his numbers in May 1841 and Macnaghten forwarded them to the Governor General in Calcutta in July. Trevor's reforms were announced and forwarded in September. However, signs of the occupation's collapse became clearly evident by October.[36] The timing of the reforms raises questions about the fiscal integrity of the occupation and its relationship to the North Indian colonial economy. Here it is sufficient to briefly address the reforms' temporal coincidence with the occupation's demise. The reforms were intended to increase the role of brokers and revenue farmers in the fiscal regime of the Anglo-Durrani state, but that agenda was motivated less by political than by economic exigencies. Alliances with brokers involved in the trade between South and Central Asia and relationships with other communities of financial intermediaries linking producers and revenue collectors throughout North India drew the British toward Kabul. Based on successful engagement of those intermediate commercial groups, and after many years of watching Shuja mishandle his stipends, British officials exhibited feelings of confidence and relief when they assumed full revenue command of Kabul and its dependencies. Refashioning the account books was an important step in the colonial administrative and textual creation of Afghanistan.

Trevor was circumspect about the methodological integrity of the Kabul accounts, and issued a caveat that real reform results required a lengthy fermentation or gestation period before being fully evaluated. Nonetheless, he and Macnaghten, and presumably Mirza Abd al-Raziq to a certain extent, advocated a budget with a markedly increased reliance on commercial brokerage services. Indian financiers generally and subgroups therein, such as the ubiquitous Shikarpuri Hindus, stood to gain considerably from the British reorganization of the Kabul accounts, and this was arguably the most basic and consequential aspect of the colonial construction of Afghanistan. Shikarpuris and other Indians formed the primary class of brokers who were slated to become revenue farmers under the colonial fiscal reordering of the Durrani state. Although the first British occupation of Kabul was cut short, the 1841 colonial budget for Afghanistan had a lasting social and economic impact on the region. With Trevor's revision of the Kabul account books, transnational merchant capital and colonial business practices were noticeably advanced in this frontier region.

Local Experiences of the New Fiscal Regime

How the fruit-producing communities surrounding Kabul experienced the colonial alteration of the Durrani state revenue bureaucracy is the subject of this section. Records from the occupation reveal a variety of fiscal initiatives reflecting a common theme. During the brief period of British control over the Durrani state revenue bureaucracy, localities of various dimensions around Kabul experienced a decided shift toward revenue farming. The prospect of purchasing the state's sanction to collect revenue was viewed as a favorable opportunity by the extant group of large-scale commercial brokers with already broad resource bases and diverse financial portfolios. Village fort-holders and other local notables claiming dues along routes of passage (*rahdari*) were among the groups most displaced by the colonial reforms and the revenue-farming arrangements they entailed. The following deals with the impact of the colonial revenue revisions on the Koh Daman district and the villages of Istalif and Arghandeh.

The British occupation created the financial and textual space for commercial brokers to become revenue farmers and increase their stake in the fruit-producing villages nestled in the fertile valleys surrounding Kabul. It was noted earlier that revenue from fruit was usually, though not always, entered in the Kabul account books as money before the British assumption of full fiscal control of nascent Afghanistan. Before Trevor's revisions in fruit-producing localities, brokers were primary agents in the conversion of agricultural produce into money form. Their services facilitated the remission of cash taxes to the state and helped fulfill smaller-scale local needs for cash currency (for a number of potential reasons including but not limited to debt payment, life-course ritual expenditure, and regular and irregular personal and household consumption needs).

Commercial brokers transformed fruit into cash at harvest sites. At the same time they also initiated the marketing processes that brought local eastern Afghan fruit to distant consumers in the dense populace of North India. After harvest, brokers arranged for one or more of the marketing steps necessary for fruit to arrive at final points of consumption. For present purposes the marketing cycle consisted of the sorting, weighing, packaging, storage, and transport of fruit to retail destinations. However, it is important to appreciate that for elements or portions of a given load, this sequence could be restarted at a number of points in transit. Successful brokers of fruit may well have performed similar marketing functions for other commodities, thus making them attractive candidates to purchase revenue-farming rights in the Durrani state that were created and auctioned by the British.

Brokers operating at harvest sites likely dictated the subsequent marketing course followed by the fruit produce of Kabul and eastern Afghanistan. Such marketing activity had both local and foreign dimensions as fruit and other forms of capital handled by successful commercial brokers circulated regularly between and widely within Central and South Asia. The British reformation of the Durrani state's revenue structure is notable for providing successful commercial brokers with already diverse financial portfolios the opportunity to further expand their resource base. For example, under Trevor's 1841 budget the right to collect *dalali* or the duty on brokerage profits earned in Kabul was farmed out for 60 percent above the previous year's rate.[37] Such an increase reflects a substantially expanded role for the institution of brokerage during the colonial fiscal regime.

The tax attached to fruit brokerage specifically was referred to as *maiwadari*.[38] This was a tax levied on fruit sold in Kabul, but it applied only to fruit sold for subsequent export. Maiwadari was collected in Kabul at various rates according to the season, the type of fruit and mode of transport (via camels, donkeys, or mules). Perhaps the most common articulation of the maiwadari tax during this period was Rs. 2 charged on a camel load of grapes exported from Kabul during the fall season. Trevor's fiscal restructuring of the Kabul accounts and revenue scheme budgeted Rs. 2,500 for the rights to the maiwadari revenue farm, which was more than a 10 percent increase from the previous fiscal year's amount of Rs. 2,240.[39]

Through their revision of the government account books the British expanded the niche of brokers at the central state level. These textual transformations were intended to further concentrate the resources associated with the institution of brokerage in Kabul. From the perspective of colonial policy makers, amplifying Kabul's role as a center of interregional trade brokerage would complement the city's recent service as a political capital. The colonial attempts to develop Kabul as a brokerage center expanded on the city's historical role as a wholesale market and staging area for goods in transport between Central and South Asia. The British revision of the Kabul accounts meant significant changes in the city's relationship to surrounding fruit-producing localities.

Koh Daman was and remains the most important fruit-producing locality in the vicinity of Kabul. The district begins roughly 15 miles west of Kabul and continues to the north along the Paghman mountain range for about 30 miles. The primary plain of the Koh Daman district varies from 4 to 12 miles in length. Koh Daman is very well watered by the Ghorband and Panjsher Rivers, and the district's natural irrigation is amplified by innumerable man-made canals. For British Indian mounted troops and mobile artillery, passage through Koh Daman was a near impossibility. This lush zone of fruit production was described in colonial records as being:

> ... like a garden. It is all orchards and fields, with scattered fruit trees, interspersed with numerous villages and hamlets. ... The greater portion of the fruit brought by traders into Upper India is from the Koh Daman. Here are grown grapes of dozen different kinds, apricots of six sorts, mulberries of as many, besides endless varieties of apples, pears, peaches, walnuts, almonds, quinces, cherries, and plums ... and (it) ... may be considered the garden of Kabul the greater part of the cultivated land being taken up by orchards and vineyards. ... Koh Daman is chiefly famous for its grapes and other fruits, on which the people largely subsist, besides exporting immense quantities. The grapes are of many different varieties and are cultivated with great care. Many of the houses are built with interstices in the walls for the purpose of drying the grapes and converting them into *kishmish* (raisins) which appear to be one of the staple articles of food in Afghanistan. ... The apricot is the commonest fruit, and there are many different kinds varying considerably in colour and flavour; perhaps one of the best is a white fleshed variety called "*kaisi*." Peaches and cherries are also excellent, and large numbers of melons and watermelons are grown where the soil is suitable.[40]

The British envisioned a greater role for brokers as revenue farmers at the central state level. This aspect of the colonial agenda is also evident in the most lucrative fruit-producing district outside Kabul, Koh Daman. It was mentioned earlier that income from fruit production was generally entered into the Durrani state account books as money, and for that to have occurred bankers and brokers facilitating the transformation of crops into cash were very active in Koh Daman. The colonial intervention into Koh Daman's account with the government barely altered the gross revenue provided by the district.[41] Trevor's plan was a significant intervention in terms of the means of revenue collection he proposed for the district, not the amount per se. The main feature of Trevor's reform package for Koh Daman was to increase the farmed component of the district's revenue by Rs. 6,000. However, this increase was offset almost exactly by a decrease in revenue of Rs. 5,992. The latter sum was composed of tax remissions, dues considered unrealizable, and a restructuring of the rights of local fort-holders (foujdars).[42]

During this period, Koh Daman was a district in the Kohistan *woleswali* or administrative division of the Parwan province. There were a number of well-known fruit-producing villages in Koh Daman, including Ak Sarai, Charikar, Istarghij, and Totum Darrah. However, Istalif was clearly the most productive locality in the district. Of 6,495 houses found in the 41 villages then comprising the Koh Daman district, Istalif contained approximately 1,200 houses, leaving each of the remaining 40 villages with an average of roughly 158 houses.[43]

As a result of Trevor's reforms, revenue farming became a much more prominent aspect of Istalif's internal fiscal structure and the locality's financial relationship to Kabul and the Durrani state. The most dramatic change in Istalif's revenue structure concerned the customs and petty taxes collected in the village. The year before the British assumption of full revenue control Rs. 5,400 in customs and petty taxes were collected by local notables in Istalif. Trevor rescinded the control of local actors over the collection of that form of revenue and instead farmed out the rights to collect those dues to brokers and financiers based in Kabul for Rs. 4,000.[44]

The Durrani state's purported "loss" of Rs. 1,400 in the customs and petty taxes of Istalif was supposedly "recovered" in the land revenue generated by the village, the vast preponderance of which was derived from fruit production. Ultimately, Trevor seems to have reproduced the kind of clerical practice he had originally chastised. In this instance, Trevor's bookkeeping maneuver increased the farm of Istalif's land revenue by Rs. 3,000, while simultaneously remitting Rs. 600 to the local fort-holder and Rs. 1,000 to the farmer.[45] The result was a Rs. 1,400 increase in Istalif's land revenue, the rights to which were farmed out. This Rs. 1,400 increase in Istalif's land revenue farm conspicuously corresponds with the decrease in revenue resulting from the colonial plan to farm out the rights to collect the customs and petty taxes associated with the village. The reforms to Istalif's land revenue scheme and the customs and petty taxes collected there, when combined, do not alter the gross amount of state revenue generated by the village. For Istalif, the colonial revenue reforms had a far more consequential impact on the means of revenue collection, which affected various sectors of the local economy, than on the sheer amount of total revenue garnered by the state from the village.

The British used revenue farming as an economic centralization tactic and as a method of balancing the Kabul account books. The brokers who were able to enter the revenue-farming ranks were either based in Kabul or had close ties to and substantive resources in the city. Members of the upper echelon of brokers were most likely to become revenue farmers as a result of Trevor's reforms. Their advancement came at the expense of less-successful or smaller-scale brokers whose resources were not concentrated in Kabul. Given the intensity of fruit cultivation in Istalif, and the state's accounting of that local produce in money form, brokers were certainly very active in the village economy before the British occupation.[46] The British reforms of the Kabul account books and the revenue structure of the Durrani state were designed to expand the role of commercial brokers to include revenue-farming responsibilities in Istalif.

A significant portion of fruit harvested in Koh Daman and Istalif was transported to Arghandeh, a village about ten miles west of Kabul, to be packed for export.[47] For Istalif, Trevor's plan rearranged and farmed out rights to collect land revenue on the one hand, and customs and petty taxes on the other, while leaving the total state revenue derived from both sources combined unchanged. Similarly, in Arghandeh the colonial budget reflects an intermingling and convolution of foreign and domestic trade considerations, and the farming of rights to collect each pool of resources, without altering the total revenue derived from the locality.

The transit tax regimen on domestic goods circulating in the territory later dubbed Afghanistan was a cause of much consternation for the British.[48] Trevor's revision of the Kabul account books and revenue scheme attempted to incorporate Burnes's reformation of the customs house finances. Trevor planned to remit the Rs. 7,292 in rahdari or transit taxes paid on foreign goods moving through Arghandeh, which was in keeping with Burnes's desire to have the customs house in Kabul serve as the sole point of collecting such fees. Under Trevor's plan local authorities in Arghandeh were slated to be deprived of the right to collect this foreign transit tax revenue, while brokers in Kabul were availed of the opportunity to purchase the farm of internal transit taxes valued at Rs. 8,804.[49] The difference between Rs. 8,804 for the new internal transit tax farm and Rs. 7,292 formerly collected in transit taxes on foreign goods moving through Arghandeh is Rs. 1,511.

Trevor's plan for Arghandeh was not fully consistent with Burnes's wish to inhibit the collection by local notables of transit taxes on foreign goods moving through sites other than Kabul. Burnes intended for the Kabul customs house to receive the revenue derived from transit taxes levied on goods not produced in Afghanistan. Although it restricted the right of local authorities outside of Kabul to collect rahdari in conformity with Burnes's wishes, Trevor's plan opted to farm out the revenue derived from the movement of foreign fruit through

Arghandeh, which deprived the customs house of that revenue as planned by Burnes. Trevor's accounting linked the revenue derived from the import duty on fruit routed through Arghandeh with a market tax on flour and farmed out the rights to both for Rs. 42,708. The amount of the farm Trevor proposed was Rs. 1,511 more than was collected locally during the previous fiscal year. This Rs. 1,511 mirrors the difference mentioned in the previous paragraph.

As with Koh Daman and Istalif, Trevor's plan for Arghandeh involved a concerted move to revenue farming from Kabul as opposed to the collection of taxes on local grounds. Trevor's revisions were an attempt to balance the Kabul account books and involved a reconfiguration of existing sources of revenue. His reforms resulted in opportunities for successful commercial brokers to insinuate their resources even further into the economies of these three localities that figured so prominently in the export fruit trade.

Trevor's reforms were announced at the beginning of September 1841, in time to take effect for the duration of that year's bountiful fall fruit-harvesting and marketing season. By the end of November 1841, the large-scale export of fruit to India was nearly complete. The preponderance of the financial activities, exchanges, and transactions associated with the harvesting, sorting, weighing, packaging, and transport of local fruit from eastern Afghanistan to markets in North India (particularly Peshawar, Kohat, and Dera Ismail Khan) had occurred. By the end of that fall's fruit-marketing season commercial brokers such as the Shikarpuris, including the more prosperous among them who became revenue farmers for the colonial state, had made the majority of their profits deriving from the British attempt to manipulate the lucrative Afghan fruit trade. While some of the economics of the colonial occupation had been completed by this time, its political life was effectively over and the Army of the Indus would evaporate in about two months.

PART II

The New Outdated Colonial Political Economy

Capital Concentrations and Coordinations: Peshawar Subsidies and Kabul Workshops

———•◆•———

The British Subsidization of Durrani Rulers

During the eighteenth century the "eastern *wilayats*" or Indian provinces of the Durrani empire provided the bulk of the revenue received by Ahmad Shah (ruled 1747–73), Timur Shah (ruled 1773–93), and Zaman Shah (ruled 1793–1800).[1] The Indian provinces including but not limited to the Punjab, Sirhind, Kashmir, Multan, Dera Ismail Khan, Dera Ghazi Khan, and Shikarpur, formed the core of the revenue-base of the early Durrani empire. The Indian provinces contributed approximately 40 lakhs of rupees annually to the Durrani polity during the late-eighteenth century, whereas the "western wilayats" of Kabul, Peshawar, Jalalabad, Bangasht, Ghazni, Kalat-e Ghilzai, Charikar, Panjsher, Qandahar, Farah, Herat, Bamian, and the Hazarajat provided only about 17 lakhs of rupees to the early Durrani dynasts.[2] By the turn of the nineteenth century, Durrani control over the Indian provinces was waning, and in 1809 when Elphinstone arrived to establish British contact with the Durranis, the Indian provinces had been permanently detached from the receding and increasingly Kabul-centered polity.

Shah Shuja (ruled 1803–9 and 1839–42) received Elphinstone, but the host's tenuous hold over the Durrani throne collapsed toward the end of his European guest's stay with him. Shuja's first reign ended rather ignobly with him having to accompany Elphinstone and the British entourage out of Peshawar, after which he journeyed to Kashmir and Lahore before petitioning the colonial government for permission to reside in British India.[3] In 1816 colonial authorities reluctantly agreed to Shuja's request and allowed him to reside in Ludiana. The British granted Shuja an annual stipend of Rs. 50,000, and his wife who was known as "the Wuffa Begum" was allowed Rs. 18,000 annually.[4] Shuja and his wife received British stipends throughout the twenty-three years they remained in Ludiana, and while residing there both parties continually petitioned colonial authorities for ever-greater volumes of pecuniary assistance and additional forms of material aid, such as improvements to their respective residences.[5]

Shuja's dependence on colonial capital while he resided in Ludiana was maintained and intensified during the first Anglo-Afghan war. The British invasion of Afghanistan was commercially motivated and a subsidiary element in the colonial Indus navigation project. The British did not restore Shuja to the Durrani throne in Kabul because of his political merits. Rather, Shuja's pliability and attachment to colonial capital made him an attractive surrogate authority and public figurehead for the occupying Army of the Indus. It is important to distinguish between the stipends Shuja received from the British in Ludiana and the subsidies he received while serving the British in Kabul. The stipend resembles a common form of domestic redistribution of capital, and in this regard the British were doing something the Durrani state also practiced.[6] The state-to-state dimension of the subsidies distinguish them from domestic stipends, but the British used each form of financial support to monitor and influence the political and economic activity of their client Shuja.

As noted, while in Ludiana and receiving a fixed stipend, Shuja continually petitioned the British for additional funds. The same insatiable clamoring to the British for ever more pecuniary assistance also characterizes Shuja's second term as the Durrani sovereign in Kabul. On being stationed in British-occupied Kabul in the fall of 1839, Shuja was given full control of the Durrani state's resource base, and during the occupation the British deployed a number of financial statistics in an attempt to demonstrate the revenue gains resulting from their "superior protection of merchants and cultivators."[7] Despite his renewed access to and control of the allegedly increasing Durrani state revenue, Shuja continued to appeal to the British for further infusions of cash. In May 1841 he asked for an additional Rs. 50,000 per month, which alienated his patrons to such an extent that they assumed full revenue control of the Durrani polity.[8] By August Shuja was borrowing money from local bankers in Kabul to support his family and retainers.[9] The first colonial occupation of Afghanistan became a legendary military disaster for the British, and Shuja expired shortly after the demise of the Army of the Indus.

The extensive Durrani empire of the eighteenth century had already been truncated when the British began to reconnoiter the Indus and its north-western flank in the 1830s. The first Anglo-Afghan war further shrank, isolated, and restricted the flow of capital to, through, and within the fledgling state. Similar to Shuja during his hiatus from the Durrani throne, Dost Muhammad (ruled 1826–39 and 1842–63) sought and received a British pension during the interim period between his tenures of rule in Kabul. The British did not provide Dost Muhammad a cash subsidy immediately on his second accession, but he did successfully petition colonial officials to fund his military defense of Herat in 1856. The British subsidized Dost Muhammad to rectify his claimed inability to repel a Qajar military threat on Herat. Arguing in favor of this subsidization of the Durrani state, the Governor General of India then reasoned:

> I believe that one of the best securities for success and harmony in our present dealings with the Afghans, and for the avoidance of embarrassments hereafter, consists in our having as few points of contact with them as possible.[10]

In 1856 the British conceived the Durrani subsidies to be a short-term tactic in a longer-term anti-Russian strategy in Afghanistan, Iran, and Central Asia. By convincing the British that Herat was in jeopardy of being taken by the Persians who were at least tacitly supported by Russia, Dost Muhammad was granted an annual cash subsidy of not less than Rs. 10,00,000.[11] For not agitating against the British during the Indian Mutiny of 1857, Dost Muhammad's subsidy was increased and regularized into monthly allotments of Rs. 1,00,000, but the funds were still conditional on his defense of Herat from Russo-Persian threats.[12] Dost Muhammad died in 1863 while defending Herat from another Iranian advance on the city.

The British subsidization of the Durrani state continued after the death of Dost Muhammad. Sher Ali (ruled 1863–66 and 1868–79) occupied Kabul immediately after Dost Muhammad died, but he had to contend with a number of other claimants and competitors to his authority there and in other cities, and in 1866 he was driven out of Kabul. From 1866 to 1868 Kabul was occupied by Muhammad Afzal (ruled 1866–67) and then Muhammad Azam (ruled 1867–68), but Sher Ali retook the city and the Durrani throne in 1868 and retained his position there until he died in 1879. From 1863 to 1869 the British provided Sher Ali with a number of subsidy payments totaling Rs. 12,00,000.[13] Until this point the British subsidies had been dispensed to shore up the Durrani rulers in Kabul against internal dissent and external threats that were invariably deemed to be inspired by Russia. In the 1870s Sher Ali petitioned the British for additional

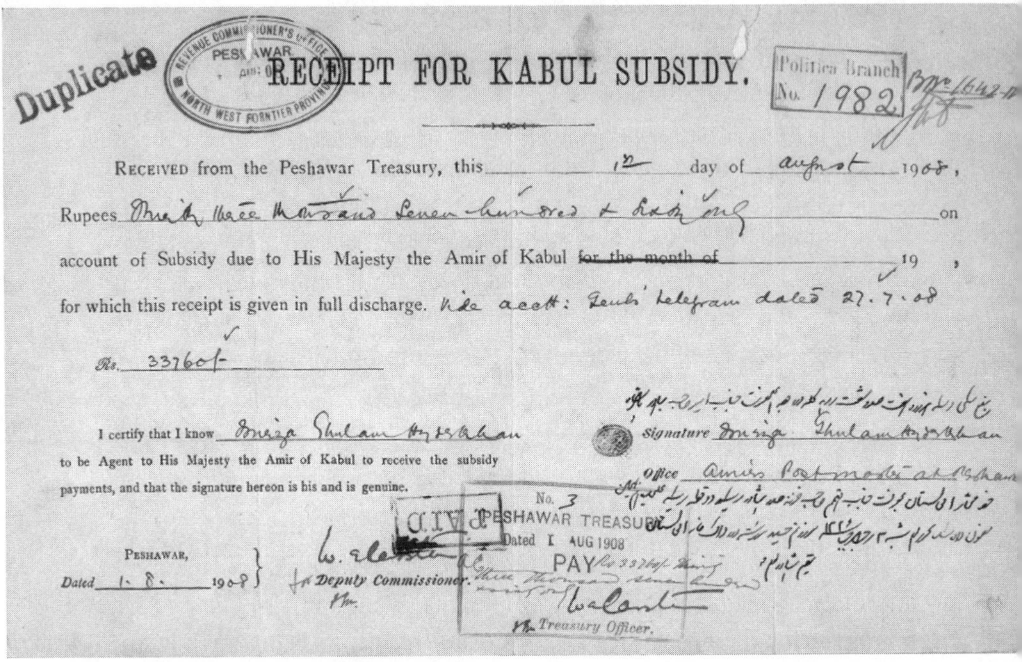

Duplicate

REVENUE COMMISSIONER'S OFFICE PESHAWAR NORTH WEST FRONTIER PROVINCE

RECEIPT FOR KABUL SUBSIDY.

Political Branch No. 1982

RECEIVED from the Peshawar Treasury, this 12 day of August 1908,

Rupees Thirty three thousand seven hundred & sixty only on

account of Subsidy due to His Majesty the Amir of Kabul ~~for the month of~~ 19 ,

for which this receipt is given in full discharge. Vide acctt: Genl's telegram dated 27.7.08

Rs. 33760/-

I certify that I know Mirza Ghulam Haidar Khan to be Agent to His Majesty the Amir of Kabul to receive the subsidy payments, and that the signature hereon is his and is genuine.

Signature Mirza Ghulam Haidar Khan

Office Amir's Postmaster at Peshawar

PESHAWAR,
Dated 1. 8. 1908

for Deputy Commissioner.

No. 3
PESHAWAR TREASURY
Dated 1 AUG 1908
PAY Rs 33760/- Thirty three thousand seven hundred sixty only
Treasury Officer.

FIG. 4.1. Kabul Subsidy Receipt, 1908

subsidy funding. His intent was to erect forts and garrison them with troops in a number of areas he wished to subjugate on the eastern and northern flanks of his realm, namely, Chitral, Bajour, Wakhan, Shignan, Maimana, and in the Waziri Pashtun tribal territory in the vicinity of Bannu and Dera Ismail Khan. British policy makers balked at this request because Sher Ali did not intend to use the subsidy to repel external aggression on his territory that the British also perceived as threatening their position in India. Colonial officials expressed the viewpoint that Sher Ali was asking for money to pursue an agenda that would not provide them any advantage.[14]

Unlike his Durrani dynastic predecessors, Abd al-Rahman (ruled 1880–1901) received regular and large cash subsidies from the British throughout his reign. The ongoing and increasing colonial subsidization of Abd al-Rahman draws attention to an important area of routinization in Anglo-Durrani relations. Compared to the experimental period of Anglo-Durrani relations covering the period between Elphinstone's mission to Shuja in 1809 and the end of the first war in 1842, and the interim period of restricted contact between the two states until the second war (1878–80), Anglo-Durrani relations appear quite routin-

TABLE 4.1

British Cash Subsidies Granted to Abd al-Rahman from His Appointment to the Durrani Throne in July 1880 to December 1881

I. Rs. 10,00,000. Paid through Chief Political Officer, Kabul, on 20 July 1880.
II. Rs. 9,65,000. Left in Kabul for Abd al-Rahman from Yaqub Khan's treasury, fall 1880.
III. Rs. 5,00,000. Paid through Peshawar Commissioner, on or about 10 January 1881.
IV. Rs. 5,00,000. Paid through Qandahar Resident, on or about 16 April 1881.
V. Rs. 5,00,000. Paid through Peshawar Commissioner, on or about 13 May 1881.
VI. Rs. 3,00,000. Paid through Colonel St. John, Qandahar, at the end of September or beginning of October 1881.
VII. Rs. 2,00,000. Deposited at Quetta (but not paid as of) December 1881.

Source: N.D.C., Photocopy Accession number 291, p. 123 (in one pagination series of many; this citation appears to correspond with the India Office Library and Records citation L/P+S/20 B258.) All rupees are the British variety (see Chapter 1 for more on the relationship between the Kabul and British rupees). These figures exclude Rs. 50,000 paid monthly to Abd al-Rahman's Governor in Qandahar from April to July 1881, or a total Rs. 2,00,000.

ized around the subsidy during Abd al-Rahman's reign. After the second war the issue in question for colonial policy makers became not whether to subsidize the Durrani state, but rather to what extent.

In the spring and summer of 1880 the second colonial occupation of Afghanistan was devolving in ways similar to the unraveling of the first occupation forty years earlier. The appointment of Abd al-Rahman was made to facilitate the evacuation of colonial forces from Kabul and Qandahar and thus avert a siege, massacre, and the taking of British hostages as experienced by the Army of the Indus and its followers. Abd al-Rahman's accession to the Durrani throne in Kabul required the political collusion and material support of the British.[15] During negotiations over his prospective role and service to the British as the Durrani sovereign in Kabul, Abd al-Rahman repeatedly clamored for guns, money, and a formal treaty from the British.[16] In accepting the colonial appointment to the Durrani throne in Kabul, Abd al-Rahman agreed to two points contained in the 1879 Gandamak Treaty between the British and Sher Ali's son Muhammad Yaqub (ruled 1879). The first element was that the Durrani state's foreign relations be conducted through British India. The second item was that a British Agent be given access to Abd al-Rahman's public court.[17] The subsidies were granted in return for these two key points of "friendship" between Abd al-Rahman and the British.

Table 4.1 indicates that in the eighteen months after being recognized as the Amir of Kabul in July 1880, Abd al-Rahman received Rs. 39,65,000 in cash subsidies from the British, which averages out to Rs. 2,20,277 per month. During

their second occupation the British estimated the annual revenue of Afghanistan to be Rs. 73,30,677.[18] With the monthly revenue of the Durrani state estimated at Rs. 6,10,890, the British monthly provisioning of Rs. 2,20,277 to Abd
al-Rahman during the first eighteen months of his reign was roughly 33 percent
above the estimated internally generated revenue of the polity.

In 1882 British policy makers resolved to transform their extensive but haphazard subsidization of Abd al-Rahman into regularized and predictable dispersals. In July Abd al-Rahman began to receive a standardized subsidy of 12
lakhs per year to be disbursed in equal monthly payments of Rs. 1,00,000. Between 1882 and 1893, or about one-half of Abd al-Rahman's reign, he was privy
to a cash subsidy of 1 lakh of British Indian rupees per month. This was more
than 16 percent above the estimated monthly revenue of the Durrani state immediately before Abd al-Rahman's colonial appointment in Kabul.

Two boundary agreements concluded between Abd al-Rahman and the British led to even greater dispensations of subsidy funds. The Durand agreement
of 1893 was an attempt to establish a permanent border between Afghanistan
and British India. Although the Durand boundary remained imprecise and
contested in a number of important respects, it resulted in Abd al-Rahman's
subsidy being augmented by 50 percent or six lakhs per year, bringing the annual total to eighteen lakhs. The additional six lakhs of rupees resulting from
the Durand agreement were paid in a lump sum once per year on 12 November.
In 1895 as compensation for consenting to the British desire that he assume
administrative responsibility for the Wakhan corridor, a region separating the
Russian and British empires in Central Asia, Abd al-Rahman was granted an
additional Rs. 50,000 per year to be paid on March first.

The seven irregular subsidy dispersals made during the first eighteen months
of Abd al-Rahman's reign were prompted by urgent and near-emergency pleas
to his colonial patron-sponsors for cash. However, accusations of impropriety,
reprisals, and general confusion, as illustrated later in this chapter, prevailed
during the reception and handling of these early subsidy dispersals. Such cha-
otic conditions impeded Abd al-Rahman's ability to receive let alone use the
subsidy money in a timely fashion, and as such destabilize the dire character of
his "needs" in the first instance.

The changing patterns of reception and redistribution of the subsidy provide useful information about Abd al-Rahman's economic restructuring of the
Durrani state. At the beginning of his reign there were significant areas of continuity with earlier Kabul-centered Durrani fiscal regimes, but Abd al-Rahman

soon and thoroughly transformed the personnel, institutions, and practices comprising the Durrani state's financial and commercial bureaucracy. Early in his reign Abd al-Rahman relied on Shikarpuri bankers to handle the subsidy, but he quickly moved to displace that group in favor of commercial agents he personally appointed and controlled.

Subsidy documents generated less than a year into Abd al-Rahman's reign indicate the Durrani state's inherited dependence on the financial services provided by a resident corps of Shikarpuri and other Indian bankers and merchants and their agents in Kabul. Collection of Abd al-Rahman's fifth intermittent subsidy dispersal (Table 4.2) resulted in a group of "Peshawar bankers" assuming responsibility for more than two of the five lakhs of rupees made available in May 1881.[19] In this instance, Abd al-Rahman deputed two people to Peshawar to collect the Rs. 5,00,000 of subsidy funds, but he subsequently replaced that pair with a single person, and a quarrel developed between the factions.[20] The new agent and a fourth individual then tried unsuccessfully to deposit over Rs. 50,000 with the two original appointees.[21] Nearly three months after the five lakhs became available to Abd al-Rahman, his Envoy with the Government of India, General Amir Ahmad Khan, ordered all parties to deposit a total of Rs. 2,07,000 with a collection of unnamed Peshawar bankers.[22] Their roles in the resolution of such extraterritorial conflict among Durrani state officials and in the routing of subsidy money to Kabul indicate the Peshawar bankers' knowledge of and familiarity with the fiscal conduct of Abd al-Rahman and his budgetary officers.

The Peshawar bankers' intimacy with Abd al-Rahman's financial practices arose from the long-standing implication of their capital in the Durrani state's resource base. Early in his reign Abd al-Rahman regularly borrowed or extorted money from the Shikarpuris in Kabul, and on certain occasions he repaid those individuals or their representatives from the subsidy.[23] For example, sixteen months after the regularization of the subsidy into monthly installments, Abd al-Rahman wrote the Government of India to state:

> As regards the allowance for November 1883, I find it desirable to realize it from the Peshawar Treasury through certain bankers, and by bills of exchange . . . I have just received Rs. 42,229.4 of the English currency from the following sixteen Hindu Bankers at Kabul.[24]

Abd al-Rahman mentions a second group of Shikarpuris in another letter to his colonial sponsors about the redistribution of this single month's subsidy:

TABLE 4.2

Shikarpuri Hindu Bankers/Merchants (of Kabul) Paid (in Peshawar)
from Abd al-Rahman's November 1883 Subsidy

Name	Amount (Rupees.Annas.Paisa)
1. Lekhu	1,909.4.0
2. Chur	2,212.8.0
3. Dheru	1,331.0.0
4. Asa	8,711.2.0
5. Lalu	6,175.0.0
6. Jassu	3,972.8.0
7. Hira, son of Manku	768.12.0
8. Birij	2,350.0.0
9. Taliya	2,673.8.0
10. Mishar Ganran	3,075.0.0
11. Dilaram	1,468.4.0
12. Hira, son of Taku	997.8.0
13. Ramu	3,768.12.0
14. Kishan	1,008.8.0
15. Santu	256.4.0
16. Mangu	1,451.6.0
17. Kundun	2,954.15.9
18. Manwi (Nanoo)	510.2.6
19. Jangal	612.3.0
20. Alwi (Hotoo)	469.2.9
21. Sharbat	111.9.0
22. Asa	238.0.0
23. Notan	1,219.10.0
24. Nainban (son of Jaltu [Dilta])	496.3.6
25. Mango	1,456.7.6
26. Brijdas (Moorj)	631.14.9
27. Shewal	10,004.2.0
28. Tharu (son of Khotu [Paman])	401.10.0
29. Mishar Amar Singh	358.2.6
30. Ram Kishen	598.4.0
31. Naru	4,101.3.0
32. Mula son of Gulab	1,515.6.0
33. Muhammad Sharif	1,397.0.6
34. Naina, son of Maraj	1,344.2.9
35. Asu, son of Laila	595.0.0
36. Lukrooma (Pokar)	867.6.0
37. Daulat	1,230.0.6
38. Moola, son of Rukko	490.0.0
39. Mishar Kalua (Jagua)	2,381.4.6
40. Mishar Thakur (son of Ram Das)	163.10.0
41. Harji, Goldsmith	298.9.0

Source: "Disbursement of the Subsidy of the Amir of Afghanistan," NAI, Foreign A Political E, February 1884, Proceeding Nos. 34–53.

"I now beg to ask you to kindly pay Rs. 30,450.4 to twenty-five merchants of Shikarpur, of whom twenty-four are Hindus and one a Muhammadan."[25] The British-appointed Durrani ruler in Kabul requested a further redistribution of his November 1883 subsidy, making a total of three separate communications to ensure that forty-three people received payments from this single subsidy allotment. The final breakdown of this monthly lakh of subsidy was Rs. 42,229.4 to one group of Shikarpuris, Rs. 30,450.4 to a second collection of the same, Rs. 24,520.8 to Haji Asad Khan, Abd al-Rahman's commercial agent in Bombay, and Rs. 2,800 to a merchant named Haji Saleh.

Unequal Reciprocity: Durrani State Commercial Agents in Peshawar and English Firms in Kabul

It was complicated and time-consuming for British officials to continually redistribute such small portions of Durrani subsidy funds to so many different Shikarpuri and other bankers and merchants. Colonial authorities therefore proposed a number of alternatives to remedy Abd al-Rahman's "inconvenient and dangerous" habit of handling his cash grants in that manner. At least five suggestions were proffered to help alleviate some of the confusion and imprecision characterizing these unwieldy Durrani subsidy redistributions. The British proposed that Abd al-Rahman write in words the payment amounts, provide accurate and full descriptions of all payees (not just a father's name, if anything), send triplicate copies of all requests, appoint one agent in Peshawar to receive the funds, and/or send separate checks directly to the individuals without the mediation of the Indian Government.[26] Although Abd al-Rahman may have heeded some of these suggestions, the effect desired by colonial officials was achieved largely through a series of domestic economic initiatives undertaken by the Durrani ruler independent of the British proposals about streamlining the subsidy redistributions.

Abd al-Rahman's establishment of trading monopolies and his confiscation of local merchant capital devastated the community of Shikarpuri Hindu bankers residing in Kabul at the outset of his reign.[27] By 1886 it was reported that only eight British Indian subjects active in the trade between India and Central Asia remained in the city.[28] Abd al-Rahman's initial dependence on Shikarpuri and other interregional bankers and traders based in India was soon transformed into competition with and then decimation of them. The practice of borrowing multiple small sums of money, on the order of a few hundreds or thousands of rupees, from the Shikarpuri bankers in Kabul that were repaid from single month subsidy dispersals began to fade away in the mid- to late 1880s. By 1890 a clear shift had occurred as the preponderance of redistributions became much larger, on the order of multiple lakhs of rupees. Furthermore, the redistributions became far more intermittent, often occurring after multiple months of subsidy had accrued, and they went not to private bankers but rather to a handful of expatriate Durrani state officials Abd al-Rahman stationed in Peshawar and other Indian cities.

Transformations in the structure of subsidy redistributions occurred processually, not abruptly, and the transition period can be estimated as covering the years from 1884 to 1889. During this period Abd al-Rahman's ongoing and rapacious domestic confiscations of capital appear to have allowed for the subsidy installments to accumulate over months. After multiple months of subsidy accrual, Abd al-Rahman would write his patrons with requests detailing which portion of which month would go to whom, where, when, and how. Communication of these instructions among Durrani authorities, between them and British officials, and within various British bureaucratic units was fraught with the potential for misunderstanding. The gradual change in subsidy procedures was demonstrated between April 1888 and March 1889 when Abd al-Rahman was privy to twelve lakhs of British Indian rupees. During this twelve-month period Abd al-Rahman requested fourteen separate subsidy dispersals to be made in four different cities, Peshawar, Bombay, Calcutta, and Simla.[29] Abd al-Rahman directed Rs. 5,70,000 to his almond agent or *badami* in Peshawar, Rs. 5,60,000 to his mercantile agent in Bombay, and Rs. 70,000 to his Envoy with the Government of India.[30]

At this time there were still many lines of communication within and between the Durrani and British Governments about the subsidy. In general, to convey his wishes about subsidy funds to the British, Abd al-Rahman wrote to his primary agent, his Envoy with the Government of India, who would transmit the requests to the Foreign Department of the Government of India. The Foreign Department would in turn usually correspond with the Comptroller General of India, and the Punjab and other provincial administrations, particularly those in Bombay and Sind. Colonial bureaucrats at the central and provincial levels of British Indian government ultimately had to communicate about the subsidy with the Commissioner and Superintendent of the Peshawar Division through the Punjab Government. This was so because the subsidy money and goods purchased with those resources (see later in this chapter) were accounted for in and transmitted through Peshawar, which was then a part of the Punjab Province. In some instances, but far less frequently, Abd al-Rahman corresponded directly with the Viceroy and Governor General of India and/or the Foreign Secretary about the subsidy. It was standard practice for Abd al-Rahman to reiterate his wishes about subsidy redistributions, often using different words and calculations than deployed in his correspondence with his Envoy and/or British officials, to his *badami* or almond agent and/or his postmaster in Peshawar. The badami and/or postmaster would then transmit those instructions to Peshawar Treasury officials through the office of the Peshawar Commissioner.[31]

The communicative web generated by the subsidy extended deep within and between the Durrani and British Indian states, and was fraught with the potential for confusion, uncertainty, and misinterpretation. For example, between April 1888 and March 1889, archival records indicate Durrani requests were not honored by the colonial government as a result of a lack of signatures and proper seals, and an even more problematic incongruence between Durrani and British calculations as to how much subsidy remained collectable after certain payments.[32] Solving such problems was bureaucratically time-consuming and required both sides to retrace communication paths in all directions. Durrani and British officials then had to meticulously review and compare documents detailing multiple arrangements in various locations at all levels and stages of the process. Subsidy correspondence between Abd al-Rahman and his Envoy to the Government of India regarding the payment of a Durrani state-contracted European engineer contains superfluous information and contingency details that represent one small set among many possible loose ends in the long tangles of a much larger body of subsidy correspondence:

> Be it known to you that Mr. Pyne, an officer of the God-granted Government, has got leave from us for the winter season, and has been entrusted to do certain things in connection with State matters. After passing the winter he will come and join his appointment at the capital. We therefore write to you that he has received his pay for January 1891; that we empower you to get Rs. 4,000 (Rupees four thousand), out of my due for the second half of October 1890, from the Government Treasury, and make the money over to Mr. Pyne in lieu of his payment for two months, viz., from 1st February 1891 corresponding to 21st Jamadi us-Sani 1308 H., to the last day of the month of March 1891, corresponding with 20th Rajab 1308. If he be engaged in State business after the expiry of two months, you will be authorized to give Mr. Pyne his

monthly salary, otherwise he will start for the capital. For the present make over this Rs. 4,000 to the said Mr. Pyne in lieu of his pay for two months. Consider this correct and approved by us.[33]

This quote is contained in a review of subsidy redistributions totaling fourteen lakhs that accrued between September 1889 and October 1890. The vast preponderance of this amount, Rs. 12,00,000 covering the period from September 1888 to September 1889, was redistributed in eight installments between May and September 1890 to Abd al-Rahman's *badami* or almond agent in Peshawar. The final in a series of disbursements to the *badami*, then Abd al-Khaliq Khan, occurred on September 22 and was for five lakhs of rupees.[34]

To obtain the subsidy cash from the Peshawar provincial treasury, the *badami* was required to match the details of Abd al-Rahman's written order to him with what British officials there understood of the transaction based on what they knew of the central Government of India's communication with the Durrani Envoy. The coinage likely came in boxes containing twelve bags, each of which held Rs. 2,000.[35] To transmit the twenty or twenty-one boxes of money to the *mashin khana* and the new minting machines there, the *badami* communicated with the *qafilabashi* or Durrani caravan official in charge of transporting state goods from Peshawar to Kabul through the Khaibar Pass.[36] The transmission of such a large amount of subsidy coinage to Kabul was an infrequent occurrence because Abd al-Rahman's standard practice was to use *hundis* or bills of exchange to redistribute subsidy funds to Durrani state commercial agents and other recipients in India. The *badami* was the most important facilitator of subsidy-related communication between Abd al-Rahman and his expatriate commercial agents. The *badami* held primary responsibility over the subsidy account. His duties included the relatively infrequent arrangement for subsidy cash transmissions to Kabul, and, more commonly, the redistribution of those funds via *hundis* to Durrani state commercial agents based throughout India.

In addition to the *badami*, the Durrani postmaster stationed in Peshawar was also an important handler of the subsidy.[37] Less than one year after he was appointed by the British, in the spring of 1881 Abd al-Rahman deputed Mirza Baiza Khan to serve as the Durrani state postmaster in Peshawar. The British not only accepted the unique presence of this Durrani state institution in their territory, they supported the foreign post office by providing office space for it. After appointing Abd al-Rahman, the only official British presence in Kabul was an Agent whose communication with Durrani officials and access to other local sources of information such as Indian merchants was heavily controlled and restricted.[38] The British therefore believed that a Durrani postmaster in India would facilitate their communication with Abd al-Rahman, increase their access to data about conditions in Kabul and greater Afghanistan, and heighten their ability to disseminate information to their contacts inside the country.[39]

Like the subsidy itself the postmaster was a key institutional node in the communication scheme integrating, however loosely, these two asymmetrical state powers. Partly as a result of his connection to the subsidy, the postmaster communicated on behalf of Abd al-Rahman with a plethora of British and Durrani officials, and Indian and Afghan traders in Peshawar and throughout India.[40] The badami and the postmaster provided intelligence to and disseminated a wide variety of information for Abd al-Rahman, not only in Peshawar but also by extension from there throughout India. There was a good deal of overlap between the subsidy-related duties of the Durrani postmaster and the badami, and this arrangement was Abd al-Rahman's method of obtaining mutual oversight of the two individuals he deputed to manage the extensive pool of subsidy resources the British made available to him in Peshawar. In practice, however, joint oversight of the subsidy created mutual intrigue and inefficiency between these two Durrani officials in Peshawar.

For reasons related but not limited to intelligence gathering, promotion, or punishment, Abd al-Rahman commonly circulated his official appointees between posts domestically and in India. The ongoing circulation of Durrani state personnel had the effect of impeding subsidy collection and redistribution. One such occasion appears to have been on June 19, 1898, when the recently appointed Durrani postmaster, Mirza Khalifa Ji Khan, went to the Peshawar Treasury to collect Rs. 5,58,954 in cash from the subsidy account.[41] In this instance, a quarrel broke out between the Durrani postmaster and his entourage, and British officials and their staffs, regarding the exact form of the coinage's packing in bags and boxes. Apparently to support his claim of entitlement to a particular configuration of bags and boxes, Khalifa Ji Khan made a series of unusual and extraordinary statements that Peshawar Treasury officials quickly forwarded to their superiors in Lahore and Calcutta. Denying any ability to remedy the local level confusion about subsidy packaging in Peshawar, the Foreign Secretary of the Government of India actually compounded the quandary by punting the question back to its askers: "(p)lease instruct the Treasury officials to act in accordance with the usual practice, *whatever that has been*" (emphasis added).[42]

It is striking that after nearly two decades of Abd al-Rahman receiving his first subsidy payment, and more than fifteen years of being granted monthly allotments, Durrani and British officials were still quibbling about such details. However, communication between Durrani and British officials about this somewhat petty point is interesting for a number of reasons, particularly because it reveals the unequal weighting of the subsidy in each government's ordering of priorities. British officials received this and many other Durrani communications about the subsidy with an air of nonchalance and a tone of distance and disinterest that reveals an inverse proportionality of the importance of the subsidy to each government. For Abd al-Rahman, the subsidy was crucially important to the financial structure of the state, and it therefore consumed a large amount of his and other Durrani officials' time and attention. For the British the subsidy was far less important and consequential, and colonial authorities viewed matters related to the subsidy as increasingly pestering and trivial as Abd al-Rahman's reign wore on.

Among the Durrani officials in Peshawar and greater India, knowledge of Abd al-Rahman's unstable temperament and proclivity for violent reprimands evoked a tangible and well-founded fear of harsh reprisals for any misconduct or failure to execute orders, particularly insofar as the cherished subsidy was concerned. Their acute awareness of quite possibly life-threatening punitive sanctions from Abd al-Rahman for any real or perceived malfeasance is reflected in the anxious and agitated tone of the Durrani appointees' communication about the subsidy. The alarm and desperation often expressed by Durrani officials in India about the subsidy and matters related to it become more palpable when set against the colonial bureaucratic tone of voice, and might account for some of the exaggerated and confusing claims made by these expatriate state functionaries. For example, as leverage to help him rectify the problem he encountered at the Peshawar Treasury in June 1898 that was mentioned earlier, Mirza Khalifa Ji Khan made an unfounded assertion concerning the displacement of a higher ranking, indeed the highest ranking, Durrani state official in India. The Peshawar-based Durrani postmaster announced he had "received orders from the Amir that His Highness's subsidy will be remitted through the Postmaster and not through the Amir's Envoy with the Government of India."[43] This bewildering declaration contravened past practice and elicited the following dismissive response from the Assistant Foreign Secretary of the Government of India:

> No importance need be attached to the report that future payments on account of the subsidy are to be made through the Postmaster, and "not through the Amir's Envoy" (to the Government of India); for, in the first place, there is no Envoy just at

present, and in the second, payments on account of the subsidy for a long time past have been more often paid to the Amir's Agents at Bombay and Karachi than to the Envoy.[44]

The Durrani Envoy to the Government of India was Abd al-Rahman's main commercial and political representative outside of Afghanistan.[45] Similar to the subsidy-generated practices exhibited by the badami and postmaster in Peshawar, the Envoy redistributed subsidy funds to Durrani commercial agents stationed throughout India, in addition to making direct purchases and payments with those resources. The Envoy's subsidy-related activities can be distinguished from those exhibited by the badami and postmaster because they occurred on a wider and larger scale, and because he retained ultimate political responsibility for the subsidy as a result of his duty of overseeing all other Durrani state officials in India. The Durrani Envoy was based near the Governor General of India, so he resided primarily in Calcutta but spent summers in Simla. As the political representative of a foreign government, the Durrani Envoy's movement in India independent of the Governor General's travels required him to be monitored. In 1899 George Curzon was the Governor General and he advocated such surveillance when the Durrani Envoy Sardar Muhammad Ismail Khan sought permission to travel to Lahore to buy Rs. 70,000 worth of *pashmina* or woolen goods. Curzon sanctioned the commercial excursion provided the Envoy not be "allow(ed) to conduct a political or religious propaganda [*sic*] under our very noses."[46]

The Envoy's redistributions of subsidy funds compensated primarily two categories of people, either Durrani commercial agents stationed in various Indian cities, or English firms whose services Abd al-Rahman contracted. The subsidy transfers to English firms involved noticeably large sums. For example, during the summer of 1893, Messrs. Walsh, Lovett & Co. requested to be paid Rs. 4,00,000 in Calcutta, which prompted the Durrani Envoy to take hasty and unusual action on this matter from the Governor General's Simla retreat.[47] Another illustration comes from 1899 when the Envoy facilitated six deposits totaling Rs. 13,35,814 from the subsidy account into the account of Messrs. J. Buchanan Guthrie & Co. at the National Bank of India in Calcutta.[48] This substantial sum comprised almost 75 percent of Abd al-Rahman's annual subsidy, then Rs. 18,50,000. The firm of J. B. Guthrie & Co. was arguably the most prominent of all the trading companies commissioned by Abd al-Rahman to build and supply his workshops, courts, and palaces (see later in this chapter).

Whether through the Envoy, other expatriate Durrani officials such as the

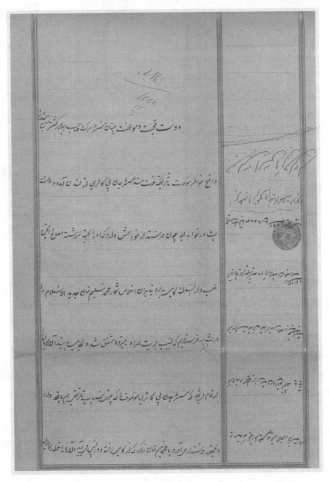

FIG. 4.2. Abd al-Rahman Document for John P. Guthrie, 1898

badami or postmaster in Peshawar, or directly by Abd al-Rahman, subsidy funds were regularly redistributed to Durrani commercial agents stationed in various cities throughout India. Subsidy payments were made to Durrani commercial agents stationed in or traveling to Calcutta, Delhi, Amballa, Lahore, Quetta, and Peshawar. However, subsidy payments made to Durrani commercial agents appear to have been made most often to individuals based in Bombay and Karachi. Table 4.3 provides a glimpse into some of the subsidy transactions at these two primary South Asian port cities.[49]

These figures show how nearly a year's worth of subsidy funds at the end of

TABLE 4.3

Select Subsidy Redistributions to Durrani State Commercial Agents in Bombay and Karachi

Agent	Transaction date/s and Location	Total RS.
1. Haji Asad Khan	December 1883, Bombay	24,520
2. Mullah Abu Bakr Khan	July, September, and October 1888 and May and September 1889, Bombay	3,70,000
3. Ghulam Rasul Khan	September and October 1890, Bombay	1,00,000
4. Mullah Muhd. Azim Khan	June 1892, Bombay	73,949
5. Mullah Dost Muhd. Khan Tokhi	June 1897, Bombay	40,000
6. Mullah Dost Muhd. Khan Tokhi	June, October, and November 1897, and January, and March 1898, Karachi	11,70,000
7. Mullah Dost Muhd. Khan Tokhi	September 1899, Karachi	15,000
8. Mullah Muhd. Azim Khan	July and December 1899, Bombay	50,000

Total Rs. Paid: 18,43,469 (Rs 6,58,469 in Bombay and Rs 11,85,000 in Karachi)

Sources: This table is distilled from the following archival citations: "Payments Made to the Amir's Agents in India on Account of His Highness's Subsidy," NAI, Foreign Frontier K.W., May 1890, Proceeding Nos. 5–24. "Disbursement of the Subsidy of the Amir of Afghanistan," NAI, Foreign A Political E, February 1884, Proceeding Nos. 34–53. "Payments Made to the Amir's Agents in India on Account of His Highness's Subsidy," NAI, Foreign Frontier K.W., May 1890, Proceeding Nos. 5–24. "Payments Made to the Amir's Agents in India on Account of His Highness's Subsidy," NAI, Foreign Frontier K.W., May 1890, Proceeding Nos. 5–24. "Payments made on account the subsidy of His Highness the Amir of Afghanistan," NAI, Foreign Frontier A, March 1891, Proceeding Nos. 8–16. "Establishment of a Post Office in Peshawar by the Amir of Kabul," NWFPA, TARC. Afghanistan Index I, File No. 205 (records from the Chief Commissioner's Office, 1881). "Misappropriation of Money Belong to Amir of Kabul by Jawahir Mal alias Jaru," NWFPA, Records from the Office of the Peshawar Commissioner, Bundle No. 60, Serial No. 1545. "Statement Showing the Payments Made to His Highness During 1897–98 and the Balance At His Credit on the 1st March 1898," NAI, Foreign Frontier A, August 1898, Proceeding Nos. 48–57. "Payments Made Out of the Amir's Subsidy. Statement Furnished to the India Office of Arms, Ammunition, and Money Presented by the Government of India to His Highness the Amir During the Year 1899," NAI, Foreign Frontier B, January 1900, Proceeding Nos. 171–201. "Payments Made Out of the Amir's Subsidy. Statement Furnished to the India Office of Arms, Ammunition, and Money Presented by the Government of India to His Highness the Amir During the Year 1899," NAI, Foreign Frontier B, January 1900, Proceeding Nos. 171–201. "Complaint by the Amir's Officials against the Peshawar Municipality in Connection with His Highness's Goods. Letter to the Amir about the Continued Collection of Afghan Dues and Tolls in British Territory," NAI, Foreign Frontier A, August 1901, Proceeding Nos. 34–40. "Payments Made to the Amir's Agents in India on Account of His Highness's Subsidy," NAI, Foreign Frontier (K.W.), May 1890, Proceeding Nos. 5–24. "Purchase of Articles for Amir of Kabul in Peshawar," NAI, Foreign Political B, September 1881, Proceeding Nos. 178–79. N.D.C., Photocopy Accession number 291, p. 123 (in one pagination series of many; this citation appears to correspond with the India Office Library and Records citation L/P+S/20 B258).

Note: The invocation of identity adjectives and markers in the table deserves brief attention. Use of core Islamic terminology such as "Haji" or "Mullah," and the regional Indo-Persian-Turkic titulature such as "Khan," "Mirza," and "Sardar" abound in the correspondence between Durrani and British officials in India. Colonial bureaucrats and scribes reproduced and eliminated these indigenous honorifics in inconsistent and seemingly arbitrary ways. The difficulties of precisely identifying "Shikarpuris," "Hindus," or "Peshawar bankers" in nineteenth-century Kabul and Peshawar were addressed in Chapter 1. Likewise, concrete and thorough understanding of the identity packages of Durrani state agents in India proves illusive at a variety of levels including cultural background, ethnicity, linguistic attributes, intra-religious distinctions (Shias and Sayyids among Muslims; Khattris, in particular, among Hindus castes), territorial affiliation, and tribal membership.

Abd al-Rahman's reign, or Rs. 18,50,000, was distributed through time to various agents stationed in or passing through Bombay and Karachi. They do not represent the cumulative total or complete record of subsidy transactions in either city. Table 4.3 also draws attention to the fluid structure of the Durrani state's presence in British India. There was an ongoing circulation of Durrani commercial agents between posts, as well as a tendency for appointees to experience short tenures in each position. The rapid cycling of individuals into, within, and out of this network of commercial agents in India mirrors a structural flaw in the Durrani state's domestic bureaucratic architecture as viewed by Abd al-Rahman's contracted European surgeon.[50]

Subsidy funds were also redistributed to Durrani state brokers who heavily influenced commercial traffic between Peshawar and Kabul. In 1899 a redistribution of two lakhs went to the joint receipt of Mirza Muhammad Rahim, Mirza Muhammad Ishaq Khan, Mirza Allahdad Khan, and Diwan Baghwan Das.[51] Subsidy documents identify these three last-mentioned men as "Commission Agents of Afghan merchants residing in Peshawar." Elsewhere the same three men are described as Durrani state brokers of the trade from Peshawar to Kabul through the Khaibar Pass:

[Mirza Muhammad Ishaq Khan, Mirza Allahdad Khan and Diwan Baghwan Das] are the men through whom all trade with Kabul must pass. They will either buy goods for merchants in Kabul charging 1/40th as brokerage, or if a merchant comes to Peshawar himself to trade, he must first, before his goods can be forwarded to Kabul, go to these men and pay 1/40th of the cost of the goods as brokerage and get a pass from them without which his goods will not be sent on by the kafilabashi. The pay of these men is Rs. 1,000, 800, and 800 respectively, and the whole of the brokerage is sent to the Amir.[52]

The subsidy funds allowed Durrani and British agents of Abd al-Rahman to make considerable purchases of Indian and European commodities in Peshawar and throughout the subcontinent. The primary items bought with subsidy funds were raw materials destined for finishing in Kabul.[53] The aforementioned Mullah Abu Bakr, who retained Abd al-Rahman's confidence for a considerable period of time through a number of different postings, was involved in an ongoing series of subsidy-generated purchases. For at least two years he received a lakh of rupees every third month with which he purchased brass and copper in bulk form.[54] At that rate, subsidy expenditures for the import of brass and copper alone consumed at least 5 percent of the Durrani state's total income.[55]

The Mashin Khana

The first dispatch of a Durrani state commercial agent to British India to purchase goods with subsidy money came less than four months after colonial authorities appointed Abd al-Rahman to the Kabul Amirate on July 20, 1880. Abd al-Rahman immediately received Rs. 10,00,000 as a result of his colonial appointment, and on or near December 14 he wrote to the Peshawar Commissioner to ask for logistical help and tax relief on the portion of that money which would soon be spent in India. Abd al-Rahman requested that the *kotwalis* or local magistrates of Peshawar, Amritsar, and Delhi be given official notice that Durrani state commercial agents would be traveling to and through their jurisdictions to make purchases on his behalf.[56]

The commodities purchased on Abd al-Rahman's first subsidy-induced state shopping excursion in India were broken down into two categories, iron and other articles. Under the former heading were "metal bars, sheets, steel, files, vices, screw making machines and metal presses." The other articles included "brass sheets, copper, tin, blankets, shirts and pantaloons."[57] This list indicates that early in his reign Abd al-Rahman used subsidy funds primarily to import relatively inexpensive raw materials, a large portion of which were refined and redistributed to his military forces. More expensive finished military products such as guns, rifles, cannons, cartridges, and ammunition are not represented in the records of Abd al-Rahman's inaugural spending spree in India.

Most of the raw materials imported at the beginning of Abd al-Rahman's reign were transferred to craftsmen populating the Kabul bazaars who were contracted by the Durrani state for the labor-intensive finishing process. In the early nineteenth century, Elphinstone reported that each of the thirty-two artisanal groups in Kabul was represented by a *kadkhoda* who managed the given labor community's transactions with the Durrani government.[58] At the end of the century each community of craftsmen was noted as having an elder spokesman or *kalantar*, and master artificers or *ustads*, as well as apprentices or *shagirds*.[59] The mashin khana or Durrani state workshops established by Abd al-Rahman significantly transformed the institutional leadership and demography of Kabul's local labor communities.

The weapons workshops established by Durrani rulers in Kabul before 1878, including those constructed by Sher Ali, were destroyed by the British during their second invasion and occupation of Afghanistan. The second Anglo-Afghan war wound down far less dramatically than the first conflict that was a re-

FIG. 4.3. Mashin Khana Aerial Photograph, c. 1960s

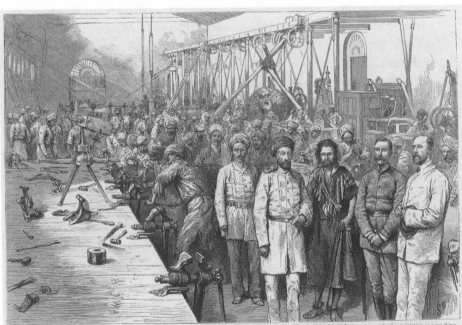

" When the British Army withdrew from Kabul in 1880 it is not too much to say that throughout the whole country of Afghanistan there was no such thing existing as a machine working by steam. At the present day the Ameer has a complete arsenal in full swing, turning out cannon, Martini-Henry rifles, and solid-drawn brass cartridges in large numbers; minting-machines capable of coining 60,000 rupees per diem; a new workshop with all the necessary machinery for rolling metal into sheets; a soap-factory, and, in fact, a mass of machinery such as is scarcely to be found in India ".

THE AMEER OF AFGHANISTAN'S WORKSHOPS AT KABUL: THE INTERIOR OF THE ARSENAL

FIG. 4.4. Mashin Khana Interior Illustration, 1893

sounding military humiliation for the British. Abd al-Rahman facilitated a safe and orderly British retreat from Kabul to begin a sufficiently noble end to the second unsuccessful Anglo-Afghan war as far as colonial policy makers were concerned. After suppressing the most threatening local revolts against his colonially ascribed position, Abd al-Rahman began to divert the bulk of his subsidy funds to resuscitating and significantly expanding on the state workshop concept.[60] Abd al-Rahman's state workshop complex became known locally as the mashin khana, and Pyne was employed by Abd al-Rahman to oversee the technical aspects of the enterprise.[61]

At a ceremony marking the inauguration of the workshops' construction on 7 April 1887, Abd al-Rahman reportedly told Pyne: "This is the happiest day of my life . . . (b)efore these workshops can be finished there are three essentials required: 1. God's help; 2. My money; 3. Your work. God's help and my money without your work, and your work and my money without God's help are equally useless."[62] Beyond daily oversight and managerial responsibilities over the Kabul workshops, Pyne's duties included traveling to India and England to purchase machinery, materials, and supplies, and to locate Indian and European specialists to employ at the mashin khana.

The mashin khana was initially organized around machinery for the production of weapons and military supplies, and by 1891 separate workshops were producing rifles, cannons, ammunition, and boots. However, the workshops were continually expanded to encompass activities far beyond the production of military supplies alone. During Abd al-Rahman's reign the mashin khana was broadened to include stamping, dyeing, minting, lithographic printing, and weaving equipment, as well as flour mills, saw mills, distilleries, tanneries, steam hammers, and lathes. New machines constantly arrived in Kabul, and existing ones were continually upgraded and refurbished.[63] In the late 1890s about one hundred machines, between four and five thousand local workers, and dozens of European and Indian experts and foremen employed at the mashin khana were churning out agricultural implements, candles, carpets, clothes, coats, coins, food, glass, soap, kilns, liquor, needles, paper, and soda pop, in addition to weaponry, most of which imitated European models.[64]

As local craftsmen were incorporated into the mashin khana the chains of authority and gradations of prestige within Kabul's artisanal communities were transformed in significant ways. Europeans contracted by Abd al-Rahman were grafted over the local social hierarchies and institutions mentioned earlier. Indian *mistaris,* the subcontracted assistants to the British mechanics and

TABLE 4.4

Commodities Purchased with Subsidy Money by Durrani State
Commercial Agents Based in India and Conveyed Duty-Free
from Peshawar to Kabul through the Khaibar Pass in 1898

Animal Conveyance:	Camel	Bullock (a/o cart)	Donkey	Mule
Commodities:				
Bricks (Pucca and other)	1139.5	85	184	1
Charcoal	121			
Copper	79			
Iron (sheets and melt)	587			
Kerosene Oil	95			
Machinery (of all kinds):	404	255	1	
Miscellaneous items:				
Bottles	1			
Boxes	1		1	
Candles	10			
Cartridges				5
Empty gunny bags	23½			
Glasses	5			
Harness	½			
Ink pens	2			
Lime	12	9		
Liquid	1			
Miscellaneous	½			
Musical instruments	1			
Lemonade bottles	14			
Packages				2
Paper	1			
Parcel			1	
Piece goods			12	
Pipes		1		
Rice				2
Rifles and cartridges			1	
Snuff				1
Soap			1	
Spices				1
Stationery	1			
Stirrups	15			
Tents		32		
Treasure	5			26
Wearing apparel	6		1	4
Zakhdan (portable ice chest[s])			1	1

Source: "Tolls Realized from Khaibar Pass," NWFPA, List of Foreign Frontier Files 1880–1900 (indexed in the list of files transferred to TARC), 1898 Serial No. 958, File No. 102 (corresponding to Punjab Government Civil Secretariat, Foreign Department, April 1898, B Proceeding Nos. 95–96). The statistics cover the eight months from April through November, the Khaibar being infrequented by commercial traffic from December to March.

Note: This file indicates Rs. 11,110 were collected as Khaibar Pass tolls from April 1897 to March 1898, compared with Rs. 46,545 in 1896–97, and Rs. 51,163 in 1895–96. The Khaibar tolls deserve separate treatment and will not be considered through time or in depth here. Road tolls and transit taxes are usually termed *rahdari* in Iran and generally *arat* in Afghanistan during this period. There were a wide variety of terms used in colonial records to identify an array of road and transit taxes in Afghanistan during Abd al-Rahman's reign. Kakar (1979), p. 209, notes three kinds of tolls applied to Khaibar Pass traffic alone, *goshi*, *rawanagi*, and *badraqagi*.

engineers employed at the mashin khana by Abd al-Rahman, were also inter-posed over and within the existing chains of authority, expertise, and resource management of local artisanal groups. The Europeans, Indians, and Afghans appointed by and responsible to Abd al-Rahman also influenced the residual Kabul bazaar production regimen by periodically siphoning human, techni-cal, and material resources from those labor communities that were not fully encompassed by the workshop project. The mashin khana was the institutional locus for the reconfiguration of social relations within and between the various local labor communities in Kabul and beyond, as well as between those profes-sional networks and the Durrani state.

At the beginning of Abd al-Rahman's reign raw iron, steel, brass, copper, machinery, and military clothing were imported with subsidy funds. Table 4.4 illustrates subsidy purchases during the latter stages of Abd al-Rahman's tenure were also characterized by the import of relatively high volumes of machinery and raw materials such as iron, copper, and bricks. However, at the end of his reign various European novelties and commodities destined for mass reproduc-tion at the mashin khana, ceremonial display, or consumption at the palaces, courts, and homes of the supra-elite of Kabul, were also imported from India with subsidy funds.[65] Like the subsidy itself, the mashin khana was oriented to-ward satisfying the state's needs. The majority of the popular classes of Afghans in Kabul and elsewhere did not benefit from the European and Indian imports to the mashin khana. Rather, ordinary people were generally adversely affected by the workshops' transformation of the mercantile social order and its output of coercive implements that were deployed by the Durrani state against them. Instead of functioning as a socially integrative institution, the mashin khana

---

The bricks were for palace, workshop, road, and other government buildings' construction. According to Kakar (1979), pp. 199–200, major construction projects completed during Abd al-Rahman's reign include: the *Arg* or new palace-fort complex which enclosed the kotwali offices and was modeled on a church Abd al-Rahman had seen in Tashkent; the Gulistan and Boston serais near the Arg, and other caravanserais on the principal roads throughout the county; the Bagh-i Bala palace, the Chilisutun (Hindki) palace (for a distant picture of which see McChesney [1999], p. 12), and the Qala-i Hashmat Khan palace in Kabul; the Paghman summer palace (the "Simla of Afghanistan"); the new Jalalabad Palace; and the Pul-i Chishti mosque, Eid Gah mosque, royal mosque and Shahrara tower in Kabul.

The copper was primarily used for the production of state coinage (which included silver, copper, and brass coins), and cooking, dining utensil, and storage container production for the court and palaces. The iron was largely consumed and transformed in the weapons workshops where rifles, artillery guns, and cartridges were produced (separate rifle-barreling, cannon foundry, and cartridge workshops existed). The donkey load of rifles and cartridges were either destined for the workshops to be evaluated for potential mass reproduction, or possessed more of an ornamental value than a coercive purpose for Abd al-Rahman. Conspicuously absent from this accounting are any heavy guns, artillery pieces or cannon. This is significant because most analyses of Durrani state formation place very heavy weight on the importation of arms by Abd al-Rahman. Rubin (1996), p. 48, is an explicit proponent of the position that 'weapons aid allowed Abd al-Rahman to pursue a coercive-intensive path the state formation.'

contributed to the growing gap in state-society relations in nineteenth-century Afghanistan. The mashin khana was the prized and most emphasized component of this Durrani ruler's state formation agenda, and to his credit Abd al-Rahman recognized its alienating effect on at least some sectors of Afghan society:

> The difficulties that I had to encounter on first opening the manufactories and workshops were enormous. My people knew nothing of modern inventions and appliances, and were consequently opposed to all these new ideas ... (w)hen I first opened the workshops my people made all kinds of remarks; they said that I did not know that the work could be much better done by hand than by machinery. They accused the officials who were working at the factories of being enemies of the Government, who wanted to send the money out of the country under the pretense of buying machinery. I was tired of all this nonsense and opposition, but, all the same, I would not give up my determination to proceed on the road I had marked out for myself ... (t)here is no doubt that it took a very long time to reap the fruits of all this expenditure on machinery; all these large amounts had to be paid by the Government Treasury, and I could not help calculating the interest on the money which was paying nothing for years, being all sunk in the factory and workshops. But I did not lose heart. I continued to buy every year as much machinery as I could find the money for, and as the machines increased I had new factories built to receive them. This I continue to do year by year ...[66]

CHAPTER 5

New State Texts and Old Commercial Flows

The Textual Dimensions of
Anglo-Durrani State Formation

Abd al-Rahman relied on three categories of accountants, collectors, and revenue officials to execute his rapacious commercial tendencies at all levels and in all sectors of the Afghan economy. The power of these groups of state financial operatives was decidedly textual. At the highest level, individuals known as *diwans* presided over the central state account books. Those responsible for provincial revenue records were usually termed *sarishtadars*. This is not an absolute distinction as diwans were also active in the provinces and sarishtadars were found in Kabul. Regarding the social origin of these institutional categories, diwan appears as a title reserved almost exclusively for Hindus, but Hindus often received the sarishtadar label. However, this, too, is a blurred rather than clear division because a variety of Muslim groups were represented among the sarishtadars. Hindus could circulate between the kinds of state fiscal service designated by the two terms, while Muslims do not figure into the diwan category. Diwans and sarishtadars can be considered the central state and provincial revenue officers.

Compared to diwans and sarishtadars, the *mirza* title is much broader and subsumes a wider variety of individuals who filled financial and textual niches within and outside of Durrani government service. Mirzas were patronized by a variety of government officials and local elites. There were no Hindu mirzas. Among the various Muslim groups found in this cosmopolitan frontier setting, the Qizilbash, an ethnically Turkic group of Shia Muslims who spoke Persian and were brought to Kabul by Nadir Shah Afshar, were noted as serving as mirzas for "every man of rank."[1] Mirzas were the most numerous of the Durrani state's financial operatives at all levels of government. They were the rank-and-file of the accountant corps and performed the majority of the financial audits and investigations into the offices and officers comprising the Durrani state bureaucracy. They could investigate diwans, sarishtadars, and members of their own constituency. The mirzas handled the majority of smaller, everyday, and ordinary bureaucratic and clerical tasks, but they could also be assigned to delicate and important matters by Abd al-Rahman or other superiors.[2] The mirza label connotes generic literacy because literacy could be either numerical or narrative. To be designated as a mirza one had to be functionally literate in the accounting or scribal sense of the term, or both. The position of secretary may best capture the written-word component of the mirza title, and accountant is perhaps the most appropriate way to conceptualize the numeric-service aspect of their duties. The labels bookkeeper and clerk apply well to mirzas whose duties subsumed both forms of literacy.

Mirzas were the primary executioners of Abd al-Rahman's aggressive fiscal policies, but diwans and sarishtadars were also prominent and active in the area of fiscal audits.[3] The three groups shared the abilities to create, interpret, and manipulate financial letters and account books, and as a result these revenue functionaries wielded enormous power over the merchant class, state bureaucrats and officials, and each other in late nineteenth-century Afghanistan. Their opinions, decisions, and judgments almost invariably resulted in revenue gains for the state, and once rendered, could only be challenged or revoked in the context of another larger and more lucrative case that would have been even more difficult to appeal. Once a mirza or another auditor was assigned to a targeted person or office, an outcome favorable to the state was essentially predetermined, only the amount of the state's bounty and the means of compensation or collection remained to be determined.[4]

It was not uncommon for targets of audits to be killed, and many of those who survived had been imprisoned and physically tortured. A large number of those audited were financially ruined and left as economic pariahs on their family, other associates, and neighbors whose resources also became vulnerable to state confiscation through textual means. In a similar vein, when diwans, sarishtadars, and mirzas replaced one another, accusations of past fraudulent activity regularly ensued. Factionalism was pronounced within and among each of the three groups of state revenue functionaries. The divisions found in and between the diwan, sarishtadar, and mirza categories were often created and perpetuated by the individuals and alliances operating in the political realm, i.e., among the officials and office-holders who were both the instigators and targets of the audits. During Abd al-Rahman's reign nobody in Afghanistan, including deceased officials and those serving in the religious establishment, was immune from the kind of textual terror he and other political elites wielded through their ability to unleash any one of a number of state-contracted auditors.[5]

The textual dimensions of the nineteenth-century Afghan economy were evident in a number of areas beyond generic auditing, including in the scheme of prices used in private bankers' and the state's account books. There were three types of prices associated with different but overlapping sectors of the economy, namely, retail prices, prices fixed by bankers and moneylenders, and government prices.[6] Ordinary consumers could be affected by all three price forms. For example, fruit producers experienced retail pricing in rural bazaars frequented to fulfill household and various personal consumption needs, and encountered bankers' and government prices at production sites, especially during harvests. But more important for our purposes, the common fruit producer was likely indebted to one or more members of the groups of brokers and bankers who financed the production of that commodity group and whose resources were heavily imbricated in the given locality. As demonstrated in Chapter 1, it became increasingly common for brokers of fruit and other commodities to become government revenue farmers and as a result function as state tax collectors in the localities associated with the given commodity.[7]

The typical scenario of a common fruit producer who was indebted to a banker, broker, or any other provider of credit including the state which garnered its revenue in the form of either produce or a form of "money," reveals at least two possible realms where those circumstances were textualized. The first set of texts that subordinated the average debtor to a creditor or group of the same were documents used by local Hindki bankers who extended various forms of credit to ordinary producers and the state. The Hindkis were themselves a diverse group whose accounting techniques remain largely unknown. The various forms of bookkeeping competence and literacy necessary to manage the active and purposefully open-ended accounts may not have been mutually intelligible among all the various groups of Hindki bankers.[8] It is necessary to again mention that Hindki bankers and creditors could serve the Durrani government as revenue farmers or in a number of other capacities. Irrespective of that important possibility, the state tax collectors used a form of pricing and set of accounting practices that were probably related but certainly distinct from those employed by the Hindki banking communities in Afghanistan.

Government prices and the form of pricing employed by local bankers were set for bookkeeping purposes. They were not equivalent, although both types of prices existed as functions of account management. Durrani government and Hindki bankers' prices represent monies of account and not hard cash.[9] Each signifies a textual form of money or book money that did not have an independent tangible existence apart from government and private banking account records. For state and private bankers book money pricing was based on unique and imaginary units of measurement. There is very little data to work from regarding the records maintained by Hindki bankers and firms such as the Shikarpuris in Afghanistan so we do not know what forms of book money accounting were used in the private sector. However, archival and published sources indicate the form of book money used in the Afghan state account books was known as the Kabuli *kham* or raw rupee. A document generated by the second British occupation of Kabul and eastern Afghanistan refers to the kham rupee as "merely one of account; it bears no tangible existence."[10] The kham rupee was based on but distinguished from the ordinary or "real" rupee known as the Kabuli *pukhta* rupee, the ripe or cooked rupee.

Braudel's argument that book-money prices represent a form of temporary credit that is convertible into real money when an account was settled through a final payment of some sort is useful here.[11] Accepting that premise, the significance of government and bankers' price schemes were that they revolved around credit, a form of money theoretically distinct from cash. The textual course of any private or state-sponsored credit cycle was basically unknown to ordinary debtors, but it was in the financial documents of the firms and the state that the prevalence of debt characterizing Afghan society was most consequentially reflected and maximized.

It is important to recognize the lack of data concerning the accountants within the Hindki community, and how that absence of information instills a high degree of conjecture about their fiscal practices and career histories. However, based on the circulation of bureaucratic knowledge in other state contexts and the patronage patterns of mirzas in Afghanistan specifically, it is reasonable to postulate that at least some Hindki accountants rotated their services between private businesses and firms, and that their knowledge and skills regarding textual debt-management, however rudimentary or refined, were relatively rare, income-generating, and transferable.[12] There is another significant and necessarily speculative area of inquiry regarding the personnel movement or bureaucratic demography of the accountants working among the Hindkis in Afghanistan during Abd al-Rahman's reign. It deals with the question of whether the kinds of textual literacy necessary to function as an accountant for a Shikarpuri or Peshawri firm would have sufficiently enabled those with such knowledge and skills to function as a diwan or sarishtadar or mirza for the Durrani state. The question as phrased begets an inverse line of inquiry about employment or contractual movement in the opposite direction, that is, from the state bureaucracy to the private sector. If such cross-sectoral employment migration existed, it begs a number of other queries about the circulation of debt among firms and between them and the state, and about the origin and available labor pool for the diwan and sarishtadar institutions in the Afghan state fiscal structure.

Abd al-Rahman's reformation of the fiscal infrastructure of the Durrani state involved more than just a greatly increased reliance on audits conducted by a diverse and growing body of accountants and financial operatives. Data limitations prohibit a definitive assessment as to the statistical expansion of the various types of state auditors during Abd al-Rahman's reign, but a certain swelling of their ranks did occur. However, any increase in the sheer number of bureaucratic personnel is less significant than the greatly expanded scope of their collective textual authority and reach. Abd al-Rahman offered clear opinions on the state account books in his autobiography.[13] He describes the poor condition of the state financial records as he encountered them on his accession, and describes his innovative approach to solving the problem as he viewed it.

Abd al-Rahman claims to have completely revised state financial record keeping practices and the texts produced by and defining such activity. The new bureaucrats, and their practices and texts, had an interactive relationship that fostered a new type of fluidity within the fiscal infrastructure of the Durrani polity. Abd al-Rahman claimed to have heightened bureaucratic efficiency because he solved the problem of pandemic graft and corruption by government office-holders who formerly could easily manipulate their office finances for personal aggrandizement. However, for merchants, officials, and society-at-large, the elimination of one type of text-based financial corruption brought another. Abd al-Rahman's textual reforms resulted in another version of widespread economic malaise, one with a coercive literati using innovative state documents and records to mulct merchants, extort office-holders, and extract inordinate amounts of resources from the general population. In essence, the Durrani government's reliance on documentary ambiguity was revised in favor of the state's commitment to textual specificity. In Abd al-Rahman's words:

The old system of keeping offices in Afghanistan was, that there were no books for entering any of the accounts, small sheets of paper, about eight inches long and six inches wide, being used. Each of these sheets was called a *fard* (single leaf). These small pieces of paper were half filled by writing at the top, the name of the office, the year and date, and various unnecessary things, and the other half contained three or four words, then the sheet was full. What could have been entered in two sheets of a book took 100 of these small scraps of paper. In consequence, when a certain item was required for reference, it was necessary to go through thousands of these scraps, which was a very great waste of time. The worst fault of all was that any official or accountant who had embezzled Government money, could easily take a few sheets or one sheet away, and either write another or tear them up all together. I have introduced books, and on the first page the numbers of each page or sheet are written and sealed with my seal to the binding of the book, so that no one can take a sheet out of the book without breaking the seal. At first some people played tricks and tore out some sheets, for which their fingers were cut! Now every one, at the time of taking a book, writes on the first page with his own hands that he promises to have his hands cut off if he cuts the book![14]

In addition to his reliance on diwans, sarishtadars, and mirzas, who were personally responsible for these refashioned account books, Abd al-Rahman used other means to exert his textual authority over a largely illiterate populace. Another example of textual oppression concerns the non-recognition of documents issued under previous regimes that were retained by merchants precisely to validate past financial action. In this regard, it appears Abd al-Rahman used rulings issued by his panchayat, or commercial council, a body appointed to legitimize his own and other officials' commercial conduct, to invalidate receipts and transform other exonerating evidence into incriminating conduct.[15] If practiced on a wide scale, discounting the validity of receipts would result in mercantile flight and devastate the economy where it occurred, and this appears to have happened in Afghanistan during Abd al-Rahman's reign.

Abd al-Rahman used paper texts as pillars of his domestic intelligence architecture. For example, petition boxes were kept under secret surveillance to learn the identities of those depositing supposedly anonymous opinions.[16] In another expression of texts as intelligence, a clarified butter-seller or *ghi furosh* in Qandahar who was severely indebted to his clients began to call on the government mirza stationed at the local granary to pen unsolicited intelligence reports directly to Abd al-Rahman. These voluntary textual offerings were apparently received favorably, as not only did local creditors ease their demands on this wily character, others actually began to present cash gifts to him in hopes of receiving favorable mention in his uniquely inspired and profitable intelligence reports.[17]

There were direct and indirect intelligence benefits from Abd al-Rahman's increasing dependence on the written word generally and state texts in particular, but the revenue function of these documents deserves special notice. In his own hierarchical ordering of the sources of Durrani state income, Abd al-Rahman mentions the Post Office as a source of funds after revenue generated from the "land and fruit trees, and duties on export and import and various customs money."[18] The post office produced a substantial income for the state from the "sale of various kinds of stamps for promissory notes, forms of contracts, bills of exchange, etc."[19] Elsewhere in his autobiography Abd al-Rahman opines even more explicitly about the income-generating aspect of his new textual regimen:

> I introduced hundreds of different stamps and forms of paper for contracts, deeds, promissory notes, marriage settlements, passports, which bring in revenue, and were never even heard of before my time in Afghanistan.[20]

Abd al-Rahman's textual interventions were felt in all regions and sectors of the Afghan economy and among all social strata. For example, to revise the local brokerage practices in Qandahar from Kabul, Abd al-Rahman armed a Hindu named Jita with a written pamphlet outlining the new state policy on this important commercial service and dispatched him to the former Durrani capital city. Jita carried a kind of text referred to as a *dastur al-amal* or regulation on the subject of brokerage that was signed by Abd al-Rahman.[21] Even the tribal *maliks* or chiefs in Qandahar province, the majority of whom were Durranis and therefore ethnic affiliates and political favorites of Abd al-Rahman, were subjected to the new forms of state-paper oppression. Formerly, district and subdistrict administrators for the Durrani government would disburse between four and five rupees as annual cash stipends directly to certain local chiefs. In this regard, Abd al-Rahman's textual innovations on these allowances triggered spatial movements by these local Durrani chiefs and contributed to their being monitored by and accessible to the central Durrani state. For their allowances Abd al-Rahman made the Durrani maliks come to Qandahar, and some maliks had to travel six or seven days' journey to that city. In Qandahar, checks were issued to them by an accountant or secretary. Each malik then had to carry the new state paper money back to the given locality and present it to the government administrator for the check to be cashed on the district's

FIG. 5.1. Landowners and Laborers in Kabul, 1878

or subdistrict's account.[22] A final expression of the revenue-earning potential of state-issued paper also comes from Qandahar where to collect the recently imposed marriage tax Abd al-Rahman distributed stamped forms to *qazis* or religious court judges on which marriage contracts were to be written. The fee of 10 rupees per marriage, or more specifically per new marriage contract, was decreed to be collected from all those who were married in Qandahar during the past three years.[23]

Abd al-Rahman's textual policies and practices were primary catalysts of the social transformations that occurred in Afghanistan during his reign. Through a heightened reliance on auditors and an increasing production and dissemination of revenue-generating texts, Abd al-Rahman carved out a prominent niche for documentation in his state formation agenda. The wide array of state texts produced by Abd al-Rahman had profound implications on relations between the Durrani government and Afghan society. The technology most implicated

FIG. 5.2. Public Execution, 1913

in these developments was that of machine printing. Abd al-Rahman appears to have imported printing press machinery to Kabul sometime between 1885 and 1890. His own comments on these powerful devices demonstrate that the expertise and knowledge required to use the new European machine technology was also imported:

> Before my accession to the throne there were no typewriting or printing press throughout the whole dominion of Afghanistan . . . (now) thousands of copies of various books furnishing information on various subjects, forms of papers, stamps, promissory notes, etc., are printed and published by the Kabul Press . . . the man who deserves the greatest praise for opening the press at Kabul was the late Munshi Abdul Razak of Delhi; he died of fever, but the printing and press work are being carried on by many Kabuli men taught by him . . .[24]

State Monopolization of the Export Fruit Trade

The Durrani state under Abd al-Rahman intervened substantially more directly and farther into fruit production and marketing processes than any previous Durrani political regime. At the end of the nineteenth century the colonially appointed Durrani Amir Abd al-Rahman monopolized the fruit export trade by inserting his own state agents as the sole brokers of the commercial trafficking in this important commodity group. The tactic of using state brokers to monopolize the export trade in fruit and other commodity groups was a primary element of Abd al-Rahman's state formation agenda.[25] The fruit monopoly resulted in the re-routing and refinancing of a significant portion of this abundant commodity that was harvested for export. The terms of the monopoly also reflect Abd al-Rahman's intention to displace an existing community of Indian brokers whose resources and investments in the fruit trade were advanced during the first British occupation. Forty years later, and after a second Anglo-Afghan war concluded by Abd al-Rahman's accession, Indian merchant capital appears visibly if not dominant in the harvesting and marketing processes associated with the export of eastern Afghan fruit.[26] However, by the end of his reign a large number of Indian brokers, bankers, and traders had left Kabul and re-routed and reallocated their resources to avoid the city. They departed due to a series of alterations to the export and transit-trade activities hinged on the burgeoning capital city.[27] Abd al-Rahman's commercial policies and practices regarding the movement of fruit and other goods ultimately restricted Afghanistan's entry into a maturing global economy.

The first British occupation of Kabul and eastern Afghanistan unraveled during the fruit-marketing season in the fall of 1841. The expulsion of the British resulted in a hiatus in the supply of data generated by colonial officials about and from within this region. For roughly forty years after the first war it is difficult to determine how much or what portions of Trevor's budgetary and revenue reform package survived in places like Koh Daman, Istalif, and Arghandeh.[28] The second Anglo-Afghan war renewed the flow of information about social and economic conditions in eastern Afghanistan.[29] During the reign of Abd al Rahman colonial officials generated a prodigious supply of data about the precipitously declining state of trade through Afghanistan. British documents relating to Abd al-Rahman's trading monopolies reveal another dimension to the relationship between revenue farming, commercial brokerage, and the Durrani state's involvement in the export of fruit from Kabul and its vicinity.[30]

When compared to the experimental period, political relations between Afghanistan and India were markedly stabilized by the British appointment of Abd al-Rahman to the Durrani throne in Kabul in June of 1880, an event that signaled the end of the second Anglo-Afghan war. On the economic front, the scheduled British disbursement of cash subsidies to Abd al-Rahman for the duration of his reign defined and regulated interaction between the two unequal state powers. The term routinization is therefore used here to characterize Anglo-Afghan relations during last two decades of the nineteenth century, but it is important to note that the notion of a subsidy-based routine applies to the realm of state-to-state interaction. When compared to his predecessors, Abd al-Rahman's relationship to the community of interregional traders and brokers linking his polity to those surrounding it, particularly to British India, were exceptional, unexpected and decidedly non-routine in a number of important respects.

Abd al-Rahman's monopolization of the export fruit trade was executed by farming out the right to collect the "brokerage and weighmen's fees" of the fruit that "Afghans and others export from Kabul to Peshawar."[31] The privilege to collect such fees was leased for one year at a time. The farmer or leaseholder agreed to pay Abd al-Rahman Rs. 1,20,000 within one year from the date of the deed of partnership.[32] Furthermore, the leaseholder was responsible for another Rs. 50,000 of Abd al-Rahman's money that was to be advanced to the carriers of the fruit when they reentered Afghanistan in the spring. The Afghan tribal traders, known locally as kochis, advanced that cash to cultivators as loans that secured future claims on their fall harvest (see later in this chapter).

After the Rs. 1,20,000 and the Rs. 50,000 were repaid, Abd al-Rahman and the fruit farmer agreed to split any further profits evenly, and both parties certainly eagerly anticipated such opportunities for additional revenue gains.

The first expression of this monopoly arrangement came in 1892 at the beginning of the annual fall exodus of Afghan traders, merchants, and laborers to India for the winter season. On September 4, 1892, the fruit monopoly era began with Abd al-Rahman issuing a deed of partnership in the export fruit trade to Nur Muhammad, a Taraki Pashtun from the Jalalabad district. The monopoly arrangement covered an array of dried and fresh fruits, certain nuts, assorted other foodstuffs, and two dyes. The list included fresh grapes packed in boxes, all kinds of raisins (long, small, red, green, etc.), two types of melons (watermelons and *sarda* or musk melons), seedless pomegranates and pomegranates with seeds, dried apricots, kernels of apricots, dried kernels of apricots, apples, pears, dried curds, ghi, gram, dried chick peas, madder, pine nuts, dried roses, tobacco, *zira* (a seed used in the cooking of rice), an edible vegetable garnish known as *samaruk*, asafetida, and a dye for silk made out of the pistachio tree, *buz ganj*.[33]

The monopoly was designed to induce a certain routing for the kochi carriers of the specified fruits. The kochis were the primary carriers of the abundant supplies of fruit from the Kabul environs to the vast consumer markets of North India. Most of the kochis entered the subcontinent by way of Ghazni, the Gomal Pass, and Dera Ismail Khan, although other routes were also used by commercial caravans carrying Afghan fruit. The fruit monopoly had the effect of shifting the fruit traffic north from the Gomal route to the Khaibar mountain passage linking Kabul and Peshawar. In order to encourage the kochis to use the Khaibar route Abd al-Rahman ordered security deposits to be collected from them, preferably at Dakka, the last Durrani state transit-trade post in the Khaibar corridor. While Dakka was the prescribed site for security deposit collection, such fees could also be paid along any other route in eastern Afghanistan where government toll posts existed.[34] To recover their security deposits, the kochis first had to take their loads to the fruit monopoly leaseholder Nur Muhammad in Peshawar who directed them to a subcontracted broker (Jit Mal, see later in this chapter) who signed their security deposit receipts. The second step toward recouping their security deposits compelled the kochis to re-enter Afghanistan in the spring via the Khaibar wherein at Dakka they could present their signed receipts for reimbursement.[35]

Returning to the commercial activities occurring in the fall season, on arrival in Peshawar laden with their fruit cargo, the kochis contacted Nur Muhammad who directed them to a subcontracted broker and the weighing facilities provided by that broker. In Peshawar an individual named Jit Mal provided brokerage services. Jit Mal's brother was responsible for weighing, and together the siblings presumably influenced the decision about additional packaging, short-term storage facilities, and the subsequent transport of the greater portion of the fruit out of Peshawar. According to petitions filed with the British Indian Government, the rates Jit Mal and his brother charged the kochis for handling their fruit were double and in some cases triple the amounts charged for similar services provided by the remaining brokers and weighmen in Peshawar.[36] Furthermore, Jit Mal was instructed to inform Nur Muhammad of any kochis carrying fruit who evaded the monopoly. The names of kochis caught without the proper paperwork were forwarded to Abd al-Rahman who required little instigation and seems to have thrived on such contrived opportunities to inflict retributive confiscation and imprisonment, or worse, on those disobeying his directives.

A community of about thirty brokers and weighmen of Afghan fruit in Peshawar were cut out of the Afghan fruit export market by the Durrani state-appointed monopolist Nur Muhammad and his partners Jit Mal and Jit Mal's brother. The disenfranchised Peshawri brokers and weighmen petitioned the British government. They claimed Abd al-Rahman's monopoly constituted an unfair business practice predicated on the very real threat of coercion faced by the kochis in Afghanistan should they be caught avoiding Jit Mal and dispensing their fruit on the open market at the best available price. The ousted middlemen argued further that the kochis were now paying exorbitant fees to the monopolist that would ultimately generate inaccessible prices for the Afghan fruits consumed by the popular masses throughout northern India. The circumvented brokers and weighmen envisioned the declining fruit trade would also be reflected in diminishing Peshawar municipal octroi receipts. Colonial officials concurred with the Peshawri brokers' assessment of the Afghan fruit monopoly's detrimental effect on their community, and reiterated an anticipated imposition on the popular consumer masses in North India:

> It will be readily seen what a serious effect so extensive a monopoly of what are almost necessaries of life will have not only upon the business of the local trade, but on the people generally . . . (the monopolized items) are articles of daily consumption by even the poorest classes of Northern British India . . . (that) can be obtained only from Afghanistan, ghi and tobacco excepted . . . There is practically no limit

to the point up to which the monopolist can drive up prices thereby causing much hardship and discontent.[37]

British officials researched the current market rates for brokerage and weighing services and determined the monopolist Nur Muhammad and his subcontracted broker Jit Mal charged the kochis artificially high prices for handling the exported Afghan fruit in Peshawar. As a result, some colonial bureaucrats opined that in practice Abd al-Rahman's fruit monopoly was actually a new form of Durrani state tax that was being collected in India. Other British Indian officials argued that:

> What he (Abd al-Rahman) is doing, namely, giving advances to growers and dealers and appointing agents in whose hands the whole trade is being concentrated, is very much like that is done in this country by large exporting firms who keep their agents at all large places, and through them give advances to cultivators and dealers, and thus concentrate the trade in grain and seeds in their own hands ... He also knows probably about our opium monopoly, which resembles this one he has taken up in the way of agents, advances, and so forth.[38]

Despite the variety of interpretations of Abd al-Rahman's fruit monopoly, there was colonial bureaucratic unanimity regarding the difference between it and the commercial monopolies or monopoly-like arrangements executed by the large exporting firms of India and the colonial state itself regarding opium and other commodities. For colonial bureaucrats the distinction lay in the degree of coercion employed. About monopoly practices generally British officials felt that in India "there is no compulsion in the matter whereas he (Abd al-Rahman) compels." Although this statement lacks nuance and makes too bold a contrast, Abd al-Rahman's penchant for mulcting the commercial classes in Afghanistan was well known to British officials. British officials were rightly convinced that whomever Nur Muhammad mentioned to Abd al-Rahman as evading the monopoly would be financially ruined through confiscations and fines (as would people immediately related and distantly connected to the original "violator").

During the first season of the monopoly's existence the brokers and weighmen in Peshawar who were cut out of the Afghan fruit trade repeatedly petitioned Abd al-Rahman and the British Government about their plight. On December 14, 1892, Abd al-Rahman wrote to the brokers directly in response to their collective claims against Nur Muhammad and the alleged unfair business practices associated with him:

Nur Muhammad is a monopolist of fruit exported from this territory to Peshawar, on the same system as the monopolies which commonly exist in all cities of Hindustan. . . . Nur Muhammad, who has obtained the contract for the fruit of Afghanistan, buys and sells this fruit with the consent of the fruit owners and at the price of the day, and this matter is no concern of yours.[39]

In his correspondence with the British about the matter, Abd al-Rahman justified the fruit monopoly as defending the kochis' interests.[40] He claimed the kochis were having their justly earned profits siphoned by the brokers and weighmen of Peshawar. Abd al-Rahman felt that as owners of the Afghan fruit the kochis, who were his subjects, should not have their resources diminished at the expense of the Peshawri brokers and weighmen who were British Indian subjects.[41] However, at the same time, Abd al-Rahman and his own officials corresponded with one another in full recognition that the kochis did not want to partake in the fruit trade via the terms of the new state monopoly. Durrani officials recognized that "unregistered" fruit from Kabul and its surroundings continued to arrive in Peshawar. Abd al-Rahman and his officials were completely aware that large numbers of kochis and other groups of Afghan merchants regularly evaded the monopoly's system of surveillance based on a Khaibar routing focused on Dakka and security deposit receipts countersigned by a subcontracted Sikh broker in Peshawar. In this regard, the kochis frequenting the Kohat Pass and Kohat city, and communities of carriers associated with Gomal Pass and Dera Ismail Khan, such as the Lohanis and Sulaiman Khel Ghalzi, received special attention from Durrani state officials as monopoly resistors.[42]

The British Indian colonial state viewed the kochis as vulnerable to Abd al-Rahman's fruit monopoly, but because they were Durrani state subjects and there was no apparent physical threat to them in India, the British did little to alter either the Durrani state's execution of the monopoly or the kochis' evasion of it. At least one colonial officer advocated deducting the amount lost by the Peshawri fruit brokers and weighmen from the subsidy the British provided to Abd al-Rahman.[43] However, the opposite occurred only a year after the fruit monopoly was instituted. The Durand agreement of 1893 resulted in the subsidy being increased 50 percent from Rs. 12,00,000 to Rs. 18,00,000 annually.[44] From the British perspective the negative economic consequences of the fruit monopoly clearly paled in comparison to the political imperatives of the "Great Game" period. Colonial officials therefore allowed the fruit and other Durrani state monopolies to exist until Abd al-Rahman's death in 1901, which created the opportunity to once again reconfigure relations between colonial India and Afghanistan.

The commodities monopolies were an integral part of Abd al-Rahman's state formation agenda. The fruit monopoly was particularly significant as a vehicle for displacing South Asian merchant capital from local production routines in and around Kabul. The Rs. 50,000 advanced by Nur Muhammad to the kochis was one of many steps Abd al-Rahman took to insert Durrani state resources into domestic cultivation processes in lieu of foreign merchant capital. The Afghan fruit monopoly documents indicate brokers in Peshawar had considerable resources invested in the local fruit cultivation schema in the vicinity of Kabul. The Peshawar brokers and weighmen depended on their relationships to kochi carriers in order to distribute their capital investments in those localities.[45] During the first season of the monopoly the British recognized the likelihood of ongoing exclusion of Indian merchants from the fruit revenue structure of the Kabul-centered Durrani state. Colonial officials understood the monopoly would cause the community of fruit handlers in Peshawar to lose the brokerage and weighing fees they earned from the kochis. The British also recognized the prospect of the Peshawar brokers' ongoing exclusion from the production and marketing cycles associated with eastern Afghan fruit. Such sentiment is implicit in the following British opinion, generated less than a month after the monopoly's announcement, that the brokers were now:

> ... unable to recover the large sums of money which they have been in the habit of advancing to the fruit merchants on their way to Kabul every spring, and of recovering from them when they come back with their fresh supplies in the following autumn.[46]

The establishment of the Durrani state fruit monopoly in the fall of 1892 transformed a number of social and economic relations in and around Kabul and throughout eastern Afghanistan, a few of which will be reviewed to close this section. In the first instance, the relationship between the kochis and the Durrani state assumed new textual, material, and spatial dimensions as a result of Abd al-Rahman's farming of the right to collect the brokerage and weighmen's fees associated with exported fruit. For the kochi carriers, whether in adjustment to or avoidance of security deposits and signed receipts and/or the Dakka-centered Khaibar routing, the fruit monopoly reconfigured a number of everyday spatial and fiscal practices. The monopoly also engaged the kochis as providers of Durrani state loans totaling Rs. 50,000 to fruit producers in localities surrounding Kabul. This action replaced the Peshawri brokers' investments in the same fruit-producing sites in eastern Afghanistan and highlights the important role of cash advances in the overall monopoly package. Similar to the appointment of Nur Muhammad who subcontracted with Jit Mal, Abd al-Rahman's cash advances to the kochis for local disbursement were designed to concentrate and circulate revenue from fruit production and marketing domestically, that is, with and within the Kabul-centered Durrani state. Before the institution of the monopoly the capital associated with Afghan fruit production and marketing processes was dispersed far into South and Central Asia and beyond through extensive commercial networks dominated by Indian bankers and traders and the resource consortiums they formed such as Shikarpuri family trading firms and mercantile houses. In addition to transforming relations between the Durrani state and the kochi carriers, and between Kabul and villages surrounding the city, the fruit monopoly also affected the course of Durrani state formation by modifying Kabul's association with other major regional markets. The monopoly was one in a series of moves undertaken by Abd al-Rahman that amplified the direct market-to-market links between Kabul and Peshawar through the Khaibar Pass. Such an intensification of commercial interaction between those two cities and along that route drew resources away from the economic exchanges between Kabul and other domestic and foreign markets such as Ghazni, Qandahar, Mazar-e Sharif, Bukhara, and Dera Ismail Khan, and diminished the significance of the routes linking those locales.

Commodity Monopoly Texts and the Qafilabashi

This section deals with the impact some of the new Durrani state texts had on the Afghan nomads who migrated from Central to South Asia in the fall, and returned from Hindustan to Afghanistan, Khorasan, and Turkistan during the spring. These long-distance nomad traders carried primarily Afghan fruit to North India during the fall season. Fall season profits were invested in a wide variety of other articles purchased in India during the winter and transported "back" to and marketed in Afghanistan and Central Asia during the spring and summer. Abd al-Rahman used a number of novel receipts, vouchers, passes, and certificates to implement his state monopoly of the lucrative export fruit trade. The nomadic traders who carried the large volumes of fruit from Kabul and its environs to Hindustan were especially hard-hit by the documentary aspects of Abd al-Rahman's fruit monopoly. The new fruit monopoly texts compelled a Khaibar as opposed to a Gomal Pass routing and identified the nomads to the Durrani state transport official known as the qafilabashi who was based in Peshawar and superintended the movement of all goods destined for Kabul that were routed through the Khaibar. The qafilabashi worked with a *monshi* or secretary who was responsible for a register book known as a *challan* within which the amounts and kinds of commodities and their means of animal conveyance to Kabul were recorded and manipulated.

As noted above in the fall of 1892 Abd al-Rahman leased the rights to collect the brokerage and weighmen's dues of all the Afghan fruit exported to India to Nur Muhammad Taraki.[47] The colonially appointed and subsidized Durrani dynast used multiple texts to execute his revenue-farming arrangement that served as the state monopoly of the export fruit trade from eastern Afghanistan to greater North India in practice. The fruit monopoly significantly impacted the nomads in the realm of routing. Before the institution of the monopoly, the carriers of eastern Afghan fruit generally proceeded from Kabul south to Ghazni where they congregated for passage through eastern Ghalzi country to and through the Gomal Pass and on to Dera Ismail Khan. Dera Ismail Khan was the nomads' banking center and the point from which they disaggregated to pursue various market paths leading across the Hindustan plains and Himalayan foothills. Through the use of various state texts the fruit monopoly compelled a routing for the nomads that carried them due east from Kabul, ideally through Buthak, Gandamak, and Surkhpul, before reaching Jalalabad, from where they would enter the Khaibar Pass and present themselves at Dakka before exiting the pass and proceeding to Peshawar.[48]

Nur Muhammad's contracted services as the fruit export monopolist allowed the Durrani state to extract additional taxes from the nomads while increasing its surveillance over their physical movements and fiscal practices and furthering its imposition on their human labor and other forms of commercial capital including animal resources. In the first instance, the Khaibar routing was induced in Kabul at the chabutara or customs house where the goods destined for India were itemized in a challan register book. At the Kabul customs house Nur Muhammad collected security deposits from the nomads for their goods that were henceforth considered Durrani state property. If security deposits could not be collected from the nomad traders at the Kabul customs house, the nomads were expected to make their required deposits at one of the four just-mentioned locations between Kabul and Dakka. In return for their deposits the nomads were given receipts issued by Nur Muhammad that they presented to Nur Muhammad's subcontracted broker and weighman in Peshawar, Jit Mall and his brother, respectively, who countersigned the receipts.

During their spring migrations from India back to greater Central Asia, the Afghan nomads had the incentive and need to again use the Khaibar Pass. One primary reason for traversing this corridor during the spring was because only at Dakka in the Khaibar could the nomads present their double-signed fruit security deposit receipts for reimbursement. The new forms of taxation and documentation associated with Abd al-Rahman's fruit monopoly were designed to route all nomads carrying fruit from Kabul to Peshawar through the Khaibar Pass. However, during the first year of the monopoly it became abundantly clear that many Afghan nomads were resisting through avoidance some of the important terms of the fruit monopoly including its higher taxes, new state paperwork, and prescribed routing. From Kabul the majority of Afghan nomads were accustomed to using routes to India south of the Khaibar, many of which led through eastern Ghalzi country, the Kohat and Gomal Passes, and converged on Dera Ismail Khan.

In the late fall or early winter of 1892, an influential group of nomad traders, including representatives of Lohani, Sulaiman Khel Ghalzi, and Kharoti tribal groups, petitioned Abd al-Rahman about the fruit monopoly.[49] These nomad traders claimed that the Khaibar routing caused them great inconvenience because their families accompanied the caravans and arrangements for their dependents, animals, and goods were traditionally made in the *daman* plains of the Indus River and the foothills ascending westerly into the Sulaiman mountain range. In late February or early March 1893, Abd al-Rahman responded to their plea by allowing them to avoid the Khaibar. However, the colonially appointed Durrani sovereign's apparent benevolence on this point was in fact countervailed because in the same letter he also announced the deputation of a mirza and two subcontracted agents of Nur Muhammad to collect *arat* or export commission fees from all nomads carrying Afghan fruit to India.[50]

Muhammad Akbar Khan was one of the Afghans Abd al-Rahman authorized to function as a sub-agent of the fruit monopolist Nur Muhammad Taraki. In the fall of 1893, at the beginning of the second year of the fruit monopoly, Muhammad Akbar appeared in the main market of the town of Kohat with another form of Durrani state text authenticated by Abd al-Rahman's seal. Muhammad Akbar carried a *parwana* or order from Nur Muhammad written in Persian by a mirza Abd al-Rahman assigned to the case. Muhammad Akbar claimed the state document he wielded entitled him to collect the same export commission rates in Kohat as at Dakka or any of the other official toll posts between Kabul and Peshawar.[51] Most of the Afghan nomads in Kohat had dispersed by the time Muhammad Akbar arrived, and most of those who remained and were found with fruit in their possession claimed insufficient resources to pay the required arat fees. These unsuccessfully evasive nomads were forced to sign vouchers, also a new documentary initiative, stating they would pay the export commission fees at Dakka on their return to Afghanistan the following spring. The kochis in Kohat who avoided the Khaibar in the fall but could not avoid the fruit security deposit net returned to Afghanistan via the Khaibar and Dakka in the spring because their signatures on the export fee vouchers identified them to Abd al-Rahman who was sure to act on their "mutually agreed on" intention to "contribute to the welfare of the tribes and benefit of the *khazana bait al-mal* (sic)" or public treasury.

Export fees were not the only form of state tax Muhammad Akbar realized from the Afghan nomad traders in Kohat through the application of Durrani state textual power. Salt, imported from India generally and Kohat in particular, was and remains an important commodity used and consumed by all classes of Afghan society. Abd al-Rahman monopolized the trade in a number of commodities, including local products, especially fruit, and imported goods such as salt.[52] Pursuit of fruit-trade profits for the Durrani state brought Muhammad Akbar to Kohat, and while there he pursued the derivative issue of arat fees, but execution of the salt monopoly also received his attention during his stay in the city. Abd al-Rahman intended for Afghan nomads to purchase passes identifying them as participants in the Durrani state salt scheme, and while in Kohat Muhammad Akbar invoked government texts requiring the nomads to invest in the "public good" in this manner. The nomads were accountable for salt passes that were acquired at rates of Rs. 1.8 per camel load, Rs. .8 per mule or bullock, and Rs. .4 per donkey load.

Similar to their view of the various taxes associated with the fruit monopoly that Durrani state officials collected from textually captive Afghan nomads in British India, colonial bureaucrats unanimously interpreted the activities associated with Abd al-Rahman's salt scheme as illegal extraterritorial taxation. British officials did little to support the nomads' redresses to the colonial courts that they were being oppressed and extorted by Abd al-Rahman while they pursued legitimate commerce and lawfully engaged Indian markets. The British did not effectively invoke the colonial state's umbrella of territorial and legal protection over the Afghan nomads, but some British Indian officials did recognize and sympathize with the legitimacy of the nomads' claims. Regarding a number of commercial issues including the Durrani state's collection of taxes from Afghan nomads in British India, colonial policy makers were restricted to one primary avenue of recourse. In response to the perceived commercial misconduct of Abd al-Rahman, the British chose only to manipulate the cash subsidy issued to their appointed and fiscally dependent Durrani sovereign in Kabul.

According to the British, Abd al-Rahman's extraterritorial tax collection, especially when associated with his trading monopolies, was increasingly "demoralizing" to Indian traders. As a result, some of the Durrani state taxation practices in India were eventually reduced and eliminated. However, colonial officials conceded the legitimacy of many Durrani taxes and taxation activities, provided they were collected or conducted at Dakka in the Khaibar, which was one of many unique administrative arrangements of this strategically important mountain passage.[53] Colonial officials also consented to the continued collection of one Durrani state tax in British India proper. Partly to monitor the flow of commercial traffic from India to Afghanistan, or more precisely, from Peshawar to Kabul through the heavily surveilled Khaibar, the British allowed Durrani state qafilabashi fees to be collected and recorded in Peshawar or at Jamrud.[54]

The Peshawar qafilabashi or superintendent of caravans was the Durrani government official in Peshawar who received state commercial caravans, such as those carrying fruit, routed from Kabul and through the Khaibar in the fall. The qafilabashi was also responsible for the dispatch of Durrani state caravans from Peshawar to Kabul in the spring. The Peshawar qafilabashi determined the chronological order and size of caravans carrying commodities purchased in India that were destined for Durrani state consumption in Kabul, and the physical configuration of items within those caravans. The taxes collected by the qafilabashi, known as *qafilabashi giri* and *rawangiri Kabul*, were assessed on the animal of carriage, and for the most common transport animal along this route, the camel, the rate was Rs. 2. As we have seen, the textual terms of Abd al-Rahman's fruit monopoly resulted in his identification of many of the nomads who transported fruit from Afghanistan to India, most of whom owned their camels. During the winter, the fruit monopolist communicated with the qafilabashi who used security deposit records produced in the fall to conscript privately owned camels from Afghan nomads for Durrani state carriage purposes in the spring.[55]

The nomads could pay their qafilabashi dues at that official's office in Peshawar city or at Jamrud before embarking on their springtime procession through the Khaibar to Kabul. No matter where they paid their fees, the nomads received a pass for their expenditure from the Peshawar qafilabashi that was necessary for them to be formally received by the *darogha* or British official stationed at Jamrud, the eastern "gate" of the Khaibar Pass.[56] The nomads' textual, fiscal, and physical engagement of the Peshawar qafilabashi was ostensibly confined to the animals used to convey Durrani state property to Kabul. However, in practice the transactions between the nomads and the qafilabashi were not limited to transport animals carrying goods destined for Durrani state consumption. Abd al-Rahman ordered his Peshawar qafilabashi to collect arati or commission fees on all products the nomads brought to market in Kabul. In theory these commission fees were attached to products the nomads marketed independently of their textually coerced, state-contracted, Khaibar-centered carriage services. In factual terms the Peshawar qafilabashi monopolized the movement of commercial transport animals through the Khaibar toward Kabul. The qafilabashi's interest in and knowledge of those animals brought their cargo into his field of vision, which resulted in him charging the nomads Rs. 1 per camel load of commodities obtained with their own capital that they transported on their own behalf through the British-controlled Khaibar to market in Afghanistan and Central Asia. It is unclear how the qafilabashi documented the nomads' arati payments for the increasingly textually inclined Durrani state, but if other tax-payment practices serve as an interpretive guide, it is likely that the qafilabashi issued receipts to the nomads and that a monshi recorded those payments in a challan.

Commodities transported from India destined for Durrani state consumption in Kabul were granted tax-free status by the British during their passage through the Khaibar. This policy was one tactic in a larger strategy to induce a Khaibar routing that allowed colonial authorities to monitor the Indian and European goods Abd al-Rahman purchased and imported, especially those commodities obtained through the redistribution of subsidy money. Although it was not feasible for him to physically inspect each camel load, the *darogha* was responsible for validating all cargo's legitimate conformity with the requisite criteria for tax-free passage through the Khaibar. Like many of the arrangements between the British and their client Abd al-Rahman, the tax-free routing of Durrani state goods through the Khaibar became a contested issue after the agreement was made. Not surprisingly, the main area of contention that developed in this regard surrounded which goods were in fact eligible for tax-free conveyance. The original agreement conceptualized goods destined for Abd al-Rahman's personal consumption to be Durrani state property and therefore eligible for tax-free passage through the Khaibar. From the British perspective, especially insofar as the Khaibar tolls were concerned, Abd al-Rahman's commodities monopolies contributed to the blurring of already leniently vague boundaries between personal, state, and public consumption of Indian and European goods in Afghanistan. Certain items were particularly problematic for the colonial adjudicators of the material status and taxability of commercial goods routed through the Khaibar that were claimed and textually (re-) appropriated by Abd al-Rahman and his officials.

Abd al-Rahman's import of Indian *shakar/shakarti/shakararti* or sugar is one example among the many disputes between British and Durrani officials regarding the taxability and textual representation of commercial traffic through the Khaibar. Between February and April 1895, the British darogha at Jamrud, Gajju Mall, notified his superiors of the attempted passage of 856 camel loads of sugar weighing over 6.5 tons.[57] A pass from the Durrani qafilabashi in Peshawar had to be presented by the Afghan nomad traders to the British darogha at Jamrud for their camels to be received there. The qafilabashi arranged for the nomads to transport as much state property as possible, and the qafilabashi passes and receipts they presented at Jamrud were designed to indicate the tax-free status of the nomads' cargo to the darogha stationed there. The darogha was responsible for registering these camels as carrying tax-free goods in colonial ledgers containing Khaibar toll-payment records. The Rs. 1,712 in Khaibar tolls represented by the sugar caravans was a substantial sum that piqued the darogha's interest, especially when considered against other categories of taxable and tax-exempt goods in the account books that he managed.[58]

The tax-free passage of that volume of sugar through the Khaibar was suspect on a number of counts. First, during the three months in question the British Agent in Kabul reported to his superiors in India that Abd al-Rahman had recently taken steps to monopolize the sugar trade in Afghanistan.[59] Colonial authorities already believed that Abd al-Rahman's trading monopolies transgressed the realm of legitimate state intervention in the regional economy, and British policy was to impose Khaibar tolls on any and every commodity transported from India for trade or resale in Afghanistan. This policy applied to Abd al-Rahman's personal and Durrani state property, and the actions of the Jamrud darogha in response to the new variables in the trans-border sugar trade were manifestations of a more encompassing colonial policy. During the same three-month period in early 1895 colonial officials in Peshawar observed that Abd al-Rahman instructed his commercial agent in Karachi to make large purchases of sugar and secure arrangements with the Peshawar qafilabashi for its transportation to Kabul through the Khaibar.[60] Gajju Mall the Jamrud darogha sought confirmation from other Durrani officials in Peshawar that the sugar was in fact destined and *bona fide* for Durrani state consumption and not another object caught in the growing web of Abd al-Rahman's trading monopolies. Although he received a certificate from Abd al-Rahman's almond agent attesting to the necessary features of the sugar from the perspective of the Durrani state, the badami's certificates were "not to be trusted," according to British officials in Peshawar.[61]

The Durrani state qafilabashi in Peshawar during the sugar episode was Rustam Ali. Rustam Ali reported to the chief qafilabashi in Kabul, a post then likely held by Mullah Wais al-Din. Mullah Wais al-Din appointed a Peshawri monshi or secretary who physically handled the challan or register book that Rustam Ali was politically responsible for. The monshi during the sugar dispute of early 1895 was Tilla Muhammad, who apparently had a long tenure in that post because he served not only Rustam Ali, but also the three previous Durrani qafilabashis in Peshawar. It was noted earlier that a qafilabashi fee of Rs. 2 and arati tax of Rs. 1 was charged on all camels collecting at Jamrud for the tax-free conveyance of Durrani state merchandise through the Khaibar. In addition to those fees, Rustam Ali and Tilla Muhammad were known to extract a further Rs. 2.6, the former receiving Rs. 2 and the latter Rs. .6, on the same textually conscripted camels.

At Jamrud, two unequal states dueled over the taxes associated with the interregional nomadic tribal trade. Using a system of passes, receipts, and vouchers, the qafilabashi and his monshi wrote various forms of nomadic trade taxes into the Durrani state's expanding monopoly-based fiscal structure, and these fees were in fact collected from the nomads. However, a more determining and relatively stable structure of Anglo-Durrani political relations allowed for Abd al-Rahman's economically constrictive monopolies to be executed even in British India. This arrangement resulted in the Jamrud darogha often only inscribing in colonial record books the potential transit taxes due from the nomads for their textually coerced commercial traversing of the Khaibar, and the sugar episode indicates the British did not attempt to collect many of these fees from the nomads. Competing trade documents prompted tangible social interaction between state functionaries such as the Peshawar qafilabashi and the Jamrud darogha, and between each of those officials and the nomads, as documents from 1896 indicate. These records refer to the qafilabashi's generalized interference in the darogha's activities by "acting as if the whole place (Jamrud) belonged to him (the qafilabashi)," the qafilabashi causing a night time commotion at Jamrud when the darogha was registering some 700 to 800 camels for the next day's travel, the qafilabashi verbally assaulting Afghan nomads whom he claimed refused to carry Durrani government stores, and his "thrashing the kochis, imposing double fines and seizing their camels."[62]

Provincial Fuel for the State Mint and the Absorption of Social Debt

The annihilation of the Army of the Indus dealt a severe blow to British political and financial prestige in India. The first Anglo-Afghan war damaged relationships at the upper levels of financing involving hundi transactions between large private banking firms and colonial state treasuries in North India. However, the occupation period resulted in a large infusion of British Indian rupees into the economies of Kabul, Qandahar, and eastern Afghanistan.[63] The extension of Company capital into this region during the first occupation was relatively successful. One important method of dispersing state coinage into multiple sectors and layers of an economy is to pay local armed forces personnel in that currency, and above in Chapter 3 attention was given to Rawlinson's attempt to execute such a maneuver in Qandahar in 1840. Another direct avenue of insinuating one currency into the political space of another is in the context of minting of state coinage. In this regard, although during the first occupation a rupee struck in the name of Shuja was the official product of the Kabul mint, that currency was a veneer masking the advance of British Indian coinage. Recycling of British Indian rupees into Shuja's coinage characterized the minting practices in Kabul during the Anglo-Durrani political condominium. The following quote describes the state's hand-minting practices as Trevor witnessed them when he was deputed to revise the Kabul account books in 1841:

> [T]he material used in the Cabool coinage is almost entirely Company's Rupees about 22,00,000 of the latter having been melted down last year when the number of Cabool Rupees struck was 27,65,612 and the quantity of bullion brought to the mint equal in weight to only Company's Rupees 85,258. The process of melting and

preparing silver for the mint is carried on in the town by contract and the contractors state that their custom is to add lead in the proportion of 40 per cent and that the product of 140 Company's Rupees weight of the mixture and 94½ of pure silver or what is supposed so, and 45 of dross. Again to reduce 94½ Company's Rupees weight of pure silver to the standard of the Cabool Rupee 25 Company's Rupees are added no other alloy is used and the mass weighing 119½ Company's Rupees is coined into Cabool Rupees 147½. The whole expense of the process of melting and purification including labor, charcoal, lead, bone ashes and utensils is defrayed by the dross which becomes the perquisite of the contractor and of which one suwar khanee equal in weight to Company Rupees 3.840 produces 3½ Company Rupees weight of pure silver and 252 ditto of copper and lead mixed in the proportion of five parts of the former to two of the latter the purity of silver received by the contractors is tested by melting a stated portion on a bed of bone ashes in a charcoal fire with lead and it is rejected whenever the loss in the process exceeds a given quantity. That loss seemed to me on witnessing the process to depend not only on the purity of the silver, and on the degree of heat and the length of time it was applied both which are left to the discretion of the operator.[64]

At their core, these calculations indicate that during the first colonial occupation of Kabul British Indian rupees comprised at least 80 percent of the raw material used in the production of handcrafted state coinage. Hand-minting of Durrani state coinage prevailed in Kabul until 1890 when Abd al-Rahman imported three large minting machines from Europe.[65] The European minting machinery greatly expanded the potential production of Durrani state coinage, and Abd al-Rahman accelerated the precedent established earlier in the century of recycling British Indian rupees into Durrani currency.[66] The heightened ability to produce state coinage motivated Abd al-Rahman to take extraordinary measures to extract British Indian rupees from his subjects. As an economic institution the mint had profound social consequences, particularly in terms of the centralization of pools of merchant capital dispersed throughout the country in Kabul, a city the British were able to fiscally colonize despite two failed military invasions of it.

Abd al-Rahman's re-coining drive focused on two silver currencies, the British Indian and Durrani rupee, with the former determining the value of the latter. However, other silver coins and a variety of copper and gold-based currencies circulated regularly and widely in Abd al-Rahman's domains.[67] As more silver rupees were produced by the minting machines in Kabul the other forms of money found in Afghanistan became increasingly valued through exchanges calculated against the proliferating Durrani state coinage. Because other monies were increasingly defined in relation to the Durrani rupee, the effects of the new mint ramified throughout all currency fields, social sectors, and geographic regions of the polity.

The main external source of British Indian rupee fuel for the Kabul mint was the cash subsidy Abd al-Rahman received, and these outright grants of British rupees were never less than twelve lakhs per year.[68] For example, in March 1890 immediately after the arrival of the minting machines in Kabul a subsidy disbursement of 5,00,000 British rupees was transported from Peshawar to the Durrani capital. This transfer of subsidy funds was clearly intended for re-coining and was likely distributed to the army for broad circulation.[69] To acquire the necessary raw material for the new machine mints, Abd al-Rahman also employed the British firm of Martin and Company to import un-coined bulk silver bullion from Europe.[70] Whereas the external supply of British Indian rupees and bulk silver had discernible limits, for Abd al-Rahman the domestic sources of British money and other forms of capital were conceptualized as being nearly limitless.

Abd al-Rahman issued numerous directives that demonstrate his desire to gather and re-coin all silver currencies in circulation in Kabul, Qandahar, eastern Afghanistan, and other market settings under his de facto control.[71] For example, he prohibited bankers and traders from remitting silver abroad, directed merchants to bring their silver to the Kabul mint, and ordered the public exchange of all previously issued Kabul rupees for his new coin. The export ban and other more direct forms of silver collection comprising the larger reminting initiative targeted bankers, merchants, and traders, and, either directly or indirectly, all other participants in the Afghan economy.[72]

The measures Abd al-Rahman took to collect silver for re-coining in the capital city had important effects on the relationships between Kabul and surrounding markets, districts, and provinces. Qandahar was particularly vulnerable to Abd al-Rahman's silver confiscation tactics as a result of the high volume of merchant capital flowing to and through the city consistent with its long-standing and prominent role in the vibrant long-distance trade between Indian and Iranian markets. In 1885, well before the arrival of the new minting machinery, Abd al-Rahman's appetite for silver to re-coin led to seizures of such a magnitude that the British Agent in Qandahar commented: "If this state of things (the confiscations) continues no money will be left with anybody in the whole of Afghanistan, and Government coffers will overflow with money."[73]

In January 1889, Abd al-Rahman turned his sights on the commercial brokerage arrangements in Qandahar in order to extract cash for re-coining in Kabul. The local community of brokers had been charging merchants a 1 percent commission, but Abd al-Rahman ordered all brokerage in the city to be concentrated under the purview of a single appointee sent from Kabul, a Hindu named Jita, who would collect a 2 percent fee.[74] Local merchants viewed this as another form of confiscation by royal decree, so they planned for a week-long export stoppage that would also close the local customs house, but the local Governor dissuaded them from doing so. However, not all local officials were sympathetic to the merchants in Qandahar who were simultaneously enduring searches and seizures of sums ranging from 10,000 to 20,000 rupees by the Chief of Police, Mirza Sultan Muhammad, who regularly trumped up charges against them.[75] Another vehicle for Abd al-Rahman's drive to re-mint British Indian rupees into Durrani state currency was the office of sarishtadar or provincial revenue official. Abd al-Rahman appointed the Hindu Diwan Sada Nand to the post of Qandahar sarishtadar in February 1889. Three months later the original and primary focus of the state's confiscatory initiative, the prized British Indian rupees, known locally as *kaldar* rupees, was again emphasized:

> The Kandahar revenue Sarishtadar has prohibited merchants from remitting Indian coins (rupees) toward India. This is because no silver comes to the Kandahar mint from any other country, wherewith to coin Kabuli and Kandahari rupees. The Queen's coin known in Kandahar as Kaldar rupees is melted and coined into Kabuli and Kandahar rupees. The merchants are therefore put to much loss and inconvenience, for they have no merchandise to export at present, and have to remit cash to Bombay and Karachi where only Indian coin is current.[76]

The preceding events occurred before the installation of the machine mints in Kabul in 1890. One indication that the new minting machinery almost immediately and most dramatically increased Abd al-Rahman's penchant for silver, especially kaldar, confiscation comes from the British Agent's communiqué from Qandahar dated January 4, 1891. In this correspondence Khan Bahadur Mirza Muhammad Taqi Khan reported a substantial increase in the agricultural tax levied on Durrani state lands, from either one-fourth or one-third of the produce, depending on particular circumstances, to a uniform one-half for all properties.[77] State land managers were accountable for remitting a certain pre-agreed amount of capital just as provincial and district revenue farmers were. Durrani state taxes were not uncommonly paid in some form of cash through the mediation of Hindki bankers and commodities brokers (see above

Introduction and Chapter 1). It is fair to deduce that Abd al-Rahman expected substantial kaldar dividends to result from this greatly increased revenue imposition on government lands in Qandahar.

Greater taxation of government lands can be considered one of the more common and obvious methods of augmenting state revenue, but such a high degree of increase appears unusual and is conspicuously concurrent with the arrival of the new state minting machinery. Immediately after the installation of the machine mints in Kabul, Abd al-Rahman called for an array of other state impositions on private capital in Qandahar that can be characterized as extraordinary. A number of harsh measures were taken and bizarre justifications offered in Abd al-Rahman's quest to supply raw material for the surge in coin production resulting from the state's very much-increased minting capacity. While the following quote typifies the kind of arbitrary seizures of capital that took place in Qandahar after the new mints went into service, it is important to appreciate that all kinds of people in all other localities in Afghanistan were subject to similar random confiscatory practices:

> Heavy fines are being inflicted and recovered now-a-days for trivial offenses, e.g., a fine of rupees twenty one thousand has been imposed on some villagers, shop keepers, and a camel driver, residents of Deh-i Khwaja, on the ground that the wife of a servant of Sardar Sher Ali Khan, ex-Wali of Kandahar, has gone to Karachi without their knowledge. The camel driver's offense lay in the fact that he hired out his camel to this woman. The villagers were fined for not reporting her departure to the authorities prior to her leaving for Karachi, and the shop keepers were fined because they were related to this woman.[78]

The new minting machinery in Kabul precipitated substantive changes in the economy of eastern Afghanistan. Relations between Qandahar and Kabul were acutely affected, with the new Durrani capital city becoming enriched at the expense of the old. On January 18, 1891, the British Newswriter in Qandahar announced the closure of the local mint:

> The Governor has received orders from His Highness the Amir to the effect that no money is to be coined in the Kandahar mint in future, and that, for the future, only new coins struck by the machinery lately erected at the headmint in Kabul will be allowed currency in Afghanistan. His Highness, however, has not notified in what way the new coinage is to be introduced, and the old coins withdrawn from circulation. But the people entertain very little hope that the change will be affected without loss being inflicted on the public.[79]

Abd al-Rahman clearly recognized the new minting machinery generated profits through the re-coining of British Indian rupees and other silver-based coinage into Durrani state or Kabul rupees. In his own rendition of how the new machine mint was fueled, Abd al-Rahman recognized little difference between the re-coining of cash grants of British Indian rupees and the ongoing searches for and seizures of silver from his own subjects that are only thinly veiled in the following quote:

> Now, however, I am fortunate in possessing coining presses in my mint, made upon the same system as those employed in European countries. . . . The British Government had given me some money coined in the mint at Calcutta; these rupees I ordered to be melted down, and, after 6 per cent. of copper had been added to the alloy, they were re-coined into Kabul rupees (the value of the English rupee is 16 pence, that of the Kabul rupee 12 pence). I also commanded my officials to purchase silver from the country, to melt it down, add a considerable quantity of copper to it, and coin into rupees, in this way making some profit. Moreover, I ordered to be refunded into the Treasury sums of money which, under the former Government, had been borrowed or looted by people, as also other sums that had been entrusted to them by Government for official payments, which sums they had retained in their own hands and used for other purposes. After this general proclamation many people refunded the money they owed and, in order to get the remainder from those who would not pay, I appointed collectors, giving them instructions to force the debtors to give up these moneys. I further appointed accountants, whose duty it was to examine the accounts, and to see that all unpaid taxes were recovered.[80]

The new minting machinery in Kabul resulted in the advancement of the British Indian rupee's presence and influence in Afghanistan. The machine-minted Kabul rupee continued to be defined by and subordinate to the British Indian rupee, just as the hand-minted Kabul rupee had been. Overall, the expansion of the British Indian rupee was a prerequisite for the spread of Durrani state coinage in the fiscal colony. Durrani state minting practices during the entire nineteenth century reflect the kind of fundamental and ongoing contradiction pointed out as defining a colonial state's operative mode.[81] It served British India well enough to have its currency provide the foundation for an Afghan economy controlled by one of its appointees. However, while recognizing Abd al-Rahman as colonially appointed and funded, it is important to appreciate that the impoverishment of Afghan society had more to do with his actions than British policy. The growing presence of Durrani rupees masked the advance of British Indian coinage, but this was not the source of prevalent economic decline and the related increased need for debt servicing. The origin of Afghanistan's impoverishment lays in Abd al-Rahman's attempt to replace resources controlled by Hindki bankers and brokers with Durrani state capital in a number of economic sectors. The areas where Abd al-Rahman attempted to insinuate Durrani state resources at the expense of Indian merchant capital include cash advances to producers, and larger-scale loans and capital transfer facilities to wholesale merchants and other financiers of the transit trade with India, Iran, and Central Asia.[82]

Abd al-Rahman's assessment of the Durrani political economy failed to integrate at least two phenomena. The first was devaluation of the Durrani currency resulting from its increased production being predicated on the more fervent recycling of a more valuable coin, the British Indian rupee. For Abd al-Rahman, minting money was a goal in and of itself, and he did not seem to fully comprehend the dynamics between the use of a currency and its value in relation to others. The second area of economic miscalculation concerned credit and debt relations and Abd al-Rahman's attempt to assume some of the roles played by Indian bankers and moneylenders in the Afghan economy. In this regard, Abd al-Rahman erred in his belief that replacing Indian bankers' and brokers' capital with Durrani state resources would be profitable.

Abd al-Rahman sought to displace Indians from the generic trade of Afghanistan because he felt they sent their profits to "their own lands."[83] As we have seen, Hindki communities in Afghanistan, such as the Shikarpuris, were the local constituents of extensive interregional banking networks. By provisioning cash and credit to producers, merchants, groups of nomadic trading tribes, and state officials the Indian bankers helped integrate various sectors of the Afghan economy while also linking local resources to distant markets. For the various Indian banking communities, the hundi or bill of exchange was the primary instrument of network communication and the key vehicle for inter-market transactions. Hundis allowed Indian bankers in Afghanistan to receive various forms of currency, which would function as sources of local credit and cash advances. The debt incurred by the recipients seems to have been heavy given the ubiquity of Hindkis in Afghanistan, and before Abd al-Rahman the cumulative debt of Afghan society was both financed and widely dispersed almost exclusively through larger Indian mercantile networks via hundis.

Abd al-Rahman was not able to entirely eliminate the Hindki population in Afghanistan, and it is important to note that a number of South Asians played prominent roles in his government. However, Abd al-Rahman was able to absorb some of the clients of the Indian bankers who were driven out of the country. The profits made by Indian bankers and moneylenders by providing cash advances and larger hundi-based loans were not immediately evident and in many ways realized through the wider network, not in any given locality. Therefore, Abd al-Rahman's agenda of having the state supply cash advances, merchant loans, and some of the facilities for long-distance commercial trans-actions meant it would also have to absorb and cater to some of the widespread local social debt. Abd al-Rahman may have been successful in having Durrani state resources fill the fiduciary void he created by eliminating some of the Indian bankers in Afghanistan. For our purpose what is relevant is that he and the bureaucratic apparatus he controlled were far less able than the Hindki communities to redistribute, spread out, delay, and refinance debt burdens with the ease and fluidity of declared adversaries such as the Shikarpuris.

CHAPTER 6

Mutual Evasion between Afghanistan and the Global Marketplace

The Sethis of Peshawar and the British Recruitment of Secret Asiatic Agents

The Sethis of Peshawar are the city's most renowned and historically active family trading firm. The Sethi firm was based in Peshawar and had branches of operation throughout India, Afghanistan, Central Asia, and beyond in the nineteenth and early twentieth centuries. According to senior representatives of the family interviewed in 1995, the family migrated from the town of Bhera in the Punjab to Chamkani, a village suburb a few miles east of Peshawar, during the period of Sikh rule.[1] At that time the family is said to have dealt in karakul wool, copper, gold thread, skins, Russian crockery, dried fruit, and especially tea and timber. Branches of the Sethi family business in Shanghai and Vladivostok organized the export of Chinese tea to Central Asia via India and Afghanistan.[2] The Sethis indicate that Abd al-Rahman granted their family the right to lease the Jaji forest in the Paktia province of eastern Afghanistan from where they exported timber through Parachinar to Thal in British India.[3] In Kabul the Sethi business house and serai complex was located in the southeastern section of the city near the masjid-i hamam in Shor Bazaar and the two streets where the Hindu population was concentrated, *guzar-i kalan* and *guzar-i khurd*. In Peshawar, the center of their mercantile network, the Sethis funded the construction and renovation of many mosques and bridges. A number of Sethi families residentially congregated in a section of Peshawar now known as the *mahalla Sethian*.[4]

The Sethis employed a number of agents who resided in the cities where family business branches existed. It is unclear whether these agents were Sethi family members or contracted employees. In Kabul the Sethis' *gumashta* or trading agent was "very friendly with Amir Abd al-Rahman, and frequently visited him in the hamam" or bathhouse.[5] The head of the Sethi family, who represents the merchant capitalist known as a shah, sahukar, or sarraf in Markovits's model of the Shikarpuri firms, is said to have received correspondence directly from Abd al-Rahman.[6] The Sethis and their local agent in Kabul did not suffer the same kind of confiscations and seizures of merchant capital as experienced by a number of other Indians living and working in Afghanistan during the reign of Abd al-Rahman. Instead of being mulcted the Sethis were favored by Abd al-Rahman, and their family firm and its agents apparently prospered in other fluid political environments in Central, South, and East Asia.[7] During the nineteenth century an agent of the Sethi firm in Central Asia is said to have been in direct correspondence with the Viceroy of India.[8]

The commercial experiences of the Sethi family firm and its agents draw attention to the importance of Peshawar as a site of information collection and dissemination concerning Afghanistan. To understand why Peshawar assumed the role of a depot for intelligence about Afghanistan, a trait still very much in evidence today, it is important to appreciate the dearth of information supplied from Kabul during the reign of Abd al-Rahman. As per the terms of the agreement between the British and Abd al-Rahman, the latter received a Muslim Indian as the representative of the British Government to his court.[9] As previously noted, the British Agent in Kabul faced severe restrictions in all areas of communication outside of the rigidly controlled public setting of Abd al-Rahman's court. The Agent's movements were increasingly restricted and the people with whom he talked or exchanged correspondence were often subject to severe punitive sanctions. Colonial officials in India referred to the British Agent in Kabul, even "under the best circumstances (as) a second rate reporter."[10]

Abd al-Rahman used a variety of methods to discourage and restrict communication with the British Agent in Kabul. For example, the Agent was once visited at his residence by an uncle who was subsequently executed and dismembered and whose remains were placed in public view by Abd al-Rahman as an object lesson to others.[11] Subsequent to these events the British Agent in Kabul advised two local agents of a Peshawar merchant not to visit him for fear of such reprisals.[12] However, the intelligence needs conditioned by the "Great Game" competition between England and Russia over mutual imperial advances in Afghanistan and Persia could not be measured by merely a few non-European lives lost. Therefore, the British Indian Government directed the Peshawar merchant in question to have his agents continue to call on the British Agent in Kabul. The colonial agenda was to gain access to the networks of information converging on Kabul, and it was with great disappointment that authorities in British India noted the near stifling of commercial intelligence from that crucial site early into Abd al-Rahman's reign. For example, by 1885 estimates of the declining state of Indian exports to Central Asia had become extremely vague:

> Most of the goods which are sent to Central Asia from India go by Kabul . . . [and] it is impossible to say what portion of the goods crossing the frontier into Kabul is sent forward to the Central Asian markets. After they pass the frontier they are lost sight of, and all that can be ascertained in regard to the Central Asian trade is what is said by traders at Peshawar.[13]

In May 1884 Henry Mortimer Durand, whose name symbolizes the eastern Anglo-Afghan boundary, the so-called Durand line of 1893, commented about the state of Central Asian intelligence: "At present our information is undoubtedly very defective, and we cannot afford to let it remain so."[14] As part of the larger colonial effort to recoup lost sources of data concerning Afghanistan, Durand offered eight specific comments on a report prepared by Charles MacGregor regarding the means of procuring better intelligence from and about Central Asia.[15] One of MacGregor's seven potential sources of information fell under the heading "Secret Asiatic Agents," and Durand's first comment about MacGregor's entire report honed in on this category in the following way:

> We often get really valuable information from Peshawar. There is a large trading community, and other means of collecting information are not wanting, both with regard to Afghanistan and with regard to northern countries.[16]

In his capacity as Secretary to the Foreign Department of the Government of India, Durand commissioned the Punjab Government to prepare a list of British Indian subjects active in the Central Asian trade. This query resulted in an inventory prepared by Gulab Khan for the Lieutenant Governor of the Punjab. In this catalogue of seventy-seven possible recruits for the colonial regime there were fifteen "natives of Peshawar," four of whom were Sethi family members.[17] There are a number of indications that members of the Sethi family and/or their agents were successfully recruited as "Secret Asiatic Agents" by the British. One convincing piece of evidence supporting that conclusion is a 1914 report submitted to the Viceroy of India by Haji Karam Elahi Sethi on his life and travels.[18] In this short autobiography Karam Elahi claims his ancestors "wholly and solely carried on trade in Bukhara, Samarkand, and Afghanistan," and mentions:

> ... [a]bout 500 men from Peshawar, Attock, Nowshera, Makhad, and Shahpur district conduct trade mostly in tea in this city (Bukhara). They have started a No. of banks in the country, thereby giving impetus to trade in various forms.[19]

In addition to this commercial intelligence on Bukhara, Sethi's travelogue also provides a glimpse into the flows of various currencies across Afghanistan's boundaries. Chapter 3 of this work discussed the movement of British Indian rupees into Afghanistan, but Sethi here describes a reverse movement of Durrani currency into British India. Sethi journeyed from Kabul, "a beautiful valley and fit for being the metropolis of Afghanistan in every respect," to Parachinar in British territory and commented that:

> ... [t]he route passes between hills and occasional villages where food &c., is easily procurable. Along the way the lands appeared well cropped and cultivated. My halting station, viz., Para Chinar is the last British town resided by a political Agent. It is a great market for fruits, etc. and bartering (sic) often takes the form of Cabul coin.[20]

Local commercial lore in late twentieth-century Peshawar relied heavily on the image of Russian rubles held by the Sethi firm filling the streets as confetti would after the 1917 Soviet Revolution was said to have rendered those paper notes nearly worthless. However, quite a different image of the Sethis' relationship to Russian rubles emerges from colonial documents produced in 1920.[21] In this archival file we find Haji Karam Elahi Sethi carrying the new title, Khan Bahadur, a status achieved in large measure by providing commercial and other forms of intelligence on Afghanistan and Central Asia to colonial authorities. Sethi contacted the Chief Commissioner of the North-West Frontier Province, Hamilton Grant, to seek permission to import 29,22,500 Russian rubles from Kabul to Peshawar.

Sethi claimed the Bukhara branch of his business dispatched the ruble notes to Kabul on or about January 1, 1920. Prohibition on the import of Russian rubles was imposed between then and September 1 when Commissioner Grant wrote the Government of India on Sethi's behalf in pursuit of having the new law waived. Arguments about the security of the ruble notes in the Peshawar Treasury and their serving as payment for goods supplied were to no avail. The Government of India rejected Sethi's plea to import Russian rubles from

Afghanistan into India. The denial was based on a stated desire not "to grant any facilities for the movement of ruble notes, which might have the effect of establishing an exchange value for them in Afghanistan."[22]

This aspect of imperial Britain's anti-Russian policy toward Afghanistan was designed to impede the Durrani state's ability to profit from inter-currency exchanges involving rubles, but in practice it also negatively affected bankers in the country whose livelihoods were closely associated with such transactions. The colonial contradiction in this instance was that the bankers were an important source of intelligence for the British, but British monetary policy deprived them of the kind of business that kept them in Afghanistan. In other words, the British policy of inhibiting the movement of Russian rubles through Afghanistan impaired the business presence of Peshawar-based inter-regional traders like the Sethis and their agents in Kabul. But at the same time, the dearth of information about the region prompted an increased reliance by colonial officials on Peshawri merchants and firms for commercial intelligence about Kabul, Afghanistan, and greater Central Asia.

North Indian Tea Trade Circumventions

We have seen how the Sethi firm shifted its base of operations and the focus of its diverse activities through time. The family firm moved its headquarters from Bhera to Chamkani to Peshawar, and in each location the focus of their enterprise changed from indigo, to tea and wood, to currencies, and finally to fur. It stands to reason that at each stage of its development the firm revised its associations with the various types of agents who served it away from the home base. The Sethis and a number of other merchants and firms based in Peshawar were heavily involved in the tea trade from China and India to Central Asia through Afghanistan. This section concerns the response of a collection of North Indian tea traders and their commercial associates based in Peshawar to Abd al-Rahman's policies and practices regarding the movement of foreign commodities through Afghanistan.

The period of colonial rule in India gave rise to a number of tea plantations in the Himalayan foothills north of Delhi. The tea trade was a blossoming global enterprise during the nineteenth and twentieth centuries that had a substantial impact on producers, merchants, and consumers in a number of regions of the world including China, India, Central Asia, Iran, and England.[23] Before Abd al-Rahman's rule in Afghanistan, a consortium of tea planters from

Kangra, Kumaoun, and Dehra Dun were engaged in a lucrative export trade of their products overland through Peshawar and Kabul to Bukhara. They valued their export business at 30,000 maunds per year which, at 95 pounds to a maund, comes to two million seven hundred thousand pounds. Estimating a camel to carry 450 pounds, six thousand camels would have been employed for the long-distance transport of this product to market. First quality Kangra tea sold for 4 annas per pound at the point of production, which meant a cost of approximately Rs. 140 per camel load, and a total investment of Rs. 8,40,000, at the start of the marketing cycle.[24]

It is necessary to consider the variety of transit tolls levied by Abd al-Rahman on goods moving through Afghanistan before addressing the tea traders' response to them. In the first instance, the amounts of the transit fees varied, as did the locations of their collection in Afghanistan. Despite the limited information received from and about the country, colonial officials produced two estimates of the transit duties and carriage costs imposed by Abd al-Rahman on the North Indian tea caravans traversing his realm. The first involved five separate impositions the sum of which was Rs. 120 per camel load, and the second comprised eight fees totaling Rs. 106 per tea-loaded camel.[25] In both cases, the transit taxes on camels carrying tea came to over 80 percent of the purchase cost, and it is important to reiterate this was only for the Afghanistan portion of the route. A notable difference between the sums is the varying amounts, methods, and locations of their extraction, which collectively reflect a wide and expanding range of techniques employed by Abd al-Rahman to reap dividends from the transport of foreign goods through his territory. In addition to the array of transit taxes levied at various locations in Afghanistan, Abd al-Rahman imposed another set of charges on the overland conveyance of commodities from India to Central Asia. The second category of exactions included:

> . . . kafilabashi at Peshawar, octroi duty from Dakka to Kabul, customs duty on arrival at Kabul, *goshi*, state brokerage, customs duty on leaving Kabul, kafilabashi for Turkistan, octroi duty from Kabul to Kahmard, *Tangi Khalam* duty, *dahana kocha* Khulum, sarai Mazar, kafilabashi Bukhara.[26]

Regarding these charges, the qafilabashi fees and state brokerage were the most remunerative for Abd al-Rahman.[27] The Durrani Government Caravan Office was overseen by the head qafilabashi or superintendent of caravans.[28] Other state-appointed qafilabashis were found in many villages and towns and in all cities in Afghanistan, and, perhaps most significantly, in Peshawar in British India. The qafilabashis were responsible for arranging, documenting, and taxing commercial traffic to, from, and throughout Afghanistan. Qafila-bashi fees were assessed by the animal and varied widely. There were different amounts charged depending on what kind of animal was carrying what type of commodity, and according to the distances, trajectory, and route segment covered. State brokerage was another distinct claim made by Abd al-Rahman on goods in transit through Kabul. A colonial document addressing Abd al-Rahman's perceived strangulation of commercial traffic between Peshawar and Bukhara noted "[t]he precise amount of state brokerage (is not) counted in adding up the total amount of [transit taxes and customs] dues of the whole length of the road."[29] Another source points to a working relationship between Afghan state brokers and octroi officials in Kabul:

> ... when goods arrive in Kabul their value is fixed by those "dalals" who are servants of the Octroi Department, and they add 50 per cent (i.e., things valuing Rupees 100 are considered worth Rupees 150) and the owners have to accept this arbitrary assessment; afterwards the Octroi officials add another 20 per cent making 170 per 100, and tax them accordingly; at the time of the same goods leaving the city an extra duty of different rates is levied on loads. In levying this duty indigo and tea are weighted with their boxes, wrappers, etc. and their value is fixed according to the weight of each load ... these goods can be divided into three parts, one part consists of piece-goods and pushmeena, another tea, and of the third part half consists of indigo and half peddler's wares. In exchange for these goods one-third or one-fourth of the sale proceeds is brought in gold coins of Russia and Bokhara, and the remainder mostly in silk, horses, charras, and silk clothing made in Bokhara.[30]

The transit taxes, state brokerage dues, and qafilabashi fees imposed by Abd al-Rahman on merchandise moving through Afghanistan were pronounced departures from the commercial scenario envisaged by the British when they appointed their client in 1880. The British opinion about Abd al-Rahman's transit-trade policies and practices reflected some aspects of the reforms Burnes and Trevor made to the Kabul customs house and fiscal registers during the first colonial occupation of Kabul (see above, Chapter 3). British officials hoped for, but did not receive two commercial concessions from Abd al-Rahman. First, they wanted to replace the multiple toll posts found throughout Afghanistan with single collection points on each border. Colonial officials also called for a simplification of various rates of taxation then levied according to the kinds, volumes, and method of animal transport with one fixed tax of not more than 5 percent based on a pre-agreed and consistently applied tariff value for the commodity or commodity group in question.[31] Compared to the approximate 80 percent of purchase cost paid in transit taxes on tea moving through Afghanistan, the 5 percent maximum called for here was rather unrealistic. Ultimately, British officials wound up having to vent among themselves about the state of the Afghan through trade. The benign colonial reflections on this matter included:

> The Amir might be shown from the returns of trade from the last 10 years that trade has practically not advanced in that period although peace has prevailed on the whole and the pulsing of our railways right up to the Afghan frontier has greatly cheapened merchandise and should have much facilitated trade. This stagnation must be attributed to the heavy transit duties and even still more to the uncertainty of traders as to changes which may at any moment be made to their detriment, and the harassment and extortions to which they are subject by repeated examinations of their goods at various stages in transit.[32]

Such a rational presentation to Abd al-Rahman never occurred, and colonial officials consistently chose not to attempt to effect any real change regarding the transit trade of Indian tea or any other commodity through Afghanistan until after his death in 1901.[33] However, in response to Abd al-Rahman's rather unbridled taxation and confiscation impulses, Indian tea traders diverted their consignments away from the traditional path through Peshawar, Kabul, and Tashkurgan to the sea route via Bombay and Bandar Abbas in the Persian Gulf, then overland through Iran to Mashhad and then Bukhara.[34] Peshawri Muslim merchant firms such as the Sethis were prominent as brokers of the North Indian tea trade with Central Asia. No longer relying on their commercial agents and agencies in Kabul, Peshawri Muslim traders and firms arranged for an entirely new routing and handling of tea from the production sites in the Himalayan foothills north of Delhi to Bukhara and the markets of Central Asia.

In Bukhara, Muslim traders and the firms they formed, such as the Sethi trading house, dealt with Hindu merchants such as the Shikarpuris to dispose of North Indian tea routed by sea, seemingly quite far away and immunized from claims emanating from Kabul.[35] The cash garnered by the Hindus in Bukhara from their handling of the tea was remitted to Jews in the city. These Jewish merchants sent the money they received from Hindus in Bukhara to Moscow by telegraph. From Moscow the cash acquired through the sale of North Indian tea in Central Asia was wired to Bombay for payment to the Peshawri Muslim brokers.[36] In this way, the various forms of merchant capital associated with the Central-South Asian tea trade completely circumvented Afghanistan. A significant feature of this arrangement was the cooperation displayed by Hindu, Jewish, and Muslim mercantile communities in Bukhara.

The Peshawar merchants' redirection of their tea consignments to the more circuitous sea route was designed to avoid the enormous exactions made by Abd al-Rahman on the flow of goods through his territory. The northwesterly flows of items such as tea were not the only commercial streams subject to heavy Durrani state impositions. An equally wide array of taxes and duties applied to the southeasterly flow of commodities, and various forms of money received in Central Asia as payment for Indian and other products imported through Afghanistan were particularly targeted by Abd al-Rahman.[37] Abd al-Rahman regularly seized gold and silver bullion and coins or forced unfavorable terms of sale on those holding it, so carrying more than trivial sums of hard cash from Central Asia to India through Kabul would have been financially irresponsible. Iranian merchants also shipped North Indian tea from Bombay to the Gulf and then on to Bukhara. The Peshawris claimed Iranians in Bukhara were able to sell the same product for 24 to 26 tillas per package, while as a result of Durrani state tax burdens and the need to avoid them they were compelled to charge 36 tillas per package of tea in order for their venture to be cost-effective.[38] The new sea routing removed the Peshawris' competitive advantage over Iranians in the Bukhara tea market.

Abd al-Rahman did not express any reservations about the various forms of taxes imposed on Indian goods carried to Bukhara through his territory. In 1885 he communicated with certain Peshawri merchants through their agents in Kabul about the transit-trade situation.[39] Abd al-Rahman expressed entitlement to a share of the profits merchants transferred back to the subcontinent, despite the facts that the tea never entered his territory and the money received for the tea moved from Moscow to Bombay by telegraph without traversing his realm! In 1887 it was reported that Jan Muhammad Khan, the *sandukdar* or Durrani State Treasurer, issued the following directive to the agents of certain Peshawar merchants residing in Kabul:

> If you send your merchandize to Moscow by this route you should bring your money also by this way. Before this you entailed a loss of 40 lakhs of rupees on the State. If you agree to what I have proposed, then well and good; if not, do not send anything from Peshawar by this road.[40]

Durrani state officials made it clear to the Peshawar merchants that if they wanted to maintain any commercial activity or presence whatsoever in Afghanistan they would need to remit their cash earnings in Central Asia to India through Kabul. In December of 1887 Abd al-Rahman reiterated his demand for two years of back transit duty from thirteen Peshawar merchants.[41] Furthermore, Abd al-Rahman rejected their pleas for compensation for goods stolen in Afghanistan and justified the admitted theft on the grounds that the merchants were allowing someone other than he to profit from business conducted outside his territory. His letter to the Peshawar merchants concludes with the following ultimatum:

> You have one of the two alternatives: —Either discontinue sending your light merchandise by way of Moscow and bring it via Afghanistan, so that Afghanistan may benefit a little or much, or do not claim compensation for any goods that may be plundered in my territory. You should consider how unjust it is that you should receive compensation from the revenues of Afghanistan for your things, which may be looted while you pay duty on your goods to a foreign Government. You send your heavy things by this way but light ones by that way. It is evident that you make mere excuses and that you are unjust. I cannot repeal my order. If you want to trade by this route, you should send your heavy goods by this route and bring your light articles, such as *tilas*, &c., also by this route. If you wish to give up this route and use the other, you are at liberty to do so. But if you want to send only your heavy goods by this way, give an agreement to the effect that you will not ask for compensation when your goods are robbed. Until you do so the former order shall not be revoked.[42]

In this letter, Abd al-Rahman implies admittedly plundered goods were justly confiscated. He seems to consider the commodities moving through his territory to the north, such as tea, indigo, and textiles to be heavy goods. The only item mentioned as moving south, the gold tilla currency, is considered light. The distinctions being muddled here are between bulky and relatively cheap commodities on the one hand, and compact and generally valuable goods on the other. The caustic tone used toward the Peshawar merchants reflects Abd al-Rahman's pangs of foreign currency deprivation as a result of the Peshawri merchants' cessation of remitting cash from Bukhara to India through Kabul. Concerning his attitude toward and treatment of these merchants, Abd al-Rahman was warned by one of his high-ranking accountants, Monshi Ahmad Jan, that "such usage does exist in any other country (and) Your Highness will get a bad name by introducing such dues." Abd al-Rahman was undeterred by the prospect of being branded with a poor commercial reputation, and continued to press his uniquely construed claim for multiple years of back taxes from the Peshawar tea traders.[43] In order to execute his intentions in this matter, Abd al-

Rahman relied on a cadre of accountants, bookkeepers, and clerks sometimes referred to as *daftaris*, but most often termed mirzas (see above, Chapter 5).

Abd al-Rahman assigned Mirza Jafar to pursue the claim against the Peshawar merchants labeled remiss for transferring money earned in Bukhara to Moscow and then Bombay.[44] The Peshawri "firm of Mian Muhammad Amin, Fazl Kadir, and Abdur Rashid" sold tea and other Indian and European commodities in Central Asia. Although they went to great lengths to avoid Afghanistan on both legs of their annual interregional trading cycle, Abd al-Rahman was intent on securing a share of their capital and profits. As discussed in Chapter 5, dispatching a mirza to conduct a fiscal audit was a very common practice during Abd al-Rahman's reign, and the outcome was almost without exception devastating for the targeted person or consortium of people. In April 1889 the Kabul-based agents of the Peshawar merchants approached Haji Asad Khan, one of Abd al-Rahman's closest confidantes, with a letter from their superiors or "principals," identified here as Muhammad Amin and Mir Ahmad.[45] The letter dealt primarily with the closure of some shops the Peshawris owned in Qandahar, but in that correspondence they also claimed Mirza Jafar's case against them for remitting money from Bukhara to Bombay through Moscow was "groundless." Referring specifically to the latter matter, Haji Asad responded to the Kabul agents of the Peshawar merchants as follows:

> I am not going to hear all these excuses. Write to your masters to say that it is my order that they should employ somebody whom they can trust and send him to this place, otherwise I will confiscate their firm which is here and imprison their agents.[46]

Most likely because all available capital had been extracted from the existing agents of the Peshawar merchants, and their relatives, friends, associates, and neighbors in Afghanistan, Haji Asad again instructed the firms to appoint new agents to manage the claim being enforced on their firms by the Durrani state. The Peshawar merchants replied that their existing agents would suffice, and reiterated their belief that Mirza Jafar's case lacked both merit and a factual basis. They also said they were fully prepared to pay not only the principal amount claimed, but also the interest on that sum, if documents could be produced to support the Durrani state's claim on their resources.[47] This information comes from the British Agent in Kabul who witnessed Haji Asad's reception and reading of this mercantile letter from Peshawar. Continuing with his report, the Agent indicates:

Previous to his receipt of this answer the Haji received a letter from the Amir (Abd al-Rahman). It stated as follows:—"Do not show any indulgence to the Peshawar merchants or be slow in the matter of Mirza Jafir's case, for the Mirza is ill at Peshawar. Should he die these liars will give another turn to this case and spoil it. You should therefore decide the case soon." On receipt of this order the Haji became audacious. In short, seven lakhs of rupees are being demanded from the above named merchants.[48]

Evidently quite gleefully, on May 8 Haji Asad dispatched *mohassils* or armed men deputed to execute state orders, that is, bill-collectors, to the local agency houses of the Peshawar firms of Muhammad Amin and Mir Ahmad in Kabul.[49] The Kabul agents of the Peshawar merchants responded that the claim against them had nothing to with Islamic law based on the *sharia*, which was a lobbying point proffered in order for the case to be referred to a panchayat council convened by Abd al-Rahman to resolve commercial disputes.[50] The local agents also offered a written guarantee to pay the principal with interest, provided the case against them could be proven in accordance with commonly accepted mercantile regulations which they mistakenly thought would be enforced in Abd al-Rahman's panchayat.[51]

The Peshawar merchants and firms possessed a number of contacts in the political and fiscal infrastructure of the Durrani state. The Peshawris availed themselves of these associations and wrote about their plight to an unnamed Durrani state official who appears as either a competitor or superior of Haji Asad. The accused merchants were successful in using that local network leverage to get Haji Asad to withdraw the muhassils he had earlier placed at their agents' homes.[52] However, Haji Asad merely reassigned the muhassils to the task of getting the local agents to "execute a bond" or give him and Abd al-Rahman "something so they might purchase their liberation."[53] In effect, this was a ransom demand for the Peshawar agents who had become commercial hostages of the Durrani state. Extortion of mercantile firms by taking their local agents hostage was not an uncommon occurrence in Abd al-Rahman's Afghanistan, and a later report from the Peshawar Confidential Diary provides another example of this practice:

Ahmad Gul and Mir Ahmad, bankers of Peshawar, have sent orders to their Agents in Afghanistan to return to Peshawar whether any book debts are realized or not, but the Amir (Abd al-Rahman) has directed them to furnish security before obtaining passports (so) that they will return to Kabul. As no individual believes that these men will go back (to Kabul) from Peshawar, they are unable to find security, and

Conclusion:
Deflecting Colonial Canons and Cannons—
Alternate Routes to Knowing Afghanistan

The windfall reaped by the Sethi family through their intimate commercial connections with Abd al-Rahman stands in stark contrast to the more usual experience of mercantile flight from and avoidance of Afghanistan. Abd al-Rahman temporarily reversed the trend of Indian capital's penetration of Afghanistan, but he could not eliminate the dependence of Afghanistan's exports on India's mass consumer markets. Geography is the primary structuring variable in the long-term economic connection between Afghanistan and India, and state politics are important determinants in the precise articulation of this commercial relationship between two unequal but interdependent economic zones. Interactive social and cultural histories blend geographical constants and political fluctuations into a multidimensional holograph of market life on the frontier between Afghanistan and India. This book explored a limited set of market relationships on this frontier during the nineteenth century when colonialism was globally ascendant.

The lens of colonialism can be adjusted, however problematically, to accommodate both macroscopic and microscopic vantage points. The oeuvres of Chris Bayly and Bernard Cohn capture those two complementary scopes of colonial analysis as each author recognizes local and global "polarities" to make their own points and positions more potent and convincing.[1] A two-tiered vision of what can be called the local and the global is at the same time an integrated one, and as such it is perhaps the primary connection at work in the preceding pages. Other connections that are equally basic, and similarly complex in their dialectics, have been necessary to consider in order to approximate what really happened on the ground and not what is imagined to have occurred from distant vantage points during the articulation of modern Afghanistan. Colonial connections between Afghanistan and British India were addressed through relations between states and markets in their own right and in relation to one another, social communities and commodity groups independently and interactively, and through texts and money again as multifaceted but singular units of analysis as well as an analytical pairing. It has been necessary to do a bit of disentangling along the way toward making social and economic connections between states, markets, people, money, and texts. This feature of the analysis highlighted important elements of distinction, on the one hand, and continuity, on the other, which were occurring within and in many ways articulating the larger and smaller colonial connections just described.

The connections between colonialism and capitalism are metaphorically electric and can be viewed as productively synergetic, but those same connections can also be simultaneously and literally explosive and destructive. Capitalism and colonialism each have their own conceptual turf, but when combined those two rich fields of inquiry yield a fertile terrain to cultivate a study of Afghanistan.

Fernand Braudel's historical analysis of capitalism, which tacks between the micro-local and macro-global levels through a layer of regional markets, has arguably yet to be surpassed.[2] The nomadic trading tribes who were central in the foregoing analysis capture the distinctions and links between what appear in Braudel's scheme as material life and market activity, the former geared toward basic subsistence and existence, the latter involving "surplus" goods and their exchange. For Braudel capitalism arises out of market activity and generates connections between formerly un-integrated markets. The agents of those connections and the agency employed to make them correspond in many important ways to the mobile Hindkis and their hundis that paired with the commercially precocious nomads to form the fluid base over which political authorities must raft and camp rather than permanently settle. Braudel's view of complementary geographic, fiscal, and social variables facilitates an understanding of the imbalanced market relationships between Kabul, Peshawar, and Qandahar. His insights about market "pulls" and polarities magnify the colonial data used here, allowing us to see distinctions and interactions between those three market settings. His global model prompts a view of our three seemingly geographically marginal markets as much more central to the functioning of larger, again separate but interactive interregional and global commercial networks.

Braudel is also a beacon for those lost at sea when trying to navigate toward an understanding of how large-scale debt is accrued and circulated, its roles in the genesis and demise of market and political structures, and its perpetual impact on ordinary debtor folk who are not fully aware of all the variables conspiring to undermine their relative fiscal buoyancy. Braudel demarcates debt through the interactions of commodities, cash currencies, and bookkeeping practices. His consideration of financial texts and accounting practices is amplified by Jack Goody who conveys the basic importance of literacy for bureaucracy and therefore in a more complicated way for governance. While attending to literacy's state locus, Goody also demonstrates that scribal groups and textual practices transcend cultural and political barriers. Together, Braudel and Goody illuminate the cavernous debt associated with Afghanistan and help to conceptually substantiate the data-driven arguments about debt presented in this book. Among the conclusions reached here are that the origins of Afghanistan's current poverty are found in late nineteenth-century state policies and practices, that the articulation of Afghanistan's debt burden transpired via state paperwork handled by certain scribal and bureaucratic classes, and that ordinary consumers experienced this state-created and -managed debt via the marketplace where Afghan state currency was increasingly less favored and devalued in relation to surrounding exponentially stronger state monies.

Capitalism's advance often signals the emergence of "new" social groups and the transformation of "old" social relations, but this does not mean that before capitalism time stood still for "traditional" societies who lacked a familiar form of history. Eric Wolf highlights how capitalism produces new global migrations of laboring classes associated with new production regimes and circulations of old commodities. Arjun Appadurai sees tension between consumers and state authorities emerging from new commodity flows and finds those conducting the new commercial movements to have a distinct form of knowledge transcending single market settings to geographically span full commodity trajectories from points of production to consumption. Appadurai identifies an important distinction between customary and diversionary commodity paths, the latter involving a larger reconfiguration of social and political relations along the way. For Appadurai and Wolf, global historical change is propelled by these new circulations and movements of certain key marketers, laborers, and commodities. In the markets of Kabul, Peshawar, and Qandahar these two authors allow us to see that the emergence of a far more robust bureaucracy signaled a new state fiscal regime that transformed labor and commodity traffic patterns and revised social and political relations in and between the three locales.

Within the vast rubrics of colonialism and capitalism we have been striving for a way to manage fundamental but fundamentally complicated relationships that constitute human economic strategies, as well as other complex associations such as those between the ideological constructions of political space and the material realities and inequalities that uncooperatively represent and belie so-often hasty reasonings about Afghanistan and everything it involves. These independent but integrated explorations of capitalism and colonialism have involved histories of populations within, on the borders of, "passing through," and at varying distances outside of the territory in question. What we have been searching for is the political economy of a permeable zone characterized by multiple kinds of barriers and crossings. In other words, we have had to reckon with, on the one hand boundaries, borders, and frontiers, and, on the other hand, interregional, indeed global exchange networks, trans-Eurasian commodity and cultural circuits and patterned migrations transgressing the limits of the analytical units being deployed.

David Akin's and Joel Robbin's enlarged spheres of exchange model generates a basic set of questions that were posed at the outset of this journey through nineteenth-century market relations between Kabul, Peshawar, and Qandahar. We are now able to answer those basic questions. Regarding the market actors themselves, we have seen Hindkis and the trading tribes as primary and interactive communities. In terms of commodities, we have focused primarily on the wide assortment of fresh and dried fruits and nuts produced in the fertile Hindu Kush valleys, but a number of other popularly consumed goods such as tea and sugar were also addressed. We have learned that multiple varieties of cash coinage, especially silver rupees, as well as paper money hundis and other forms of textual money, and various private and state monies of account were involved in market transactions in these three cities. We now also know that relations between state currencies and accounting practices are subject to wide fluctuation and manipulation as parts of wider credit-provisioning and debt-servicing networks. It is clear that there have been two states, and therefore two large and diverse sets of state actors, operating in Kabul, Peshawar, and Qandahar. It is also clear that tension between the respective state commercial agents in each market diluted the potential influence of state agents on local market practices. Arguably the most basic point about the relations between these three markets is that they are dynamic and interrelated.

The growing concentration of commercial and other forms of capital in Kabul through the agency of colonialism increasingly transform the city's market relationships with Peshawar and Qandahar, intensifying connections between Kabul and Peshawar and diluting commercial interaction between Kabul and Qandahar.

The organization of this study has necessarily left a number of areas either unexplored or undeveloped. In the first geographic instance, this has been a study of markets on the eastern "side" of Afghanistan and primarily only one route between Afghanistan and India. Markets in northern and western Afghanistan have not been addressed directly, and it is certainly the case that the market connections between Qandahar and Herat had an impact on the Kabul-Qandahar route, for example. Similarly, market relations between Mazar-e Sharif and Kabul had an effect on the commercial traffic and trafficking through the Khaibar Pass to Peshawar. And the market functions of the central Hazarajat highlands are important, in different ways, for understanding the economic and social fabric of Qandahar and Kabul. The cultural and historical influence of Persia on Afghanistan and the Russian strategic presence in British Imperial and Indian colonial visions have also not been engaged. The market analysis itself has perhaps been unconventional in treating markets in relation to one another rather than as isolated loci of social and economic activity. The connections made between Kabul, Peshawar, and Qandahar did not address market hierarchies, periodicities, and network patterning in play in each location. The small-scale, short-distance pastoralism practiced in relation to rural markets that is common throughout the region of our concern did not receive attention due to the nature of the sources consulted for this project. The result is a large gap or missing connection in this work, namely urban-rural relations between our three urban market settings and their respective hinterlands.

The rigorous use of archival records was at the same time partial because smaller district archives in localities such as Dera Ismail Khan and Quetta were not consulted, nor were larger imperial repositories of textual and material colonial data found at such institutions as the Royal Asiatic Society in Calcutta or the Imperial War Museum in London. Afghan state source materials held at the National Archives of Afghanistan and perhaps other government repositories in Kabul and elsewhere in the country could shed considerable light on this study of market relations between Kabul, Qandahar, and Peshawar. Municipal records from three cities and private business records from individual traders and family firms also hold considerable promise as sources of data for future researchers interested in delving deeper into the connected histories of these three markets. And finally, the economic aspects of comparative and theoretical treatments of gender, Islam, and war have the potential to complement and enhance this study of markets in nineteenth-century Afghanistan.

The foregoing notice of gaps in and areas of augmentation for this study indicate a number of conceptual mechanisms and data pools that have the potential to provide a more complete understanding of the market relations addressed in this book. Ultimately this has been a spatially and chronologically limited, largely demilitarized, and relatively secular social history of markets and the economy in Afghanistan. The determining influence of British Indian colonialism on the country, despite the outcomes of the two Anglo-Afghan wars, may be the primary realization that is gained from this book for some readers. In the end, it is hoped that for all readers this work forms a springboard into new ways of understanding the country. After all, the routes between Kabul, Peshawar, and Qandahar do not begin or end in those markets; rather, they have origins and lead elsewhere.

The only route of history is toward the present, which is of course just a small gateway into a large future. It is therefore worthwhile to close with a few words on the status of these markets in the early twenty-first century, with a clear understanding that a full comparison of the nineteenth century with events in the historical present requires consideration of the twentieth century that is not possible here.

Whereas nineteenth-century British colonialism favored the Khaibar Pass route between Kabul and Peshawar, the current colonial or neo-colonial project in Afghanistan in the early twenty-first century privileges the Kabul-Qandahar highway. At first glance, this represents competition between Peshawar and Qandahar for Kabul's favor. However, today, as always, there is more complexity to the relationship between these three cities than any single dyadic market connection can explain. Beyond the highly contingent interaction between Kabul, Qandahar, and Peshawar, cultural, political, technological, and military considerations and relationships extending far beyond the market triad are also involved in the economic relationships between the locales.

Today, Kabul is again the object of local colonial occupation, the subject of distant colonial strategizing, and a staging point for larger colonial intitiatives. The current Kabul regime continues a pattern of colonial dependence Abd al-Rahman and his British Indian patrons implanted in the Afghan state structure. Abd al-Rahman's dependence on colonial resources has been transformed into today's political culture of entitlement expressed by current regime officials in their dealings with aspiring and declining global colonial powers.[3]

A flagship project of the current colonial regime, the Kabul-Qandahar highway, has failed to meet its primary goal of integrating the markets of Kabul and Qandahar. The highway itself is a useful index of the sheer magnitude of capitalism underlying the current colonial presence, however qualified with para- or neo- or international or multilateral, in Afghanistan. For the first phase of resurfacing 242 miles of the 300-mile road in September 2002, the U.S. government through its Agency for International Development awarded a contract of $190 million and ultimately committed $270 million to the Louis Berger Group of New Jersey, which employed approximately two thousand Afghan nationals and five hundred Turkish and Indian nationals for the work that was completed in December 2003.[4] The Berger group has successfully bid on work commissioned by the U.S. government in the area categorized as "Rehabilitation of Economic Facilities and Services." For its projects in Afghanistan, the Berger group works with multiple hundreds of companies from the Americas, Europe, the Middle East, South Asia, and South East Asia.[5] Through U.S. government contracts alone, there are hundreds of organizations like Berger that are profiting from the current colonial cycle in Afghanistan. The Kabul-Qandahar highway was opened with great fanfare as the flagship project of the new regime, but it quickly reverted to being a patchy and dangerously insecure road, and the expected burgeoning of market activity in and between Kabul and Qandahar has not materialized.

In addition to the United States, there are a handful of major countries that directly fund the systematic "kinetic" destruction of Afghanistan and benevolently claim credit for its economic and social reconstruction that together with about a dozen smaller countries host most of the several thousand non-governmental organizations funded to execute a variety of "development" projects in the country. Although the current activities in Afghanistan are distinct in scale and context, they are not very much unlike "urban renewal" in the West in practice, and these destroy-to-rebuild paradigms represent both capitalism and colonialism and the influence of state policies on those combined processes.

In the markets of Kabul, Qandahar, and Peshawar, Afghan and Pakistani state currencies still compete with each other, with the Pakistani rupee winning that particular exchange battle. Both local and state currencies are losing value in relation to more powerful international currencies, such as U.S. dollars, Euros, and Iranian and Saudi riyals. Enlarged subsidies and the reform and revaluation of cash currencies and book monies of account were important elements of nineteenth-century colonial activity in Afghanistan. Similarly, the current regime in Kabul instituted dramatic fiscal changes by issuing a new state currency, now with all denominations entirely in paper, revaluing it against other state monies, and opening up a brand new formal bureaucratic space for the state to receive its subsidies.[6] Afghan state currency continues to diminish in absolute and comparative value and is now explicitly unwanted outside of the country while also experiencing declining circulation inside Afghanistan. Foreign currencies increasingly dominate the economic space of Afghanistan.

In the historical present, there is very limited if any exchange of coinage, and paper currency is still ultimately controlled by new forms of accountants' book money. Small-scale credit and debt may be settled by large wads of various paper monies, but now electronic money transferred through a growing number of banks and paper money forms circulated through informal hawala-based networks have become increasingly prominent.[7] The textual and technological dimensions of money and its accounting draw attention to the general importance of literacy, and currently a number of new literacies are exerting their influence in the markets of our concern, sometimes from great intercontinental distances. Computer and cell phone literacies of various kinds, accounting and clerical literacies, English, Pashto, Persian, and literacies in other languages, technical and industrial literacies, and literacy in drug production, financing, and smuggling are all vying for market space.[8]

As was the case in the nineteenth century, today the communities and markets of Kabul, Peshawar, and Qandahar, and the Afghan state itself are all differentially affected by new technologies and technical literacies necessary to engage them. As in the colonial past the privileges and disparities of literacy continue to be evident in Afghanistan. In the neo-colonial present, imposition of new literacies is inconsistently and unevenly transforming pre-existing state bureaucratic practice and public sphere literate communities while also exacerbating residual class, ethnic, and geographically based tensions that were produced during the British colonial period. The relationships between spoken languages and various forms of textual literacy through which market transactions occur and state intervention is expressed are complex and fluid, and perhaps designed to be elusive and ambiguous to outside observers.

During the experimental period (1809–42) of Anglo-Afghan relations in the nineteenth century culminating with the demise of the Army of the Indus, a small group of experts who wielded influence in Afghanistan for the British, such as Alexander Burnes, are identified in colonial literature as "men on the spot."[9] During the routinized phase of Anglo-Afghan relations that began after the second Anglo-Afghan war and the reign of Abd al-Rahman (1880–1901), scores of specialists and experts, ranging from piano tuners to engineers and medical professionals, were contracted to service the Amir personally, his court more broadly, and the state workshops specifically. Today, a much larger and more diverse body of experts, numbering in the tens of thousands, who collectively possess a much wider range of skills and literacies than comparable individuals and communities in the nineteenth century, are active in the country.

Elements of continuity between the nineteenth- and twenty-first-century generations of foreign experts on Afghanistan include the general lack of local language skills, both written and oral, involving but not limited to Persian and Pashto, the overwhelming concentration of their experiences in Kabul to the exclusion of other locations, and an expressed desire for financial profit.[10] Through the various intensive courses of Afghanistan's exposure to colonial and neo-colonial projects in the modern era, a handful of relatively well-known experts and cadres of much less visible but still very influential "Afghan specialists" with marketable knowledge about the country have emerged. The degree of continuity between the first Afghan experts and those active and influential today is remarkable for how various forms and combinations of literacies, some fashionable and specific and others more durable and transferable, are marketed in Kabul by non-Afghans and Afghans alike, with Western training commanding the upper market hand.[11] The literacy market in colonial Kabul is driven by practicality and basic functionality, with conceptualization and framing of issues, and basic questions about basic relationships devalued and undesired.

In that sense, the orientalist practices of homogenization and stereotyping that took shape during the British colonial era have been reproduced consistently to and through the current neo-colonial activities in Afghanistan. Sweeping generalizations made from great physical and cultural distance about the activities and practices of Pashtun populations and the Pashtun influence in Afghanistan are key reflections of this orientalist tendency that has resulted in a tautology of a country existing as if it were only about one single monolithic group. Today this is the most notable area where colonially inspired orientalism continues to persist and perpetuate a misleading vision of Afghanistan for Afghans and non-Afghans alike inside and outside the country. This book demonstrates Afghanistan can be discussed outside of the foiled rubric of "Pashtun domination."

It is hoped that through its focus on routing between three key markets, this book will advance knowledge about Afghanistan in ways that challenge the overtly political tone and orientalist bias characterizing classic colonialism and a great deal of contemporary scholarship and political commentary about the county. This book has portrayed Afghanistan as a remote place only if the connotations of remoteness include complexity, dynamism, and cosmopolitanism.[12] It is hoped that attention to connections between socially distinct groups of economic actors and the markets they form will contribute to conceptual reorientation for all those who engage Afghanistan and its inhabitants' alleged remoteness using exoticism, militarism, racism, and romanticism as intellectual tools.

Reference Matter

Appendix:
Commercial Vocabulary
in Nineteenth-Century Afghanistan

———•◆•———

What follows is a list of words relating to commerce and commercial transactions that would have been used in the nineteenth-century markets of Kabul, Peshawar, and Qandahar as well as a selection of concepts related to the subject matter of this book. For Persian words I have followed the transliteration system used by the *International Journal of Middle Eastern Studies*. For Pashto phonemes modified Arabic letters and their equivalent English representations including a diacritic are used as follows:

x̱ = ښ	ṟ = ړ
dz = ځ	ṉ = ڼ
ts = څ	ḏ = ډ
zh = ژ	ṯ = ټ
g = ږ	

Variations of [ی] in Pashto are generally rendered [ai] and differentiated in only a few instances below.

The large number of monetary units and textiles found in nineteenth-century Afghanistan are not incorporated here. For information about some of the metallic currencies circulating in that context readers can refer to Gregorian pp. 401–2, and Kakar (1979), pp. 216 and 236. For some of the weights and measures used in nineteenth-century Afghanistan see Furdoonjee, Gregorian, pp. 404–6, Kakar (1979), pp. 235–37, Jenkyns, pp. 21–22, Warburton, pp. 11–12, and "Memorandum of Information Available in the Foreign Department on the Government, Revenue, Population, and Territorial Divisions of Afghanistan," N.A.I., Foreign Secret (Supplementary) K.W., January 1880, Proceeding Nos. 536–44. For textile descriptions and terminology readers are directed to the Appendix in Habib, pp. 69–70.

Appendix

ENGLISH	PASHTO	PERSIAN
Account book	de ḥesāb ketāb	ketāb-e ḥesāb
Accounting	ḥesāb kawul/shmeral	ḥesābdārī/moḥaseba
Administrative division	woloswālai	woloswālī
Afghan hundi	ḥawāla	ḥawāla
Afghan Nomad Trader	kochai (plural kochi), lohānai (plural lohani), pāwenda	kochī, lohānī
Agent or Factor		gomāshta
Agricultural Field or Land	mzaka	zamīn
Alfalfa	reshqa	reshqa
Almond Agent	bādāmī	bādāmī
Almond	bādām	bādām
Antimony	rānza	sorma
Apple	mana	saeb
Apprentice	zda kawunkey	shāgird
Apricot	zardālū	zardālū
Arbitration Council	maraka	panchāyat
Bangles (Glass)	bangrey	chorī/karra
Barley	orbaxa	jao
Bill of Exchange	hundī	hundī
Bird	alotekai	parenda
Blue	asmānī/nīlī	asmānī/nīlī/ābī
Bookkeeping	ketābat	ketābat
Box	qoṭai	qoṭī
Brass	mes	mes
Bread	ḍoḍai	nān
Bridle	qaiza (for the animal) and jelao (for the rider)	qaiza (for the animal) and jelao (for the rider)
Broker	dalāl	dalāl
Brokerage Duty	dalālī	dalālī (also meaning occupation of brokerage)
Brown Sugar	gora	gor
Budget	bodeja	bodeja
Bull	ghweyai	nar gao
Business House	tujārat khāna	tujārat khāna
Buyer	akhestūnkai	kharīdār
Cadastral	daftarī	daftarī
Camel	ūx	shutor
Candle	sham'	sham'
Caravan	kārwān	kārwān
Carpet	qālīna	qālīn
Carrot	gazera	zardak
Century	pairai	qarn
Cheap	arzān	arzān
Cherry	gailās	gailās
Chief Secretary	mīr monshī	mīr monshī
Citadel	bālā ḥesār	bālā ḥesār
City	xār	shahr
Clerk	kateb/merza	kateb/merza
Clothing	kālī	kālā
Clover	shaftal	shaftal
Coat	kortai	kortī
Color	rang	rang
Confiscation	zabṭ	zabṭ

ENGLISH	PASHTO	PERSIAN
Contract	qarārdād	qarārdād
Contractor	qarārdādī	qarārdādī
Cooked	pokh	pokhta
Cotton	ponba	ponba
Countryside	aṭrāf	aṭrāf
Cow	ghwā	gao, mada gao
Crown Lands	khāleṣa	khāleṣa
Cultivator/Farmer	dehqān/bazgar	dehqān/bazgar
Cumin	zīra	zīra
Custom	rawāj	rawāj
Customs	gomrok	gomrok
Debt	qarz	qarz
Deputy	nāyeb	nāyeb/mo'īn
District	'alāqa	'alāqa
Document	sanad	sanad
Domestic	koranai/dākhelī	dākhelī
Dried Apricot	keshta	keshta
Dried Chickpeas	nakhod	nakhod
Dried Curd (Whey)	korat/qorūt	qorūt
Dried Fruit	wocha maiwa	maiwa-ye khoshk
Dye	rang	rang
Dyeing	rangawel	rangdādan
Egg	agai	tokhm
Elephant	fīl	fīl
Embroidery	golgandel	goldozī
Exchange (to)	badalawel	badal kardan
Expensive	qimatī	qimatī
Export (to)	ṣāderawel	ṣāder kardan
Exports	ṣāderāt	ṣāderāt
Fall	manai	khazān
Farming	deqānī	deqānī/zamīn dārī
Fig	anjīr	anjīr
Firewood	largī	chob
Flower	gol	gol
Fodder	wāxa	kah
Food	azoqa	azoqa
Fort Holder	qalādār/qalābegī	qalādār
Fort	qalā	qalā
Fruit	maiwa	maiwa
Fresh fruit	tāza maiwa	maiwa-ye tāza
Fruit tax	maiwa dārī/de maiwey mahsul	maiwa dārī/mahsul-e maiwa
Fruit tree	de maiwey wana	darakht-e maiwa
Ghee (clarified butter)	ghwaṛī	roghan
Goat	ūza	boz
Government	hokūmat	hokūmat
Government Bill Collector		mohaṣel
Government Contractor	teka dār	teka dār
Government Manual	dastūr al-'amāl	dastūr al-'amāl
Government Regulation (Written Order)	neẓām nāma	neẓām nāma
Grape	angūr	angūr
Green	shīn	sabz
Hair	waixte	mūī

179

ENGLISH	PASHTO	PERSIAN
Harvest	ḥāṣel	ḥāṣel
Hashish	mofarah	mofarah
Hat	khwaley	kolā
Horse	os	asp
House	kor	khāna
Import (to)	wāred kardan	wāred kardan
Imports	wāredāt	wāredāt
Indian or European Technical Expert	mestarī	mestarī
Indigo	nīl	nīl
Iron	spana	ayin/āhan
Irrigation Canal (man-made; see stream below)	wiyāla	joī
Land Revenue	mālīa	mālīa
Lapis Lazuli	lājward	lājaward
Lease (of land)	ejāra	ejāra
Leek	gandana	gandana
Lemon	laimū	laimū
Load	bār	bār
Marijuana	chars	chars
Market	bāzār	bāzār/manadanī
Meat	ghwaxa	gosht
Melon	khatakai	kharbūza
Metal	felez	felez
Mint	na'na	na'na
Money changer (and banker)	sarāf	sarāf
Money	paisa	paisa/pūl
Monopoly	enḥeṣār	enḥeṣār
Mortgage	geraw	geraw
Mountain pass	kotal	kotal
Mountain Slopes	de ghre lamen	kohdāman
Mountain	ghar	koh
Mulberry	tūt	tūt
Mushroom	samāroq	samāroq
Neighbor (economic dependent)	hamsāya	hamsāya
Orchard	bāgh	bāgh
Occupation	kesb	kesb
Oil for Lanterns	thael-e khāq	thael-e khāq
Onion	pyāz	pyāz
Opium	bang	bang
Orange	nārenj	nārenj
Peach	shaftalū	shaftalū
Pear	nāk	nāk
Pepper	mrech	murch
Pinenuts	zalghozī	jalghoza
Pistachio	pesta	pesta
Plum	ālubālu	ālū/ālubālu
Pomegranate	anār	anār
Potato	kachalū	kachalū
Price	baya	bahā/qimat
Prison	bandīkhāna/tawqīf	bandīkhāna/ tawqīf
Profit	gaṭa	fāīda
Province	welāyat	welāyat

ENGLISH	PASHTO	PERSIAN
Public Treasury	khazāna	khazāna
Quince	behī	behī
Raisin	mamīz	keshmesh
Red	sūr	sorkh
Rent	kera	kera
Residential Quarter	mahala	mahala
Rice	wrīzai	brenj
Road (for vehicular traffic)	sarak	sarak
Road-Path (for non-vehicular traffic)	lara	rāh
Rose	gol/golāb	golāb
Saddle	zīn	zīn
Saffron	zafarān	za'farān
Salt	mālga	namak
Saltpeter	nawshāder	nawshāder
Season	mosūm	maosom
Secretary	monshī/mirzā	monshī/mirzā
Security	amneyat	amneyat
Seed	dāna	tokhm
Seedless (Fruit)	baidāna	baidāna
Sheep	pesa	gosfand
Signature	emẕā	emẕā
Silk	wraixem	abrayshum
Skin	post	post
Spinach	sālak	sālak/sabzi
Spring	pesarlai	bahār
State Formation	dawlat joṟawul	dawlat sākhtan
State	dawlat	dawlat
Stream (natural; see irrigation canal above)	wiyāla	joī
Sugar	būra	būra/shakar
Sugarcane	naishakar	naishakar
Summer	dobai	ṭābestān
Tax	māliya	māliya
Tea	chāī	chāī
Timber	chartarash	chartarash
Tobacco	tambākū	tambākū
Toll	rāhdārī	rāhdārī
Transit Pass (for commoditieis)	rāhdārī	rāhdārī
Trader (Merchant, Businessman)	sawdāgar	tājer/sawdāgar
Transport (to)	wṟel/naqlawul	naql dādan
Tree	wena	darakht
Tumeric	zardchoba	zardchoba
Turnip	shalgham	shalgham
Turban	langotai	longī/langota
Valley	dara	dara
Village	kelai	deh/dehkada
Village Spokesman	malek	malek
Walnut	chārmaghz	chārmaghz
Watermelon	hendwāṇa	tarbūz
Wheat	ghanem	gandom
Wine/Liquor	sharāb	sharāb
Winter	zemai	zemestān

Appendix

ENGLISH	PASHTO	PERSIAN
Wool	pashm	pashm
Woolen Overcoat/Cape	postīn	postīn
Woolens	pashmī	pashmī
Woven	owdelai	bafta shoda/baftagī
Yellow	zaīr	zard

Note on Sources:
Abbreviations, Transliterations
and Spellings

This project is founded on archival sources consulted at five institutions in South Asia. These are the National Archives of India in New Delhi, the North-West Frontier Provincial Archives in Peshawar, the Tribal Affairs Research Cell in Peshawar, the Punjab Provincial Archives in Lahore, and the National Documentation Centre in Islamabad. Hereafter these institutions will be identified as NAI, NWFPA, TARC, PPA, and NDC, respectively.

Spellings of local names found in the colonial archives are retained in the text (for example, "Kaldar," "Muhin," and "Wuffa" remain in place of the contemporary transliterations of Kallah Dar, Mo'in or Moeen, and Wafa, respectively). Readers interested in local commercial vocabulary are invited to consult the Appendix.

Ben Hopkins's *The Making of Modern Afghanistan* (Palgrave Macmillan, 2008) appeared too late to be incorporated and engaged in this book.

Notes

————————•◆•————————

Introduction

1. See Singh, Chakrabarti, Lockhart (1938).

2. The Indian Ocean literature is growing and can be entered through Bose, Boxberger, Chandra, Chaudhuri (1993 and 1995), Das Gupta (1979 and 2001), Hill, Ho, McPherson, and Subrahmanyam (1995).

3. Timur Shah transferred the Durrani capital from Qandahar in 1775–76. Kabul and Peshawar then shared time as the dual Durrani capital cities, the former during the summer and the latter during the winter season. Elphinstone met Shuja and gathered the bulk of his data about Kabul in Peshawar in 1809. Kabul's development as the solitary capital of an Afghanistan comprised of the Kabul, Qandahar, Herat, and Mazar-e Sharif provinces resulted from the colonial encounter. Prior conceptions of the term Afghanistan, notably Babur's, did not include all the areas or social groups associated with today's polity. Timur's move of the Durrani capital from Qandahar to Kabul involved immediate political motivations. Shuja was deposed from Peshawar merely days after Elphinstone left the city, only to be returned to Kabul with the Army of the Indus some thirty years later. Shuja's return is addressed below in Chapter 3 in the context of a discussion of Sarwar Khan Lohani, who provided carriage and transportation services for the British and Shuja. See below Chapter 5 for more about Timur wanting to be closer to Qizilbash community in Kabul.

4. The Silk Road literature is also expanding. A good beginning can be made with Broadman, Christian, Kurin, Luce, Nebenzahl, and Whitfield (1999, 2004a, and 2004b).

5. See Braudel (1979), vol. II, pp. 138–53 on bill of exchange circuits and their closing.

6. R. D. McChesney has produced an English translation of Faiz Muhammad Katib's *Seraj al-Tawarikh*, or Lantern of Histories (1913–15), which will soon appear online at the Afghanistan Digital Library. See the ADL Web site at http://afghanistandl.nyu.edu/.

7. See Dale and Levi for the presence of Indian merchants along the old Silk Road

in Central Asia, and Markovits for attention to a wider dispersion of Indian merchants communities within and beyond Indian Ocean circuits. See below Chapter 1 for further consideration of these works and the diaspora model.

8. See Bayly (1988) for treatment of family merchant firms in North India and British dealings with them during the transition to colonial rule.

9. See Burnes "on the Persian Faction in Kabul" in Burnes, Leech, Lord, and Wood for the quote about the "ramifications" of the Qizilbash influence in Kabul, and Masson, vol. II, p. 260, for notice of the separate police and court system for this community.

10. See the map inserted at the end Elphinstone, vol. II, and Babur, vol. II, pp. 476–77 for one of Babur's rare uses of the Afghanistan label.

11. See al-Beruni, Bosworth (1963 and 1977), Minorsky (1937), and al-Utbi. Gommans provides a good treatment of these processes for the early Durrani polity in the eighteenth century that centers on the horse trade. His sensible starting position on historical handling of the terms Afghan and Afghanistan, p. 12, is especially relevant here.

12. See Eaton, Kumar, and Haig.

13. For Khalaj as either Turks or Afghans, see Barani, Habibi, K. S. Lal, and Minorsky (1940).

14. See Lockhart (1938 and 1958) and Singh.

15. The Suri dynasty ruled from c. 1540 to 1555. The Lodi dynasts who ruled from c. 1451 to 1526 also identified themselves as Afghans, not as Pashtuns. The Lodis and Suris used the Persian language in the bureaucracies they controlled, and each dynasty has subsequently received the Pathan label from a number of authors. Lodi and Suri historiography includes Abd Allah, Dorn, Haziya, H. Khan, K. S. Lal, Mushtaqi, Niazi, Nimat Allah, Qanungo, Sarwani, and Yadgar.

16. See the introduction to the Pata Khazana by A. H. Habibi at http://www.alama-habibi.com/.

17. See Ansari, MacKenzie, Morgenstierne (1939), Darweza, and Caroe. The Pashto Makhzan-i Afghani of Akhund Daweza referenced here differs from Nimatullah's Persian language Makhzan-i Afghani (see Dorn), a genealogical history of Pashtuns, who are dubbed Afghans by the author, that was compiled during the early-seventeenth-century reign of the Mughal Emperor Jahangir.

18. See ibid., Qandahari, and Arlinghaus. Akbar ruled from 1556 to 1605, and the Roshaniyya (literally "enlightened") movement was framed as insurrectionary by the Mughals who termed it the Tariki (literally "darkened") movement. Ansari (lived c. 1525 to c. 1585), who is also known as the Pir-i Roshan, wrote the Khair ul-Bayan before the outbreak of the revolt that the Mughals commissioned Darweza to refute. Akbar's new religion was termed Din Ilahi (literally "Godly religion"). See Rahim.

19. See Morgenstierne (1960) and Raverty (1867).

20. See Jones and Vansittart.

21. See Trautmann (1995 and 1998) for more on the comparative and theoretical is-sues raised by Sir William Jones and his work.

22. Modern Iranian Persian is known as Farsi. The Persian dialect spoken in Af-ghanistan has been referred to as Dari since the 1950s in accordance with Afghan state policy, although the term Farsi is still often employed domestically and in outsiders' references to Afghan Persian.

23. See M. J. Hanifi (2004).

24. See Cohn (1996) for an overview of Hindustani in British India.

25. See the entry for Henry George Raverty in the *Dictionary of National Biography* and Raverty (1978, 1981, 1982a, 1982b, and 1987).

26. For more on the use of the generic Hindki label, see below Chapter 1.

27. For an introduction to the Mughal economy, see Richards, ch. 9.

28. See Markovits, p. 296. Ahmad Shah was born in Multan (Singh, p. 15), and it is possible that he capitalized on connections with merchants based in that location later in the empire-building stage of his life. See Lockhart (1958 and 1993) for events in early- and mid-eighteenth-century Iran involving the Hotak Ghalzi and Nadir Shah Afshar that form a combined prelude to the rise of the Durrani empire. See Astarabadi and al-Hussaini for the two primary Persian language sources for Nadir Shah Afshar and Ahmad Shah Abdali/Durrani, respectively.

29. See Balikci, Balland, and Ferdinand (1962 and 1969).

30. See Caroe, p. 15, for one such genealogy. Pashtuns are commonly referenced as the world's largest segmentary society. Issues of segmentation are linked to ethnography of tribal societies that fall within two main subtypes in Islamic societies, egalitarian or segmentary tribes, and hierarchical chieftaincies. These issues have generated as sub-stantial literature in anthropology and history. See Khoury and Kostiner as an entrée to some of these issues and surrounding literatures.

31. Robinson identifies pawendas primarily but not exclusively as eastern Ghalzi tribes among whom the Sulaiman Khel confederation was most prominent, although a number of non-Ghalzi (p. 157–85) are also identified. See S. M. Hanifi (2004) for a brief treatment of the Sulaiman Khel.

32. See Braudel (1973 and 1979), Mintz, Wallerstein, and Wolf. Also contributing to the framing of this work is Kasaba's application and refinement of Wallerstein's world systems theory that focuses on the peripheralization of the Ottoman empire after being engaged by Eurocentric capitalism.

33. Sahlins.

34. Akin and Robbins.

35. Goody (1988 and 1996).

36. Appadurai.

37. See Bayly (1988 and 1996), and Cohn (1987 and 1996).

Chapter 1

1. Part II of the *Baburnama* (see Babur) is devoted to Kabul. N. Dupree (1977), pp. 88–89, provides brief descriptions of Babur's gardens and tomb on the slopes of the Koh-i Sher Derwaza mountain overlooking the Kabul river and the western portion of Kabul city.

2. Babur, part II, p. 266.

3. Ibid., p. 265. In the original Persian text, the citadel is rendered as the Arg-i Kabul. The citadel can be equated with the Bala Hissar complex, which was largely demolished by the British during the second Anglo-Afghan war, although it was subsequently partially rebuilt. Abd al-Rahman built a second Arg, which became the new palace complex, but it should not be confused with the original or renovated citadel or Bala Hissar in Kabul.

4. Ibid., pp. 263–64.

5. Ibid., p. 275. See Warburton and the *Gazetteer of Afghanistan*, pp. 476–500, for more on Laghman. The region begins about twenty miles east of Kabul city and runs north from the Kabul river for approximately thirty miles. The province averaged twenty-six miles in width in 1914. Jabar Khel Ghilzai Pashtuns are among the most prominent social groups in Laghman.

6. Babur, part II, p. 266. See the Appendix for Persian and Pashto terms for these and many other fruits and commodities.

7. Ibid., p. 281. See the *Gazetteer of Afghanistan*, pp. 267–68, and later for more on Istalif. N. Dupree (1977), p. 110, has a photograph of the village.

8. Habib, map sheet 1 A–B, and notes to that sheet on pp. 2–3.

9. Ibid.

10. Alam (1994), p. 210.

11. Ibid.

12. The regions of fruit production quoted here come from a reprint of Bernier's text in which the word "Bali" is mentioned as being a misprint for Balkh. See Bernier, pp. 203–4. This and the following passage from Bernier are cited in Alam (1994), p. 210.

13. Bernier, p. 249. "Dear" here meaning expensive.

14. Elphinstone, vol. I, pp. vii and 1. The mission was comprised of fourteen Europeans, one hundred "native cavalry," two hundred infantry, and one hundred irregular cavalry.

15. Ibid., 341–42.

16. Burnes, vol. I, pp. 151–52.

17. Ibid., pp. 153–54.

18. Ibid., pp. 149–50.

19. Vigne, p. 172.

20. Bellew's enumeration is quoted in MacGregor, pp. 505–7. Although Bellew spent

time in Qandahar after the first Anglo-Afghan war his comments in this regard apply sufficiently well to the experimental period.

21. Masson, vol. II, p. 282.

22. Ibid., pp. 329–30.

23. Ibid., p. 269. It is worth noting that the American adventurer Josiah Harlan petitioned the United States Government for support in schemes to import Afghan camels and fruit into the U.S. in 1854 and 1862, respectively. See Harlan (1854 and 1862) and MacIntyre.

24. Braudel (1973), p. 328. Medieval here is delineated as 1400–1800.

25. Dialects of money is my phrase, but the cue comes from Braudel (1973), ch. 7, particularly pp. 357–72. Braudel's honing in on the "theoretical frontier separating money and credit" (p. 358) is especially useful. See p. 367 for his claim about the bill of exchange.

26. The use of book money in Durrani state financial records is considered below in Chapter 3.

27. Habib, maps 1 A and B and 2 A and B, and notes, pp. 1–5. Although Akbar took Qandahar from the Safavids in 1595 a Mughal mint was not established in that city. Rather, the royal mint was located roughly 160 miles to the southwest along the Helmand river. Whereas Qandahar was a contested locality between the Mughal and Safavid empires, Herat remained in the Safavid realm until Ahmad Shah Durrani's incorporation of it in 1749 (see Singh, pp. 81–86). Akbar also established a copper mint at Attock where the royal road connecting Peshawar and Calcutta crosses the Indus. This road was completed by Sher Shah Suri, considerably improved under Mughal patronage, and became known as the Grand Trunk road during the colonial period. See H. Khan, Qanungo, and Sarwani for more on Sher Shah Suri.

28. See Habib map 4 B and notes on pp. 9–10 for a useful cartographic expression of Multan's horse market function during the Mughal period. See Gommans for a consideration of the Central-South Asian horse trade in relation to the early Durrani empire, Fattah for the seaborne horse trade between the Persian Gulf and India from 1745 and 1900, and Dale for the commercial proclivities of "Multani Afghans" between 1600 and 1750.

29. See Dale, pp. 55–64.

30. I distinguish the early Durrani empire from the later Anglo-Durrani state.

31. Singh, pp. 365–73. Every mint did not issue each type of coinage, nor were all coins within one metallic category of the same weight or quality if measured otherwise.

32. For more on Multan's market functions see Burnes et al., pp. 79–88, corresponding to Leech's "Report on Multan Commerce." See also "Mohan Lal on Multan Commerce," NAI, Foreign P.C., 9 May 1836, Proceeding No. 42, much of which corresponds with passages in Mohan Lal (1977), pp. 239–44.

33. Burnes et al., p. 83.

34. Ibid., pp. 81–82.

35. "Mohan Lal on Multan Commerce," NAI, Foreign P.C., 9 May 1836, Proceeding No. 42, corresponding with passages in Lal, 1846, pp. 240–41.

36. M. Lal (1977), p. 244.

37. Burnes et al., pp. 23–25, from the entry titled "On the Commerce of Shikarpur and Upper Sind" by Burnes. Masson, vol. I, p. 359, claims that Shikarpur "has or had the privilege of coining; and the rupee is a very good one, nearly or quite equal to the *sicca* rupee in India." This claim and the information about the hundi rates and currencies in Multan prompt a tempering of the notion that money was only coined by states. Rich merchants and aspiring rulers without a formal polity could and did have currency made in their name. It is also important to note that currency from a state or a ruler no longer in existence could continue to circulate after the ruler's death or the polity's end.

38. M. Lal (1977), p. 268.

39. The list of markets in Burnes et al., p. 24, includes "Muscat, Bunder Abbass, Kerman, Yezd, Meshid, Astracan, Bokhara, Samarcand, Kokan, Yarkund, Koondooz, Khooloom, Subzwar, Candahar, Ghuzni, Cabool, Peshawer, Dera Ghazee Khan, Dera Ismael Khan, Bukkur, Leia, Mootan, Ooch, Bhawulpoor, Umritsir, Jeypoor, Bucaneer, Jaysulmeer, Palee, Mondivie, Bombay, Hydrabad (Deccan), Hydrabad (Sinde), Curachee, Kelat, Mirzapur and Calcutta."

40. M. Lal (1977), p. 268.

41. Burnes, vol. I, pp. 168–70.

42. Burnes et al., p. 24. Writing based upon his experiences in the region over the years 1826–38, Masson, vol. I, p. 354, argued Shikarpur was on the decline and that Multan had recently surpassed it as a commercial center. Masson attributed Shikarpur's ascendancy to the fleeting political fortunes of the Durranis. See ibid., pp. 353–58. Alam (1994), p. 221, links the mercantilist ideology evident in early Sikh scriptures to the growing trade between the Punjab, Multan, Sind, and Central Asia during the sixteenth century.

43. Burnes et al., p. 24. This group of Lohana Hindus from Shikarpur should be distinguished from Lohani Afghans, but the nomenclature correspondence refocuses attention back to Lal's information about the Shikarpuri Hindus and Afghan Lohanis working together to dominate the trade between Bukhara and Multan. Levi, p. 103, footnote 66, cites a number of sources said to consider the Lohani as a bifurcated social category including the nomadic "Muslim Afghan Powinda tribe (or) a sedentary Hindu merchant caste, or conglomeration of castes, of Sind, engaged in Indo-Turanian commerce." Alam (1994), p. 219, sheds some light on the possible religious heterogeneity of the Lohani term by hinting at the commonality of Hindus converting to Islam while residing for extended periods of time in the predominantly Muslim societies of Central Asia.

44. Alam (1994), p. 211. Alam also notes the involvement of Khattris in the Mughal administration, and the participation of Mughal nobility in interregional commerce. See ibid., p. 217, and Alam (1986). In addition to Hindu Khattris, Dale includes Muslim Afghans and certain Hindu and Jain groups known as Marwaris as diaspora Multanis. See Dale, pp. 55–64. It is interesting to note that Baluch communities including the Dodai and Hot were associated with Multan in the Mughal and early Durrani periods (see Gommans, pp. 38–39 for the latter and Habib, Map 4 A, and notes, pp. 9–10, for the former epoch), but they seem not to have been a significant presence in the Multani diaspora.

45. For Jeth Mall's connection to Shuja and the latter's failed attempt to recover his former status in Kabul see PPA, Book 141, Serial No. 68. In the fall of 1832, Shuja petitioned his way to four months' advanced payment from his annual British stipend (see "Shuja Allowed to Stay at Ludiana with Rs. 50,000 Annually as Stipend," PPA, Book 9, Serial Nos. 97 and 106. This sum included Rs. 1,500 per month to his wife), which came to Rs. 16,000, and gathered an additional sum he estimated at Rs. 1,50,000 and roughly five thousand troops for the reconquest of Kabul (and what he referred to with regularity as *wilayat*). It was neither a well-planned nor impressive display. He intended to follow the Qandahar via Sind route, and in Shikarpur, the mercantile hub of Sind, he planned on being able to raise another loan of Rs. 50,000 through the agency of his Shikarpuri Hindu Finance Minister Lala Jeth Mall. Shuja was unsuccessful in raising more money and therefore maintaining his army while encamped outside of Shikarpur. However, it is interesting to note that mercenaries from North India's war labor market did appear, if only to abscond on small loans secured from the *banias* or Hindu traders traveling with Shuja. See PPA, Book 140, Serial No. 7 and later in this chapter for more on Shuja's presence outside Shikarpur on this occasion.

46. See Barth (1969), which is a benchmark in the school of thought that can be termed the situational approach to ethnic identity construction and maintenance (see also Barth, 1964). In conceptual opposition to Barth and the situationalists, Geertz speaks for the position that ethnicity is a kind of primordial sentiment, and Bentley lays out an approach to ethnicity based on Bourdieu's notion practice.

47. See Dale, pp. 55–64, and Levi, p. 103.

48. Barth (1961) discussed wealthier and impoverished nomads who leave their groups while Black-Michaud presented data about rich and poor nomads remaining in their groups. Barfield entered the debate by drawing attention to the degree of commercialization and market access for pastoral communities. See Barfield, pp. 118–22, for a summary and full citations of this debate over pastoral economic change.

49. E.g., Curtin, Dale, and Levi.

50. Markovits, p. 25, but see also pp. 181–82 for more on the circulation of information in the Shikarpuri commercial network. The circulation of capital in the form of hundis through the network was structured by a partnership, typically between a Shikar-

puri *shah* or merchant capitalist (also termed *sarrafs* or *sahukars*) who advanced money to agents contracted for a specific purpose, the gumashtas. See ibid., pp. 157–60. Both gumashtas and shahs could be found outside the network center.

51. Markovits, p. 296.

52. Ibid., pp. 256–57.

53. Abd al-Rahman's panchayat did not foster commerce as both Levi, p. 163, and Gregorian, p. 136, insinuate. Gregorian, ibid., p. 183 refers to the panchayat as a council of elders, and Abd al-Rahman (S. M. Khan, vol. I, pp. 201 and 209) refers to the panchayat as a board of commerce that was one department in his central administration (and may have been replicated provincially). See also Hamilton, p. 282, for reference to the board of commerce under Abd al-Rahman's son and successor, Habibullah (ruled 1901–19). See below Chapter 5 for an instance of Abd al-Rahman's use of the panchayat to confiscate merchant capital and drive Indian commercial groups such as the Shikarpuris out of Kabul and Afghanistan.

54. Markovits, p. 93, recognizes the distinction between Shikarpuris in Central Asia who dealt closely with Shikarpur, and the Shikarpuris in Peshawar who dealt mainly in the trade between India and Afghanistan. Levi, p. 207, quotes a twentieth-century colonial source indicating fifty Shikarpuri families in Peshawar "dominated India's trans-Khyber trade." Evidently these Peshawri Shikarpuris were affiliated with a Multani firm that was established in Peshawar during the period of Durrani control over the city (c. 1747–1834), but then relocated to Amritsar during the period of Sikh control (c. 1834–48) of the ancient and cosmopolitan frontier market city.

55. Elphinstone, vol. I, pp. 412–15.

56. The *Gazetteer of Afghanistan*, pp. 254–55. This encyclopedic source incorporates an earlier entry in MacGregor, p. 385. The primary source for both seems to be a report by Henry Bellew resulting from his time in Qandahar before and during the Indian rebellion or "mutiny" of 1857. Working with three hundred thousand Hindkis in Afghanistan in the 1850s and estimates of Afghanistan's population from the 1870s (a conservative one from 1874 is 2,535,000, and a liberal estimate from 1871 is 4,901,000) results in Hindkis comprising between 6 percent and 12 percent of Afghanistan's population. See "Memorandum of Information in the Foreign Department on the Government, Revenue, Population and Territorial Divisions of Afghanistan," NAI, Foreign Secret Supplementary K.W., January 1880, Proceeding Nos. 536–44. The estimates of Afghanistan's population come from British colonial sources, the difference between them being the inclusion or exclusion of certain trans-border tribal groups and certain portions thereof. As noted, the term Hindki is not precise, and the term Afghanistan is here defined as including "1. Afghan-Turkestan which includes the tract lying between the Hindu Kush and the Oxus from Wakhan on the east to Maimena on the west. It contains the following districts or Governorships: i. Badakshan and Wakhan, ii. Kunduz, iii. Khulm or Tashkurgan, iv. Balkh, v. Shiberghan, vi. Akcha, vii. Andkoi, viii. Maimena. 2. The

Hazarajat. The mountainous country surrounded by the territory of Kabul, Maimena, Herat, and Zamindawar. 3. Herat and the Turkoman country on the Murghab. 4. Lash Jowan and Seistan. 5. Kandahar and Zamindawar. 6. Ghazni and Zurmat. 7. Kurram and Khost. 8. Kabul, Kohistan, and Ghorband. 9. Bamian. 10. Jellalabad. 11. Kunar and Lughman. 12. Kafiristan bounded by the Hindu Kush on the north and west, by Kabul on the south, and by Chitral, Dir, Asmar, and Kunar on the east." Ibid.

57. It is equally reasonable to postulate a connection between the Hindki category in nineteenth-century Afghanistan with the current prominence of the Hindko community in and around Peshawar. However, such an association is not complete, has not been addressed to my knowledge, and may not be accurate for reasons beyond the fact that contemporary Hindkos are Muslims, which cannot be entirely explained by presence of the Pakistani state. The relatively small amounts of time and space separating the contexts where Hindkis and Hindkos are prominent, and the uncertain social and historical connection between the terms, once again highlight how treacherous it is to carry labels such as Multanis over many centuries and very much greater distances while so loosely hitched to other equally problematic categories such as Afghans and Lohanis, not to mention Peshawris and Kabulis.

58. Gankovsky (1982), pp. 84–85, and Gankovsky (1985), pp. 126–28. In both places, it is noted that a Russian traveler in the late-eighteenth century claimed an Indian merchant in Kabul to wield a portfolio worth 100 lakhs or one crore of rupees (Rs. 100,00,000).

59. Elphinstone, vol. I, p. 228. The relationship between honor and wealth in Afghan society merits substantive future research.

60. See Bayly (1988), chs. 10 and 11, for treatment of merchant family firms in North India during the eighteenth and nineteenth centuries, Levi, ch. 4, for an overview of Indian family firms, and Dale, pp. 112–20, for a consideration of an Indian "firm" (Dale's quotes) in Astrakhan in the mid-eighteenth century. See Bayly (1996), pp. 36–44, for a discussion of literacy, and Markovits, pp. 260–65, for a consideration of trust among Indian merchants.

61. Burnes, vol. I, pp. 168–70. Evenly divided these numbers give each trading house represented in Kabul, which for present purposes can be equated with the Shikarpuri family firms stationed there, 37.5 families. Abd al-Rahman also built a palace–pavilion complex that he originally named the Hindki palace. However, the structure's designation was later changed to the more Irano-Islamic sounding *chihil sutun*, literally the palace of forty pillars. See N. Dupree (1990).

Chapter 2

1. To varying degrees, Indian, European, machine-made, and handcrafted commodities were involved in Sayyid Muhin Shah's commercial experiments. Unless indi-

cated otherwise, in what follows those distinctions are subsumed in the phrasing "British Indian" "goods" or "manufactures." Tables 2.1 and 2.2 and numerous quotations in this chapter list some of the items involved in these colonial commercial speculations and considerations. The name Muhin appears in the sources and is retained in what follows. Muhin is an early colonial rendition of the Muslim name commonly spelled today as Moeen or Mu'in.

2. PPA, Book 139, Serial No. 47. The loan may have been granted by the Persian merchant Agha Ismail.

3. MacGregor, pp. 512–13 (quoting H. B. Lumsden, who wrote about Qandahar's trade in 1857).

4. Ibid., p. 512.

5. The Persian term for this rotation of royalty is *badshahgardi* or king-turning, which Caroe repeatedly applies to the intra-Durrani dynastic succession squabbles. See Caroe, pp. 262, 292, 316, *passim*.

6. Conolly, vol. II, pp. 49 and 112.

7. Incidents of nomadization such as that experienced by Muhin Shah are far less frequently discussed in anthropological literature than episodes of sedentarization. For more on nomadization specifically, see Khazanov, ch. 2. For a model of sedentarization as a processual, voluntary, and flexible response to changing local circumstances, see Salzman, p. 14, which is useful because it prompts a reciprocal characterization of nomadization and its forms as adaptive strategies rather than teleologically. Anthropologists have long recognized the importance and vitality of relationships between nomadic and sedentary societies. For considerations of this symbiotic relationship, see Nelson and a number of essays in *Pastoral Production and Society*.

8. Conolly, vol. II, pp. 48–49.

9. Ibid., p. 48.

10. Ibid., pp. 51 and 170.

11. Ibid., p. 170.

12. Ibid.

13. Conolly, vol. II, p. 232. This appears to be one segment of a longer twenty-month commercial journey between South and Central Asia undertaken by the sayyid between November 1827 and June 1829 that covered 2,337 miles of land and 1,600 miles of water. For details of this extended trading expedition see "Commercial and Political Resources of Central Asia," NAI, Foreign S.C., 25 November 1831, Proceeding Nos. 7–12.

14. Conolly, vol. I, p. 9, passim. There is a portrait of Sayyid Karamat Ali facing the cited page. A portrait of Sayyid Muhin Shah faces p. 49 of vol. II.

15. Conolly, vol. II, pp. 255–56. Conolly notes that Sayyid Karamat Ali went on to serve the British Indian Government in Kabul (and Qandahar, see later), then became the *mutawali* or administrator of a religious endowment or *waqf* property in Hooghly.

16. "Memorandum on Trade of Afghanistan," NAI, Foreign S.C., 25 November 1831,

Proceeding Nos. 1–3. The Secret Committee dispatch referenced is dated February 17, 1830.

17. Ibid.

18. See the next section in this chapter for more on the role of Mithenkote in the larger Indus navigation project.

19. See later in this chapter for more on the Ghalzi presence along and the British use of the Qandahar-Kabul road during the first Anglo-Afghan war. In practice, nomads had the ability, opportunity, and periodic need to break from planned paths, directions, or series of incremental movements. There were generally multiple routes to choose from when moving between the aforementioned cities. Temporary labor opportunities for nomads in colonial India, as road builders and canal and well diggers in particular, also make it difficult to fully and precisely chart the spatial dimensions of nomadic commercial migrations through and between Kabul, Peshawar, and Qandahar in the nineteenth century. See *Zhob District Gazetteer*, pp. 165–66, for Ghalzi Pashtun nomads as excavators of *qanats* or underground irrigation channels, and Balland, p. 209 (footnote), quoting another source about the class of nomads who entered the subcontinent for seasonal labor opportunities such as "stone-breaking, road-making, clearing jungle (*butimari*), and any sort of job where energy and strength are more necessary than professional skills." The latter quote implies a degree of flexibility and unpredictability concerning where and by what routes the nomads traveled in colonial India.

20. "Memorandum on Trade of Afghanistan," NAI, Foreign S.C., November 25, 1831, Proceeding Nos. 1–3. According to his entry in the *Dictionary of National Biography*, vol. 19, p. 1135, from 1827 to 1831 Trevelyan held the post of Assistant to the Commissioner of Delhi who was then Thomas Metcalfe. William Bentinck served as the British East India Company's Governor General of India from 1828 to 1835. Auckland held the post from 1836 to 1842, during which time he was under "the pernicious influence of his young secretary, William Macnaghten" (see Wolpert, p. 219). Auckland's "folly" in Afghanistan resulted in Ellenborough assuming the Governor Generalship of India in 1842, followed by Dalhousie from 1848 until 1856. See Wolpert, pp. 218–26, for a consideration of the first Anglo-Afghan war in the high politics of colonial India.

21. "Commercial and Political Resources of Central Asia," NAI, Foreign S.C., November 25, 1831, Proceeding Nos. 7–12. See also NAI, Foreign P.C., September 5, 1836, Nos. Proceeding Nos. 9–19, a citation associated with two titles, namely, "Trevelyan's Note on Commerce of Afghanistan" and "Trevelyan's Note on Trade of Cabul."

22. "Memorandum on Trade of Afghanistan," NAI, Foreign S.C., November 25, 1831, Proceeding Nos. 1–3.

23. "Memorandum on Trade of Afghanistan," NAI, Foreign S.C., November 25, 1831, Proceeding Nos. 1–3. The tabular account and narrative recitation of Muhin Shah's first British-sponsored commercial experiment in this file do not consider transport expenses beyond a generic "duty" category, they omit the Bombay purchase prices, and

they lack references to currencies, exchange rates, and other important transactional details.

24. NAI Foreign P.C., September 5, 1836, Nos. 9–19, cited as both "Trevelyan's Note on Commerce of Afghanistan" and "Trevelyan's Note on Trade of Cabul."

25. "Result of Muhim Shah's Commercial Speculation in Bukhara," NAI, Foreign S.C., May 8, 1834, Proceeding No. 14. See Wade's entry in the *Dictionary of National Biography*, vol. 20, pp. 411–13. Ludiana was the primary location where the British concentrated the large numbers of Afghan exiles, pensioners and refugees, which gave Wade a unique influence on British policy toward Afghanistan.

26. Ibid. However, Wade continued to communicate with Kabul through the Peshin sayyid's conveyance of information, gifts, and other resources (see later in this chapter).

27. "Result of Muhim Shah's Commercial Speculation in Bukhara," NAI, Foreign S.C., May 8, 1834, Proceeding No. 14.

28. See PPA, Book 118, Serial No. 50, being a letter from Macnaghten, then the Secretary to the Governor General of India, to Wade dated November 2, 1835: "Muheen Shah has already been furnished (with) another loan of Rs. 12,000, for the purpose of assisting him in carrying on his commercial dealings with the countries beyond the Indus, on condition of rendering an account of the manner in which it shall be employed."

29. See PPA, Book 140, Serial No. 66, for Wade's concurrence that Muhin Shah's retreat to Peshin from Kabul, which prevented him from accompanying the Company's capital to Bukhara resulted from illness and not any "neglect of Government interest."

30. Ibid.

31. Direct communication between Lohani chiefs and British officials will be explored in Chapter 3.

32. "Trevelyan's Note on Commerce of Afghanistan," and "Trevelyan's Note on Trade of Cabul," NAI, Foreign P.C., September 5, 1836, Proceeding Nos. 9–19.

33. For more on Alexander Burnes, see his entry in the *Dictionary of National Biography*, vol. 3, pp. 389–91, Norris, *passim*, and "Trevelyan's Note on Trade of Cabul," NAI, Foreign P.C., September 5, 1836, Proceeding Nos. 9–19. The early missions referred to began in 1830 when Burnes was deputed to deliver six horses to Ranjit Singh. This delivery was the context for Burnes's initial surveying of the Indus for commercial navigation. Burnes concluded the river could be navigated by large flat-bottomed commercial vessels. In December 1831, he and a small party including James Gerard and Mohan Lal were deputed to investigate the commercial potential of the territories northwest of the Indus River. Burnes, and the majority of Mohan Lal (1977) are based on this expedition. In September 1836, the Governor General of India selected Burnes "to conduct a commercial mission to the countries bordering the Indus, with a view to completing the reopening of that river on the basis of treaties lately concluded with powers possessing territory along its banks" (the Amirs of Sind, primarily); see again "Trevelyan's Note on

Commerce of Afghanistan"/"Trevelyan's Note on Trade of Cabul," NAI, Foreign P.C., September 5, 1836, Proceeding Nos. 9–19. The published results of this expedition include Burnes et al. (1839), and Wood. Burnes's 1836 mission to Kabul also had political dimensions because part of his assignment involved securing the commitment of Dost Muhammad to an alliance with the British and the Sikhs. The purported failure of the political aspect of this mission was based on the arrival in Kabul of a competing Russian Agent. The mere presence of a Russian agent in Kabul was apparently used to justify the formation of the Army of the Indus that invaded Afghanistan in the spring of 1839, marking the final stage of Burnes's career and life. He was killed in Kabul in November 1841 as the British occupation was unraveling.

34. Wade was the most consistent advocate for Mithenkote. Burnes argued Dera Ghazi Khan was superior to Mithenkote because of the seasonal flooding experienced by the latter; see "Establishment of an Entrepot for Indus Trade," dated January 18, 1838 in Burnes et al. As late as 1840, Macnaghten was voicing a qualified preference for Dera Ismail Khan, see "Macnaghten's Opinion on Trade of the Indus," NAI, Foreign S.C., March 2, 1840, Proceeding Nos. 113–17.

35. "Assembly of Lohanis at Mithenkot," NAI, Foreign S.C., May 8, 1834, Proceeding Nos. 16–18.

36. PPA, Book 118, Serial No. 7, being a collection of letters from Macnaghten to Wade. The letter quoted is dated February 11, 1835, and it was also addressed to Nawab Muhammad Zaman Khan and Sardar Sultan Muhammad Khan.

37. Ibid.

38. PPA, Book 140, Serial No. 94. The quote comes from a letter from Wade to Karamat Ali.

39. In 1833, while serving the British in Kabul, Karamat Ali was paid Rs. 150 per month in addition to Rs. 50 for expenses. After Karamat Ali was dismissed from his post in Kabul he was reassigned to Qandahar, where he served the British until 1836. Nawab Jabar Khan's service as a British Agent was betrayed by Karamat Ali, which also figured in the latter's dismissal from Kabul and reappointment to Qandahar (PPA, Book 140, Serial No. 94, and "Resources of Afghanistan," NAI, Foreign P.C., March 30, 1835, Proceeding No. 46). Nawab Jabar Khan arranged for his son, Abd al-Ghias Khan, to study English with Shahamat Ali (see Ali) at "Wade's school" (Vigne, p. 144) in Ludiana under the supervising tutelage of Mirza Muhammad. Karamat Ali likely facilitated this opportunity. Nawab Jabar Khan sent his son to India to form a "familial connection with the English" to guard against whatever might happen in Afghanistan in the future (PPA, Book 140, Serial No. 93). As a minor, Abd al-Ghias initially received Rs. 100 per month as a stipend from the British, but soon petitioned for an increase to Rs. 150 per month. Afghan adults "expected" Rs. 1,500 per month as a British pension in India (ibid., containing a letter from Wade to Macnaghten dated November 16, 1834). Because he had "not received anything" from his father, Abd al-Ghias felt compelled to borrow Rs. 3,000

from a local banker in Ludiana ("Commercial and Political Resources of Central Asia," NAI, Foreign S.C., November 25, 1831, Proceeding Nos. 7–12, containing a letter from Wade to Macnaghten dated February 11, 1835). The colonial policy of providing liberal stipends to various Durrani political elites perpetuated the *badshahgardi* or "king-turning" that was often bemoaned in British discourse about Afghanistan (e.g., Caroe). Masson, vol. III, pp. 218–19, notes the jealousy between Dost Muhammad and his brother Nawab Jabar Khan was such that the former would have detained Abd al-Ghias had he known of the Ludiana plans. Ultimately, to avoid detection by Dost Muhammad, Abd al-Ghias was secretly set on a raft and floated down the Kabul river from Jalalabad to Peshawar, his horses and attendants following. The hundreds if not thousands of these Durrani elites, their families, and entourages who received British pensions in North India, particularly Ludiana, deserve separate treatment.

40. PPA, Book 140, Serial Nos. 94 and 96.

41. Mazari tribespeople, who preyed on vessels moving through the territory they inhabited on both banks of the Indus, also were identified as obstacles necessary to surmount in order to actuate the Mithenkote plan. See paragraph nine of Burnes's instructions for his 1836 mission in "Trevelyan's Note on Commerce of Afghanistan," NAI, Foreign P.C., September 5, 1836, Proceeding Nos. 9–19.

42. Masson was intelligent and articulate, a prolific correspondent, but a deserter or fugitive from the Indian Army with criminal claims standing against him in British territory. Wade suggested his service as Newswriter in Kabul didn't have to be recognized but should certainly be encouraged, and that the quality of information he provided "merits some clemency on the part of the Government for his past crimes/conduct" (PPA, Book 140, Serial No. 96). On February 11, 1835, he was formally appointed "Agent in Kabul to report intelligence" with a monthly payment of Rs. 250 ("Resources of Afghanistan," NAI, Foreign P.C., March 30, 1835, Proceeding No. 46).

43. PPA, Book 140, Serial No. 66.

44. Ibid.

45. The revenue from the *chabutara* or customs house of Kabul was farmed for Rs. 1,40,000 in 1834. See "Masson's Observations on Kabul Commerce," NAI, Foreign P.C., November 2, 1835, Proceeding No. 56.

46. Ibid., and "Measures to Promote Trade Between Mithenkote and Central Asia," NAI, Foreign P.C., May 16, 1836, Proceeding Nos. 47–48. The first series of gift exchanges had Khair al-Din sending a Persian sword and sheepskin coat or *postin* valued at Rs. 20, and the Governor General conveying six yards of fine creped gauze (@ Rs. 1.8 per yard, totaling Rs. 9), six yards of *garnit*, a muslin (@ Rs. 2 per yard, totaling Rs. 12), six yards of flowered silk (@ Rs. 1.12 per yard, totaling Rs. 10), 2 penknives (Rs. 4), one powder flask (Rs. 4), one leather shot belt (Rs. 3.8), one box containing matches, and so on for striking fire (Rs. 5), six dozen enameled gilt buttons (Rs. 7.8), and two boxes of detonating powders (Rs. 2), the total of which came to Rs. 57.8.

47. PPA, Book 140, Serial No. 66.

48. PPA, Book 118, Serial No. 24.

49. "Measures to Promote Trade Between Mithenkote and Central Asia," NAI, Foreign P.C., May 16, 1836, Proceeding Nos. 47–48.

50. "Masson's Observations on Kabul Commerce," NAI, Foreign P.C., November 2, 1835, Proceeding No. 56 (also titled "Observations on Trade of Kabul"). The threat of a competing fair in Russian Turkistan was reiterated by Burnes two years later: "The Cabul and Bokhara merchants at the last fair at Negnei Novogorod were all presented to the Emperor Nicholas, which is much talked of here, and who gave them great encouragement and commendation" (NAI, Foreign P.C., January 31, 1838, Proceeding No. 35).

51. "Masson's Observations on Kabul Commerce," NAI, Foreign P.C., November 2, 1835, Proceeding No. 56 (also titled "Observations on Trade of Kabul").

52. Ibid.

53. Ibid.

54. Ibid.

55. Ibid.

56. Ibid.

57. Ibid.

58. Ibid. Mohan Lal (1977), p. 46, reiterates the claim: "The blue paper of Russia is found throughout the whole Afghan state."

59. Ibid.

60. See earlier and PPA, Book 118, Serial No. 24: "Agreeably to my invitation the Lohanee merchants have resorted to that mart and began to barter their goods with the merchants of Hindustan" (letter from Wade to Mullah Khair al-Din dated May 11, 1834).

61. "Lohanis Complain About Their Treatment at Dera Ismail Khan," NAI, Foreign P.C., December 12, 1838, Proceeding Nos. 34–38. In 1836, Wade requested Omar Khan Lohani to escort a British officer, G. T. Vigne, through eastern Afghanistan. The results of this experience are conveyed in Vigne.

62. "Wade's Report on the Lohanis," NAI, Foreign Political Proceedings, January 3–17, 1838.

63. Dera Ismail Khan was a key financial hub where transactions between Lohanis and their Hindu brokers occurred each fall when the former descended from the crevices of the Hindu Kush through the Gomal Pass to the daman. See "Wade's Report on the Lohanis," NAI, Foreign Political Proceedings, January 3–17, 1838. Referring to the Lohanis, Wade says: "of these meritorious merchants, the honesty of whose character is not less conspicuous than their enterprise I may observe, that in my visit to Dera Ismail Khan in 1833 I had the satisfaction in meeting the principal part of them. They were then congregated there contemplating their annual investment of indigo (likely from Multan for export to Central Asia). I explained to them as well as the Hindu merchants

of the place, who act as their brokers, the object which the British Government had in opening the navigation of the Indus."

64. Chelwashtee is a Persianized nisba adjective of the Pashto *tsalwekht* or forty. Elphinstone claimed the institution existed only among the daman tribes, the Sulaiman Khels of Katawaz, and other Ghalzi Pashtuns. He argued the institution was not found where strong khans existed and that it remedied the bad effects of hereditary chiefs. According to Elphinstone, the institution of chelwashtee was the "first step from a patriarchal government to a republic in usual form." See Elphinstone, vol. II, pp. 60–66.

65. Ibid. Sarwar Khan invoked the Pashtun concept and institution of nanawati, or asylum/mediation/protection, with the brother of his main rival. It is important to underscore that the Durrani government sent Ghalzi contingents to assist Sarwar Khan in recouping his hereditary prerogative.

66. Masson, vol. I, pp. 49–59.

67. Ibid., and MacGregor, p. 309.

68. "Burnes' Letter of Introduction for Lohanis," NAI, January 31, 1828, Proceeding No. 35.

69. See earlier and "Results of Muhin Shah's Commercial Speculation," NAI, Foreign P.C., August 17, 1835, Proceeding Nos. 70–73.

70. Ibid. Muhin Shah paid Rs. 258 for the use of six camels from Benaras to Darraband, and Rs. 84 for the same from Darraband to Kabul.

71. "Moonshi Mohun Lal's Report on the Commerce of Multan," NAI, Foreign P.C., May 9, 1836, Proceeding No. 42. This item is inexactly reproduced (e.g., Donaz for Omar Khan and the table) in Mohan Lal, (1977), pp. 239–44. Lal notes that at Darraband the Lohanis, who had congregated at Daud between Ghazni and Katawaz for collective defense, disaggregated into three groups. Those heading to Hindustan were said to go through Dera Ghazi Khan, those going to Multan went through Kohri and Leya, and the portion traveling to Amritsar were routed through Dera Ismail Khan. For adult male Lohanis to leave their women and children with Omar Khan he must have commanded a significant amount of confidence and trust from them. This socially translated into prestige and cultural capital that helped form the basis of Omar's position as a Lohani chief.

72. "Lohanis Appraised About Burnes' Deputation to Shikarpoor," NAI, Foreign S.C., November 14, 1838, Proceeding Nos. 55–67. Burnes's commercial and political mission to Kabul lasted from September 5, 1836, to October 1, 1838. During this period, the Governor General of India targeted Burnes to secure the carriage and provisioning services of the Lohanis for the impending invasion and occupation of Afghanistan and restoration of Shuja in Kabul. See "Carriage Supply Furnished by Lohanis," Governor General's Dispatch to Secret Committee, September 24, 1838, Proceeding No. 23 (contained in a large bound monthly proceedings volume).

73. "Burnes' Letter of Introduction for Lohanis," NAI, January 31, 1828, Proceeding No. 35.

74. Ibid. Wade subsequently validated Burnes's view: "I beg leave to observe that Capt. Burnes has, in my opinion, placed a just value . . . on conciliating the Lohani Chiefs to whom he has given a letter of introduction to insure their presentation to the Right Honourable the Governor General of India, in the wish of these men seeking an interview with his Lordship." See "Wade's Report on the Lohanis," NAI, Foreign Political Proceedings, January 3–17, 1838 (consulted in a large bound monthly proceedings volume).

75. "Complaints by Lohanis of Their Treatment by Maharaja Ranjit Singh's Agents at Dera Ghazee Khan," NAI, Foreign P.C., December 21, 1838, Proceeding Nos. 34–38. It is unclear whether the animals were intended as a personal gift or an "official specimen of local produce."

76. Ibid.

77. The invasion's preparation period went from November 1838 to April 1839, the former date being when the Army of the Indus gathered at Ferozpur and the latter when it entered the Qandahar province (the force left Ferozpur in December 1838 and marched through Sind and Baluchistan). In August 1839, Shuja reentered Kabul, marking the height of the occupation that began to collapse in the early fall of 1841. A large portion of the Army of the Indus was destroyed during an attempted retreat from Kabul in January 1842. During the fall of 1842, a colonial army of retribution returned to avenge the earlier losses by destroying large parts of Kabul and inflicting significant damage to the fruit-producing villages surrounding the capital city, such as Istalif and Charikar. These events represent the end of the first Anglo-Afghan war according to a military timeline.

78. "Lohanis Appraised About Burnes' Deputation to Shikarpoor," NAI, Foreign S.C., November 14, 1838, Proceeding Nos. 55–67. As part of his transfer Burnes was directed to "render all accounts of the Kabul mission" (ibid.). Accordingly, Burnes submitted data or "descriptions and quantities of articles . . . which may serve as guides to the speculator," on the commodities carried by Lohanis from India to the Kabul customs house or chabutara during 1837 and 1838. See "Taxes Levied on Indian Goods Taken By Lohanee Merchants to Cabul," NAI, Foreign P.C., September 26, 1838, Proceeding Nos. 10–11. That year, the Lohanis brought Rs. 3,89,300 of "Iamandanee, Coloured chintz, Mlwan Goolvar, Chintz of Jamugur, Jalee, Muslin, Long Cloth, Long Muslin, Half Coloured Chintz, Khasa Manee, Mushrou, Chintz of Farrukhabad, Nainsookh, Raj Mahal, Mootan Longee, Nasurkhanee Chintz, Chintz of Sona Nugur, Mbra Chaf of Bhawalpur, Timour Shahi, Gallou, Mootanee Daboo Chintz, Feringee Narouz, Lakharee Chintz, Mdrus, Hyder Shahee, Hyjuanee Chintz, Flowered Muslin, Jhora, Shalkee, Budulkhanee, Chikun, Momee Chintz, Handkerchiefs, Bhawulpur Alacha, Coarse Cloth, Juglahoo Otter Skin, and Bafta Mooltaneee." These textiles were taxed at the standard Islamic 1 in 40, leaving the state Rs. 9,732. Indigo was taxed separately from textiles in the Kabul chabutara. Ibid. See below Chapter 3 for more on Burnes's revisions of the Kabul customs house during the occupation.

79. "Lohanis Appraised About Burnes' Deputation to Shikarpoor," NAI, Foreign S.C., November 14, 1838, Proceeding Nos. 55–67. During the occupation, Burnes was placed in a subordinate role to Macnaghten, who had been removed from his influential position as Secretary to the Governor General of India in favor of a uniquely sensitive role as Envoy and Minister to the colonially restored Shuja. Burnes's salary became Rs. 1,800 per month with an additional Rs. 200 when absent from Shuja's court.

80. "Lohanis Appraised About Burnes' Deputation to Shikarpoor," NAI, Foreign S.C., November 14, 1838, Proceeding Nos. 55–67.

81. "Shikarpore Political Agent's Advance to Lohani Chiefs," NAI, Foreign S.C., July 31, 1839, Proceeding Nos. 31–32. The sum of Rs. 1,06,063.15.8 broke down as follows (near-verbatim descriptions of the amounts are attached): Rs. 1,953 as compensation for camels and property stolen at Shikarpur and Khairpur; Rs. 96 for hire of treasure camels from Sukkur; Rs. 13,700 in advance to camel man at Shikarpur; Rs. 314.15.8 in exchange on Shikarpur (rupees acquired at 2 percent commission); Rs. 90,000 as an advance to *jemadars* or camel men, totaling Rs. 1,06,063.15.8 (a sum not including Rs. 285.7.9, an amount advanced on account of Mr. Macnaghten for conveyance of articles with exchange on Shikarpur included).

82. Ibid. 1,03,700 is 97.77 percent of 1,06,063.

83. "Shikarpore Political Agent's Advance to Lohani Chiefs," NAI, Foreign S.C., July 31, 1839, Proceeding Nos. 31–32. The words mullah and Khorasan used in this receipt deserve notice. Concerning the former, this is an isolated if not the only instance in documents at my disposal where that title was attached to Sarwar Khan Lohani's name. It is particularly important as a term of self-reference. Use of the word Khorasan here indicates that the word and concept of Afghanistan had then not fully adhered in colonial and local discourses.

84. Ibid. In addition to the aforementioned cash advance, Eastwick transmitted coercive resources to Sarwar Khan. These included a matchlock "forced upon" the former by the Sind Amir Mir Rustam Khan, fifty remount horses "with permission to use them if need be, 100 muskets from the stores of Bukkur (through Colonel Gordon), and 33 matchlocks costing Rs. 8 each."

85. "Masson's Observations on Kabul Commerce," NAI, Foreign P.C., November 2, 1835, Proceeding No. 56 (also titled "Observations on trade of Kabul"). Speaking of their monopoly of the Multan-Kabul trade, Masson notes "no other men could travel even in kaffilas from Kabul to Dariband, the Lohanis pass with arms, and the camels (the beasts of burden they employ) are their own property, no other traders can afford to bring or carry merchandize at so cheap a rate, and they have therefore no competitors in the markets they frequent."

86. "Gordon's Observations on Ghiljies," NAI, Foreign S.C., October 2, 1839, Proceeding Nos. 81–82. According to the Lohani trader Lal Khan, fifteen thousand armed men were desirable when Lohanis passed through the Gomal Pass and the Waziri tribes

inhabiting its vicinity. Lal Khan said that the Sheranis, who lived further north in the area of the Tawa Pass, were friendlier to the Lohanis. Because only four thousand armed retainers would be required, Lal Khan suggested the Tawa Pass be used for the Lohani transport of British mail and supplies to Kabul and Qandahar from Dera Ismail Khan. Noting the heightened security of property held by sayyids and sufis in Sind and Baluchistan, Gordon proposed using such holy men as "shields for kafilas" passing through the Gomal and Waziri territory. He suggested placing "Bahawudeen of Mooltan, the peer most revered in Sind, Baluchistan and the Punjab (when moving) military stores through Vizeeree country." Furthermore, based on information gathered in Multan, the British were prepared to pay the Waziris Rs. 20,000 to secure the route between Dera Ismail Khan and Ghazni, which passed through their territory.

87. "Lohanis Refuse to Go Beyond Qandahar," NAI, Foreign S.C., October 2, 1839, Proceeding Nos. 59 and 62. This statement obviates the fact that not all Lohanis left their families with Omar Khan in Darraband (see earlier in this chapter) when proceeding to India during the fall trading season. This source also indicates that when Shuja was encamped in Ghalzi country local chiefs "behaved in a most unbecoming manner to (Shuja), making exorbitant demands of him. (Shuja) has maintained utmost temper and forbearance in the face of these provocations."

88. "Gordon's Observations on Ghiljies," NAI, Foreign S.C., October 2, 1839, Proceeding Nos. 81–82.

89. Ibid. It is unclear when and under what circumstances Sarwar Khan traversed the Qandahar-Kabul route. Gordon noted that in local markets it was assumed the British had unlimited funds and that prices would be driven up if merchants knew the commodities they sold, apparently to the Lohanis, were going to *farengis* or the British (farengi applies to European Christians generally). It is worth noting that rum was imported in high volume to Afghanistan during the occupation, and that in June 1839 Lohanis were identified as the only suitable carriers of such alcoholic spirits from Dera Ismail Khan to Ghazni ("Wade's Proposal to Employ Lohanees in Convoys," NAI, Foreign S.C., September 11, 1839, Proceeding Nos. 54 and 56). Wade knew of "no way whatever of conveying rum from D.I. Khan to Ghazni excepting through the agency of the Lohani merchants, unless it's escorted by a large body of troops who could force their way through the passes. Even the Lohanis are frequently obliged to effect their passage by force."

90. Ranjit Singh and the British consistently maintained cordial relations. For Sikh support of the Mithenkote scheme, see "Proclamation of Sikh Government on Trade," NAI, Foreign S.C., January 1, 1840, Proceeding Nos. 128–31.

91. "Detention of Lohani Camels," NAI, Foreign S.C., August 17, 1840, Proceeding Nos. 22–25.

92. Ibid.

93. Ibid.

94. Ibid.

95. See Hough, pp. 123–30, for scattered attention to Sarwar Khan. Refer to ibid., pp. 126–27, for the quoted passage. Hough insinuates, perhaps correctly, that Sarwar Khan could not fully control his armed caravan retainers.

96. Ibid., p. 126.

97. Ibid.

98. Ibid, p. 128. The Commissariat's circular order implies the invasion force was also a roving camel market: "Officers reminded the camels brought to Hd. Qrs. by Sarwar Khan, and other Lohanee merchants, are still in Government employ; and they are not to purchase any of them."

99. "Petition from Mushka Khan son of Sarwar Khan Luhani," NWFPA, Peshawar Commissioner's Office Records, 1893–94, Bundle No. 73, Serial No. 2049.

100. Ibid.

101. Ibid. Mushka Khan states that Sher Ali treated him and his father well, but that after Sarwar Khan's death he fell out of favor with the ruler. Mushka claims Sher Ali knew about this pool of resources, if nothing else "because everyone in Afghanistan knew (Sarwar Khan) had lent Macnaghten Rs. 1,00,000."

102. Ibid.

103. Ibid. The regional rebellion referenced is that of Muhammad Ishaq Khan in Turkistan from 1888 to 1890, for which see Faiz Muhammad, vol. III, pp. 575–625, with digressions.

104. Ibid. Mushka Khan traveled to Quetta via Bukhara, northern Iran, the Gulf, and Karachi, thus avoiding territory claimed by Abd al-Rahman. Browne's jurisdiction may have included Karachi, which is where Mushka Khan went to speak with the *madar-i wali-ahd*, or the widow of Sher Ali and mother-in-law of Sardar Muhammad Hashim Khan, at one time the heir apparent to the Durrani throne, who was said to have information about the original orders.

105. Ibid. The file is incomplete, so the exact outcome of this case is unclear. The colonial bureaucracy never directly challenged the claim that Macnaghten issued the said bills to Sarwar Khan, nor could they prove they had been cashed. However, the British mustered point-by-point rebuttals of many of Mushka Khan's subsidiary claims. The colonial bureaucracy dealt with hundreds if not thousands of petitions from various Afghans for payment for past services rendered to the British during the two Anglo-Afghan wars. Mushka Khan refers to "Lord Roberts, Sir Lepel Griffin, the late Sir Thomas Baker, and other British officers" who could vouch for his service during the second Anglo-Afghan war. Mushka also claims to have had a receipt from a British lady prisoner held in Laghman during the disastrous retreat of 1842 indicating Sarwar Khan had lent her Rs. 25.

Chapter 3

1. "Increase in Cabul Commerce and Customs Duties," NAI, Foreign S.C., 2 Aug. 1841, Proceeding Nos. 61–64.

2. See later in this chapter for more on Burnes's attempt to eliminate rahdari collection outside of Kabul.

3. Ibid. Burnes planned, perhaps unreasonably, on an almost exponential increase in the flow of these currencies as a result of his reforms. His expectations were based on the lure of a much-reduced tax charged on these moving currencies at the Kabul customs house. Burnes substantially reduced that amount from 2.5 percent to .5 percent. The rupees used in his computations were Kabul kham rupees. Kham, as opposed to pukhta, rupees in the Kabul account books are addressed below in Chapter 5.

4. Elphinstone, vol. I, pp. 333–34. Elphinstone also comments on the relationship between Hindki bankers and Durrani nobility. He identifies the bankers and Durranis as sharing the same interests, but the bankers worked in different though still symbiotic ways with the elite and petty Durrani nobility. The great nobles invested their money with Hindki bankers, while the lesser nobility had to "afford their protection to bankers, and treat them with great attention, in the hope of being able to borrow money from them," ibid., p. 335. Elphinstone, ibid., p. 334, also mentions dealing with bankers in Peshawar who would accept his bills, but only pay him secretly at night with money dug from the ground for the purpose.

5. "New Exchange Rate Between Qandahar and Company Rupees," NAI, Foreign S.C., 11 January 1841, Proceeding Nos. 58–60.

6. Frye, pp. 66–67 and 240, identifies the local variant of hundis in twentieth-century Afghanistan as hawalas, and emphasizes the bilateral debt-settling nature of the device by referring to it as a draft drawn on a trading associate. Frye also indicates a variety of credit standings entered into hawala transactions.

7. Braudel (1973), p. 358.

8. "New Exchange Rate Between Qandahar and Company Rupees," NAI, Foreign S.C., 11 January 1841, Proceeding Nos. 58–60.

9. It is unclear whether the Army of the Indus maintained a mobile mint in its treasury. It is appropriate to describe the location of the Qandahar mint because it aids the understanding of indigenous surveillance structures and information networks that would likely have borne on who came to know what and how about the planned exchange-rate change. The following description comes from "Qandahar: Account, Taxes, Duties," NAI, Foreign S.C., 30 April 1858, Proceeding Nos. 46–51: "In the Bazaar-i Shahi stands the '*kotwali*' and mint. One kotwal, a *Naib*, four *jemadars* and twenty six *chupprassies* with an additional five men for the protection of the *charsook* is the entire police force of the City. Each jamedar has his own beat extending over about 19 *muhallas* each of which has a muhalladar over them who looks after the internal management of his

own portion, but seldom interferes in police matters, and is not paid by government but receives a trifle at all births, marriages, and deaths."

10. "New Exchange Rate Between Qandahar and Company Rupees," NAI, Foreign S.C., 11 January 1841, Proceeding Nos. 58–60. These appear to be monthly interest rates, although their exact terms, such as when they commenced and how they were compounded, remain unclear.

11. Ibid.

12. Ibid. The recipient of the devalued currency was known as the provincial qafilabashi, or state-appointed superintendent of transport. The qafilabashi would have passed any received losses on to the nomadic commercial carriers it was his duty to identify, organize, and regulate. In turn these carriers, that is, the kochis, Lohanis, and pawendas, would have cycled those deficits into one or a collection of exchanges and transactions remaining for that single commercial season, or more probably, rolled the losses into a forthcoming season's calculations. See below Chapter 5 for more on the Durrani qafilabashi in Peshawar, and Burnes, vol. I, p. 173, for the involvement of a domestic qafilabashi in the export of purported contraband Korans. Rawlinson also considered ridding the Indus Army treasury of Qandahar rupees through advances to local officials and in remittance of hundis drawn on the Company treasury in Qandahar by British officers and agents in cities such as Herat and Farrah.

13. Yang, p. 238. Yang here refers to hundis as notes of credit whereas in another location, ibid., p. 257, he adopts the more common translation for hundi as a bill of exchange. Braudel, p. 368, distinguishes four possible handlers in a bill's life course, the purchaser, the drawer, the bearer, and the drawee who would accept the bill (or not, which might give rise to *protests* or a lawsuit). Of course not all individuals were required; two could suffice to complete the circuit. Levi, pp. 203–5, distinguishes hundis from bills of exchange that were written against commercial goods and could only be cashed and not deferred, transferred, or sold. For a translation of hundi he prefers the compound idea of a money order and promise of payment. Levi (ibid.) notes the bond-like function of hundis that could be purchased at a 2 percent or 2.5 percent discount, and distinguishes two types of payment promises, either by distance from the point of purchase or length of time until cashing.

14. Braudel (1973), p. 368.

15. Ibid.

16. "Instructions to Political Officers Regarding the Drawing of Bills in Cabul," NAI, Foreign S.C., 21 December 1840, Proceeding Nos. 66–68, and Foreign S.C., 28 December 1842, Proceeding Nos. 49–53. Todd's motives for using invisible ink included but were not limited to concealing financial information from local bankers and the identity of local collaborators.

17. Ibid.

18. Ibid.

19. Ibid. By this stage of the occupation's life Pottinger was not able to execute Macnaghten's orders to indicate the rate at which the hundi transaction occurred and the amount and kind of cash received. The figures given are all British Indian or Company rupees. Other British officers conducted hundi exchanges in ways that led to accusations of impropriety. See "Resources of Afghanistan," NAI, Foreign P.C., 30 March 1835, Proceeding No. 46 for Sayyid Karamat Ali's mishandling of hundis issued by Claude Wade. Wade was then the British Political Agent in Ludiana and Karamat Ali was serving as the British Newswriter in Kabul. Karamat Ali's hundi impropriety contributed to his dismissal from that post. See also N. Dupree's introduction to Lal's (1978) book on Dost Muhammad, p. xxv, where it is revealed that some of the bills Lal handled in Kabul were questioned by colonial officials and that Lal faced accusations of over-borrowing on General Pollock's account.

20. Ibid.

21. "Income and Expenses of Shuja," NAI, Foreign S.C., 24 May 1841, Proceeding Nos. 36–38. *Jezailchee* and *janbaz* are the terms used for the musketry and foot soldiers, respectively.

22. Ibid. Shuja began to receive an annual British stipend of Rs. 50,000 in Ludiana in September 1816, which included Rs. 1,500 monthly for his wife who was known as the Wuffa Begum. See PPA, Press List 2, Book 9, Serial No. 97 and Press List 3, Book 18, Serial No. 142. However, both Shuja and his wife continued to regularly ask for more and different kinds of support from the British until the former's final petition in May 1841.

23. For Mullah Shakur as a "confidential servant and pre-ceptor" for Shuja see PPA, Press List 3, Book 18, Serial No. 142. For Mullah Shakur's service in all but name as the finance minister under the British-Shuja condominium see the introductory narrative to "Resources and Expenditure of Afghanistan, 1841," NAI, Foreign S.C., 25 October 1842, Proceeding Nos. 32–35, and Appendix O therein for the large number of tax remissions he granted during the occupation. The Shikarpuri Hindu Lala Jeth Mall served as Treasurer to Shuja during the latter's aborted attempt to regain his royal prerogative in Kabul in 1832 (see PPA, Book 141, Serial No. 68), but it is unclear whether Jeth Mall continued to serve Shuja during the British occupation.

24. It is unclear whether this Mirza Abd al-Raziq is the Monshi Abdul Razak of Delhi who Abd al-Rahman credits with opening the machine printing presses in Kabul. See below Chapter 5 for more on Durrani state texts during the reign of Abd al-Rahman.

25. L. Dupree (1994), p. 398, notes the destruction of only parts of Istalif while the *Gazetteer of Afghanistan*, p. 329, indicates the entire village was destroyed during the first British invasion. The chahar chatta was an innovative architectural feat for the first half of the seventeenth century and its construction is ascribed to the patronage of the Mughal official Ali Mardan Khan. The covered bazaar had four arcades that were unique for having public squares and fountains within them. The chahar chatta formed the

principal retail bazaar complex in Kabul before being leveled by the colonial army sent in retribution of the Indus Army's annihilation. The *Gazetteer of Afghanistan*, ibid., indicates Dost Muhammad rebuilt the structure in approximately 1850. Masson, vol. II, pp. 263–69, provides a number of useful comments about seasonal price fluctuation, fruit markets and brokerage, and the location of key institutions of Kabul commerce such as the customs house, in addition to the chahar chatta, which is described quite favorably. See Burnes, vol. I, p. 145, for a notably less enthusiastic description of the chahar chatta than Masson's.

26. "Resources and Expenditure of Afghanistan, 1841," NAI, Foreign S.C., 25 October 1842, Proceeding Nos. 32–35.

27. Ibid.

28. Ibid.

29. Ibid.

30. Ibid.

31. In addition to the community of brokers, the nomadic trading tribes known variously as kochis, Lohanis, and pawendas who transported the fruit also facilitated the entry of cash currency into fruit-producing localities (see above Introduction and Chapter 1). In the fruit-based revenue regime centered on Kabul, we find brokers mediating economic relations between producers and transporters of fruit, and between those communities and the state.

32. "Resources and Expenditure of Afghanistan, 1841," NAI, Foreign S.C., 25 October 1842, Proceeding Nos. 32–35.

33. See later in this chapter and below Chapter 5 for attention to "book money" in the Durrani state financial registers.

34. Ibid.

35. Ibid., and "Increase in Cabul Commerce and Customs Duties," NAI, Foreign S.C., August 2, 1841, Proceeding Nos. 61–64. When reporting the customs house transformation to the Governor General in July 1841 Macnaghten indicated Burnes's reorganization of the most lucrative commercial institution relating to the interregional (foreign) trade routed through Kabul resulted in a 150 percent profit on Indian and European goods transported from South to Central Asia. Burnes's reforms consisted mainly of eliminating *rahdari* or transit taxes collected outside of Kabul on foreign goods moving through the country. For example, for fruit rahdari was trifurcated according to the kind of fruit being transported, by what means of animal carriage, and whether the state or "chiefs and villagers" along the routes collected the dues. There were six rahdari collection points for Central Asian fruit destined for India moving the approximate 130 miles along the route segment between Bamian and Kabul. Exported Afghan fruit paid rahdari at two stations between Kabul and Ghazni. In addition to eliminating the various rahdari tolls in favor of a single tax collected in Kabul, Burnes planned to collect taxes on an increasing volume of textiles moving from South to Central Asia, and on

the large amounts of opium, horses, and gold currencies moving the opposite direction through the capital city. See later in this chapter for more on Burnes's customs house reforms as they related to the movement and supply of money in and around Kabul and Qandahar during the experimental period. See Emerson and Floor for rahdari in Iran from roughly 1500 to 1750.

36. Burnes was murdered on November 2 and Macnaghten and Trevor on December 23, 1842. See L. Dupree (1994), pp. 369–401, and Allen, Hough, Iqbal, Kaye, and Norris for more on the first Anglo-Afghan war.

37. "Resources and Expenditure of Afghanistan, 1841," NAI, Foreign S.C., 25 October 1842, Proceeding Nos. 32–35. The British sold the brokerage profit tax farm for Rs. 16,000. The previous year's entry for that account was Rs. 9,812.

38. Ibid. The maiwadari tax was distinct from the tax on exports levied at the Kabul customs house.

39. Ibid.

40. The *Gazetteer of Afghanistan*, pp. 442–47. It is important to note that citation of sources in the encyclopedic Afghanistan Gazetteer series is vague and potentially seriously misleading. Even when they appear the sources are not well referenced. The redundancy contained within original sources is perpetuated, and problematically so, in the Gazetteer series. Nevertheless, the Gazetteer pages cited here provide useful information about the social composition of the district: "Koh Daman is a favourite country residence of the wealthy inhabitants of Kabul, and is almost as thickly studded with forts as with gardens. They are strongly built, and are, in fact, mimic representations of the old baronial residences in Europe. Babar, when he conquered Afghanistan, located a number of his countrymen in the Koh Daman, the descendants of whom are now among the most prosperous in the valley."

41. "Resources and Expenditure of Afghanistan, 1841," NAI, Foreign S.C., 25 October 1842, Proceeding Nos. 32–35. Trevor's reforms were designed to bring in Rs. 2,42,772 whereas in the previous year Koh Damn generated Rs. 2,42,764 for the state. The difference was a mere eight rupees.

42. Ibid. Fort-holders were known locally as *foujdars*. Their state-sanctioned entitlements were known as *foujdari*. Foujdari seems to have included other local fiscal privileges known as *sursat* and *purayana*. Trevor's financial plan is notable for consistently rescinding foujdari wherever such entitlements appeared in the Kabul account books. In the case of Koh Daman the foujdari amount Trevor targeted for elimination was Rs. 2,755.

43. The *Gazetteer of Afghanistan*, pp. 442–47. Two villages were estimated as having 700 houses, two villages had 400 houses, three with 300, two at 200 hundred, eight with 100, and 23 villages or over 50 percent were estimated as having less than 100 houses. The same source contains entries for all the villages just mentioned in Koh Daman.

44. "Resources and Expenditure of Afghanistan, 1841," NAI, Foreign S.C., 25 October

1842, Proceeding Nos. 32–35. Such a change was in keeping with the colonial agenda of reducing rahdari tolls collected outside Kabul (see earlier in this chapter).

45. Ibid. Trevor planned on Rs. 2,42,772 as the land revenue of Koh Daman. Rs. 30,480, or approximately 13 percent of that amount, was expected of Istalif.

46. Ibid. Trevor's reforms reduced dallali, or the tax on brokerage, in Istalif from Rs. 100 to Rs. 40. This move did not reflect a devaluation of brokerage as an institution because there was a far more dramatic increase in the brokerage tax at the central state level under the British revenue scheme (see earlier in this chapter).

47. Ibid. About the principal Afghan export, dried and fresh fruits, Trevor noted: "[b]ut little however of either kind pass through Kabul the great fruit trade being carried on from Cohdamun direct and the duties levied at Urghundee where fresh fruit packed for exportation pays three rupees per camel load and dried fruit two rupees exclusive of kishmish (raisins) on which there is some abatement."

48. Ibid. Trevor was bewildered by the various kinds and inconsistent rates (depending on the identities of the carrier and collector) of taxation by state and local authorities on the domestic movement of "everything produced in the country which is not consumed on the spot by the producer."

49. Ibid.

Chapter 4

1. Gankovsky (1982), pp. 85–96.

2. Ibid.

3. "Shuja Wants Refuge in British Territory," PPA, Press List 2, Book 8, Serial No. 39 (dated 18 June 1813), and "Shuja's Intention to Seek Asylum in British Territory," PPA, Press List 2, Book 8, Serial No. 51 (dated 9 July 1813).

4. "Shuja Allowed to Stay at Ludiana with Rs. 50,000 annually as a stipend," PPA, Press List No. 2, Book 9, Serial No. 97 (dated 28 September 1816). For Shuja's wife see PPA, Press List 3, Book 18, Serial No. 157 (an untitled document dated 7 December 1816), and "Destitute Condition of Shuja's Wife," PPA, Press List 2, Book 9, Serial No. 32.

5. "Shuja Refuses Initial Housing Offering and is Informed about His Stipend," PPA, Press List 3, Book 18, Serial Nos. 136–38 (dated 10 November 1816), and "Shuja Writes for Increased Allowance but is Informed of the Necessity of Economy," PPA, Press List 4, Book 72, Serial No. 322 (dated 1 April 1825).

6. See appendices D through L of "Resources and Expenditure of Afghanistan, 1841," NAI, Foreign S.C., 25 October 1842, Proceeding Nos. 32–35, where the allowances (*mulikana*), pensions (*jagirs, rukhshadigi*, and *mulak-i zur khurid*, which were treated more like exemptions in the state fiscal registers), stipends (*wazifa*, which were generally granted to *ulama* or the clergy), remissions (*tukhfif*), and salaries (*musarifi* and *aliosurifi mulkia*) dispensed by the Durrani state before the British occupation are listed. See

above Chapter 3 for more on Durrani state revenue documents and the British manipulation of them during the first occupation.

7. "Income and Expenses of Shuja," NAI, Foreign S.C., 24 May 1841, Proceeding Nos. 36–38.

8. Ibid.

9. "On the Finances of Shuja," NAI, Foreign S.C., 4 October 1841, Proceeding Nos. 54–56. See above Chapter 3 for attention to the British reformation of Durrani state finances after they assumed full control of those resources.

10. "Temporary Subsidy of 10 Lacs/Year to Amir of Cabul," NAI, Foreign S.C., 26 December 1856, Proceeding Nos. 7–12. The first or one of the first remittances to Dost Muhammad was for Rs. 3,00,000 and the British had difficulty securing reasonable hundi exchange rates from local bankers in Qandahar to finalize the transaction "due to the insecure and confused state of Afghanistan and Qandahar." See "Remittance of 3 Lacs to Amir of Cabul," NAI, Foreign S.C., 31 October 1856, Proceeding Nos. 58–61.

11. "Temporary Subsidy of 10 Lacs/Year to Amir of Cabul," NAI, Foreign S.C., 26 December 1856, Proceeding Nos. 7–12.

12. "Amir's Wish to Receive Subsidy Without Allowing Any Advantage in Return," and "Census of Revenue and Population in Provinces Under Amir's Authority," NAI, Foreign Secret, August 1875, Proceeding Nos. 82–86 (the title on the document itself is "Memorandum by Munshi Faiz Bux").

13. Ibid.

14. Ibid.

15. See Kakar (1971), appendices IV and VI, for revealing conversations between Abd al-Rahman and Lepel Griffith, particularly p. 268, where the former confesses to the latter: "I am really appointed by you."

16. Ibid. A formal treaty never materialized, although there were many informal agreements made between the British and Abd al-Rahman, many of which were terminated by the former on the latter's death in 1901. The British claimed the deals they had struck with Abd al-Rahman were specific to his person, not the Durrani state.

17. Abd al-Rahman succeeded in obtaining the British consent that their agent in Kabul be an Indian Muslim and not a European.

18. "Memorandum of Information Available in the Foreign Department on the Government, Revenue, Population and Territorial Divisions of Afghanistan," NAI, Foreign Secret (Supplementary), January 1880, Proceeding Nos. 536–44. Afghanistan here meant the "Kabul Kingdom (including provinces/districts of Jallalabad, Kandahar, Herat, Pusht-i Rud) and Afghan Turkistan." In these figures the category "revenue" excludes subsidies but is comprised broadly to include land revenue, and other charges payable with land revenue, a wide variety of taxes, duties, tolls and other extractions of road dues, and income from fines and forfeitures.

19. "Disposal of Money Belonging to Afghan Amir by Peshawar Merchants," NAI,

Foreign Political B, September 1881, Proceeding Nos. 79–80. These "Peshawar bankers" were also known as Shikarpuris. See above Introduction and Chapter 1 and later in this chapter.

20. Ibid. Mullah Muhammad Bakr and Muhammad Akbar were replaced by Yar Gul Khan.

21. Yar Gul Khan attempted to deposit Rs. 33,000 and Ghulam Mohiyudin Rs. 22,800 to Mullah Muhammad Bakr and Muhammad Akbar.

22. Mullah Muhammad Bakr and Muhammad Akbar deposited Rs. 1,52,000.

23. Dost Muhammad was also known to extort money from the Shikarpuri banking community in Kabul. For example, in response to Shuja's aborted attempt to recoup his lost royal prerogative in 1832–33, Dost Muhammad was reported to have levied forced contributions from "every tribe, Sunni, Shia sect, the sons and grandsons of Agha Muhammad known as Ismailoo, the *mujawer* (attendant/keeper) of the tomb of Ashiqan-i Arifan, from the sons of Dervish Khwaja Esa Khan and Khwaja Khan, . . . every district, town, village, as well as the mercantile part of the community . . . (to the point where) he is destroying Kabul" (PPA, Book 139, Serial Nos. 51–68[?]). Shikarpuri merchant capital is specifically mentioned as having been confiscated by Dost Muhammad during this period: "(t)o meet his pecuniary exigencies, Dost extorted one and one half laks of rupees in money and effects from the Shikarporees of Kabul. He calls it a loan paying at the rate of 3000 rupees per diem." See NAI, Foreign P.C., 30 March 1835, Proceeding No. 46.

24. "Disbursement of the Subsidy of the Amir of Afghanistan," NAI, Foreign A Political E, February 1884, Proceeding Nos. 34–53. The individuals referred to are the first sixteen people named in Table 4.2. One aspect of the disorder accompanying this particular subsidy dispersal revolved around Asa and Lalu, the fourth and fifth persons mentioned in the Table, arriving at the Peshawar Treasury claiming to be owed different amounts than indicated by Abd al-Rahman. Asa claimed Rs. 4,000 more and Lalu Rs. 4,000 less than indicated by Abd al-Rahman. Ibid.

25. Ibid. Persons numbered 17–41 in Table 4.2. In the cited source, the Muslim from Shikarpur is indicated to be Muhammad Sharif, number 33 in the table, but number 37, Daulat, is also a Muslim name. Concerning the second group of Shikarpuris, colonial officials resolved "the payment should not under any circumstances exceed the total amount given in the Amir's letter" (of 17 December 1883). Abd al-Rahman also wrote to the British on 2 November and 16 December 1883 about this month's subsidy.

26. Ibid.

27. See below Chapter 5 for attention to some of the state trading monopolies established by Abd al-Rahman and his seizures of merchant and other forms of capital in Kabul and beyond.

28. "Proposed Organization of an Improved News Agency on the Russo-Afghan Frontier," NAI, Foreign Secret F, March 1886, Proceeding Nos. 303–13.

29. "Payments Made to the Amir's Agents in India on Account of His Highness's Subsidy," NAI, Foreign Frontier K.W., May 1890, Proceeding Nos. 5–24.

30. Ibid. See later in this chapter for more on the Durrani badami and postmaster in Peshawar, the Durrani Envoy with the Government of India, and the commercial agents stationed elsewhere in India.

31. The subsidy files I have seen at the NAI, NWFPA, and PPA appear to have been generated by discrepancies, disputes, or other irregularities concerning the transmission or redistribution the subsidy.

32. "Payments Made to the Amir's Agents in India on Account of His Highness's Subsidy," NAI, Foreign Frontier K.W., May 1890, Proceeding Nos. 5–24.

33. "Payments made on account the subsidy of His Highness the Amir of Afghanistan," NAI, Foreign Frontier A, March 1891, Proceeding Nos. 8–16. See later in this chapter for more on Salter Pyne.

34. Ibid. This particular cash dispersal of British Indian rupees was destined to be re-coined with minting machinery recently imported from Europe and installed in the Kabul workshops or mashin khana, which was an exceptional use of subsidy funds. See below Chapter 5 for more on the impact of European minting machinery in Kabul, and later in this chapter for attention to the mashin khana. Supplying the mashin khana with Indian and European commodities, particularly heavy machinery, consumed most of the subsidy funds.

35. Such a configuration is deduced from information contained in a file generated by the theft of subsidy cash by a Shikarpuri Hindu named Jawahir Mal who was banished from Kabul during the early years of Abd al-Rahman's reign. See "Misappropriation of Money Belong to Amir of Kabul by Jawahir Mal alias Jaru," NWFPA, Records from the Office of the Peshawar Commissioner, Bundle No. 60, Serial No. 1545.

36. See below Chapter 5 for more on the Durrani state qafilabashi in Peshawar.

37. "Establishment of a Post Office in Peshawar by the Amir of Kabul," NWFPA, TARC. Afghanistan Index I, File No. 205 (records from the Chief Commissioner's Office, 1881). A partial list of the men appointed to this position of Durrani postmaster in Peshawar begins with Mirza Baiza Khan who assumed the position in 1881. Mir Haidar was the Afghan Postmaster in Peshawar in 1885, and Mirza Khalifa Ji Khan held the office in 1898. See below Chapter 5 for more on the mirzas or state-appointed accountants/book-keepers/financial clerks during Abd al-Rahman's reign.

38. See below Chapter 5 for more on the predicament of the British Agent in Kabul. It is nevertheless useful here to convey a quote from Hamilton, pp. 373–74: "The British agent at Kabul holds an absolutely thankless position. He is shunned of necessity by Europeans in order to avoid giving rise to political suspicions, and he may see the Amir only in the public Durbars or by special appointment. To all intents and purposes he is a prisoner; since, although received in Durbar, he does not visit anyone and seldom ventures into the street. If a European were seen speaking to the British Agent, or to anyone attached to his staff, he would certainly be packed off to at once to the frontier. No

Afghan is allowed to enter the British Agency and no Englishman has visited the British Agent, since Sir Salter Pyne left Kabul. Even to be found near the building causes suspicion, as several Afghans have discovered. Moreover, since in many cases punishment has not ended merely with imprisonment, it has become an unwritten law to avoid the British agent and his *entourage* at any cost."

39. When the Durrani post office in Peshawar was established "almost all" of the fifty or sixty letters sent each week between that city and Kabul were the correspondence of traders. Ibid. The same source indicates it took five days for mail between the cities to be conveyed through twenty post stops at each of which three runners were stationed. Excepting Abd al-Rahman's correspondence that came and went as needed, mail ran twice weekly, usually on Monday and Thursday. Kakar (1979), p. 33, indicates that between Kabul and Jalalabad postal runners carried spears with small bells attached while transporting mail ten miles a day, five miles in each direction, and that they lived communally in stone huts stationed five miles apart. Kakar, ibid., also indicates Sher Ali established "the modern Afghan postal service."

40. For example, in February 1884, Abd al-Rahman directed his Postmaster Mir Haidar to pay eighteen Shikarpuris through a subsidy redistribution. Abd al-Rahman had recently purchased Rs. 8,000 worth of gold the Shikarpuris carried from Bukhara to Kabul. Abd al-Rahman likely imposed his own value on and coerced the "sale" of the gold, and then issued the Shikarpuris a hundi payable in Peshawar from the subsidy account for that amount. See "Misappropriation of Money Belong to Amir of Kabul by Jawahir Mal alias Jaru," NWFPA, Records from the Office of the Peshawar Commissioner, Bundle No. 60, Serial No. 1545.

41. "Statement Showing the Payments Made to His Highness During 1897–98 and the Balance At His Credit on the 1st March 1898," NAI, Foreign Frontier A, August 1898, Proceeding Nos. 48–57.

42. Ibid.

43. Ibid.

44. Ibid.

45. The Durrani Envoy is often referred to as the Durrani Agent in India. Envoy is used here to distinguish that official from other Durrani commercial agents stationed in India (see later in this chapter). Abd al-Rahman desperately wanted to have a Durrani ambassador in London, and he took steps to debunk arguments circulating against such an appointment by claiming the subsidy did not remove but rather enhanced his perceived right to political representation in London. In this regard, Abd al-Rahman is reported to have heard of Englishmen in his employ on leave in London claiming to the Queen and Parliament they could sway him in matters of policy. Far from denying the validity of those reports, Abd al-Rahman actually deployed them to bolster arguments for having a Durrani ambassador in London by inferring a reciprocal presence of English 'ambassadors' in Kabul. See S. M. Khan, vol. II, pp. 254–57.

46. "Payments Made Out of the Amir's Subsidy. Statement Furnished to the India Office of Arms, Ammunition, and Money Presented by the Government of India to His Highness the Amir During The Year 1899," NAI, Foreign Frontier B, January 1900, Proceeding Nos. 171–201. This source indicates that from May 1899 to January 1900 the Durrani Envoy Sardar Muhammad Ismail Khan received seven subsidy redistributions in Amballa, Lahore, and Simla that totaled Rs. 2,63,100.

47. The Durrani Envoy was then Ghulam Rasul Khan, and 4 lakhs of rupees was between 22 percent and 33 percent of the annual subsidy, which increased from 12 to 18 lakhs in 1893. See "Payments Made on Account of the Subsidy of His Highness the Amir of Afghanistan," NAI, Foreign Frontier A, October 1893, Proceeding Nos. 42–50. The Walsh firm was among the most visible of foreign mercantile organizations commissioned by Abd al-Rahman to supply his court, palaces, and workshops or mashin khana (see later in this chapter). The subsidy exposed a number of Englishmen and their firms to Abd al-Rahman's fiscal conduct, and their influence over his financial practice became quite pronounced. Abd al-Rahman's notice of his sometimes-subordinate role in this relationship was noted above. Another example of that phenomenon apparently came in response to the steep rise in transit tolls and other commercial dues and tariffs Abd al-Rahman instituted (see below Chapter 5). In various ways the Government of India, and many Afghan, English, Indian, and Iranian, transnational merchants and trading houses made repeated unsuccessful attempts to persuade Abd al-Rahman to reduce his new and exorbitant impositions on Afghanistan's potentially lucrative 'through trade' between Central and South Asia. Kakar (1979), p. 212, argues that in 1890 Walsh, Lovett and Company succeeded in convincing Abd al-Rahman to reduce the heavy tax burdens imposed on the transit trade which was stifling commercial activity in Afghanistan as a whole.

48. The deposits occurred between April and December 1899. See "Payments Made Out of The Amir's Subsidy. Statement Furnished to the India Office of Arms, Ammunition, and Money Presented by the Government of India to His Highness the Amir During the Year 1899," NAI, Foreign Frontier B, January 1900, Proceeding Nos. 171–201. During 1899, and many if not most other years of Abd al-Rahman's reign, the subsidy documents contain a conspicuous "*nil*" or absence of transference of coercive means under the heading "Arms and Ammunition Presented to the Amir." But of course the presence of the heading itself is also important.

49. Although possibly not a comprehensive list, the post of Durrani commercial agent in Bombay was held by (at least): Haji Asad Khan in 1883; Mullah Abu Bakr Khan in 1888 and 1889; (possibly) Colonel Ghulam Rasul Khan Safi in 1890; Mullah Muhammad Azim in 1892 and 1893, and again in 1899 and 1900; and Mullah Dost Muhammad Khan Tokhi in 1897 and 1898. There does not appear to have been a Durrani commercial agent regularly stationed in Karachi. Abd al-Rahman apparently dispatched the Bombay agent or his main Envoy to that city on an *ad hoc* basis.

50. See Gray, p. 512–15. Gray was Abd al-Rahman's personal surgeon for a number of years. One exception to the rotation rule was Mullah Abu Bakr. This individual was one of the first two agents Abd al-Rahman deputed to assume control of his British subsidies in Peshawar immediately after his colonial appointment in Kabul, and someone who managed to retain the Durrani ruler's confidence for an extended period of time.

51. "Payments Made Out of the Amir's Subsidy. Statement Furnished to the India Office of Arms, Ammunition, and Money Presented by the Government of India to His Highness the Amir During the Year 1899," NAI, Foreign Frontier B, January 1900, Proceeding Nos. 171–201.

52. "Complaint by the Amir's Officials against the Peshawar Municipality in Connection with His Highness's Goods. Letter to the Amir about the Continued Collection of Afghan Dues and Tolls in British Territory," NAI, Foreign Frontier A, August 1901, Proceeding Nos. 34–40.

53. The raw materials imported with subsidy funds were finished primarily by the hand-craftsmen of Kabul until 1887 when the machines of the Kabul workshops began to assume the preponderance of that labor burden. See later in this chapter. The qafila-bashi or Durrani state caravan official in Peshawar was responsible for the conveyance of those raw materials to Kabul before and after the establishment of the workshops. See below Chapter 5 for more on the Durrani qafilabashi in Peshawar.

54. "Payments Made to the Amir's Agents in India on Account of His Highness's Subsidy," NAI, Foreign Frontier (K.W.), May 1890, Proceeding Nos. 5–24. The Durrani Envoy Wali Ahmad Khan followed a precedent established by his father General Amir Ahmad Khan as ordered by Abd al-Rahman: "every three months make over to Mullah Abu Bakr Khan the sum of Rs. 1,00,000 to enable him to purchase the articles (brass and copper)." Mullah Abu Bakr Khan was then the Durrani commercial agent in Bombay. It is unclear precisely how long this practice may have continued, but it lasted at least two years.

55. It was estimated earlier in this chapter that the subsidies, once regularized at 12 lakhs of British rupees per annum in 1882, accounted for roughly 16 percent of the revenue received by the Durrani state. The approximate total government revenue used in those calculations, Rs. 73,30,680, was based on statistics gathered from Durrani state sources for the years 1877–78 that were consulted during the second British occupation of Kabul in 1879 (see "Memorandum of Information Available in the Foreign Department on the Government, Revenue, Population, and Territorial Divisions of Afghanistan," NAI, Foreign Secret [Supplementary], January 1880, Proceeding Nos. 536–44). That data is organized on the basis of province. The majority of provincial revenue was derived from agricultural production and a significant amount from transit trade taxation. Both of these economic sectors and their derivative income declined markedly during Abd al-Rahman's reign (see Kakar [1979] p. 189, for agricultural decline, and ibid., p. 215, for the diminishing transit trade). Therefore, the subsidies could have been

substantially more significant than the previously indicated 16 percent of the Durrani state's gross national product, making four lakhs per year for brass and copper far more than 5 percent of the state's revenue in all its forms.

56. "Purchase of Articles for Amir of Kabul in Peshawar," NAI, Foreign Political B, September 1881, Proceeding Nos. 178–79. Abd al-Rahman wanted these kotwalis informed at least for the purpose of avoiding octroi, other municipal taxes, and transit duties on the subsidy-garnered goods as they moved through and between those primary markets in India.

57. Ibid. Without the original letters it is impossible to know if the two categories were Abd al-Rahman's or colonial bureaucratic artifacts. According to Kakar (1979), pp. 193–94, iron became the preferred metal for rifle and gun production in the Kabul weapons workshops, the *karkhana-i sultanat-i Kabul*, during the reign of Sher Ali. Gregorian, p. 86, indicates a karkhana or workshop was established solely for weapons production by Abd al-Rahman's father Muhammad Afzal, and significantly expanded on by Sher Ali.

58. See Elphinstone, vol. II, p. 336, for categories of craftsmen, merchants, and traders in Kabul. It is important to remember Elphinstone's description of the social organization of Kabul's mercantile community is not first hand. Rather, it is based on data gathered primarily through informants interviewed and information collected in Peshawar.

59. Kakar (1979), p. 193.

60. See Kakar (1971) for more on the internal revolts against Abd al-Rahman's rule.

61. Pyne was approached and contracted in 1887 through Abd al-Rahman's Envoy in Calcutta, General Amir Ahmad Khan. Sultan Muhammad Khan later became Abd al-Rahman's *mir monshi* or chief secretary, and helped author his patron's "auto"-biography. See S. M. Khan, vol. II, p. 23, for Sultan Muhammad Khan's role in bringing Pyne to Kabul. See also Yapp's Introduction in vol. I, p. xvii, for the autobiographical spuriousness of volume two of this text. The first foreigner contracted by Abd al-Rahman to rebuild and expand the Kabul workshops was M. Jerome who was given Rs. 1,41,000 to purchase European engines and machines, which he successfully arranged to be conveyed to Kabul along with twenty-one Indian workmen familiar with that technology. However, Mr. Jerome never reappeared in Kabul, which resulted in Abd al-Rahman hiring Pyne.

62. Quoted in Kakar (1979), p. 195.

63. The Kandahar Newsletters from the 1890s contain numerous reports of people being maimed or killed while transporting some of these heavy machines overland to Kabul from Qandahar. However, not all of the larger machines imported from Europe were shipped to Karachi and then transported to Quetta before reaching Qandahar. Many if not most of the disassembled and crated machines and machine parts were routed from colonial India to Afghanistan through the Khaibar using elephants. See

Table 4.4. A. C. Jewitt, an American engineer who between 1911 and 1919 during the reign of Abd al-Rahman's son Habibullah (ruled 1901–19) supervised the construction of Afghanistan's first hydroelectric plant, the *jabal as-siraj* or mountain of light, in the Kohistan district roughly fifty miles north of Kabul, provides a number of pictures of these elephants. See Bell, pp. 99, 101, and 102. Other sections in this interesting and lively series of vignettes forming Jewitt's account of his experiences in Afghanistan that bear on this study are ibid., pp. 67–70, 82–86, 196–206, and 234–41.

64. Wooden models of Hotchkiss, Maxim, Gardiner, and Gatling guns were used to mimic the authentic variety, and these wooden imitations served as the reproductive template for workmen at the mashin khana. See S. M. Khan, vol. II, pp. 29–30. Most of the weapons produced at the mashin khana were imitations of European models and notable for their uneven if not inferior quality. See Gregorian, p. 143, and Kakar (1979), pp. 193–98. Production of weaponry and all other finished goods at the Kabul workshops was constrained by a dependence on moving water, steam, and wood, as opposed to coal, for fuel. Kakar (1979), p. 196, notes the following about the volume of arms production at the machine khana for the year 1896: 4 differently sized artillery guns each week, and 15 rifles (imitations of English Martini-Henrys [*panahpur* locally] and Sniders [*baghalpur* locally], and apparently to a much lesser extent local versions of Russian designs and models) and 20,000 cartridges (10,000 for both Martini-Henrys and Sniders) daily. Quality, not quantity, was the challenge of arms production at the mashin khana. Pyne had a vested interest in the reputation of mashin khana products, and therefore praised the finished results. Observers with less personal stake in Abd al-Rahman's workshops characterized both the arms and ammunition produced in Kabul as unreliable and of poor quality.

65. Chapter 2 referenced Masson's opinion from the mid-1830s that "looking glasses and a multitude of various little articles conducive to comfort and convenience" of ordinary consumers be specifically targeted for import to Kabul from Mithenkote by the Lohanis in order to drive out similar Russian goods that were more expensive and of inferior quality. See "Masson's Observations on Kabul Commerce," NAI, Foreign P.C., 2 November 1835, Proceeding No. 56 (which is also titled "Observations on Trade of Kabul"). Chapter 2 also noted that during the same period the Governor General of India sent the Kabuli merchant Mullah Khair ud-Din gifts including pocketknives, flasks, buttons, and belts. See "Measures to Promote Trade Between Mithenkote and Central Asia," NAI, Foreign P.C., 16 May 1836, Proceeding Nos. 47–48. Similar versions of the European commodities advocated for import and mass consumption during the experimental period of the 1830s ultimately did make their way to Afghanistan during the 1890s routinization period. However, during the later period the European novelties were consumed primarily by Abd al-Rahman and the Muhammadzai Durrani political elite he catered to domestically, not the popular consumer classes of Afghanistan referenced by Masson.

66. S. M. Khan, vol. II, pp. 27–28.

Chapter 5

1. "Kuzilbash Influence in Afghanistan," NAI, Foreign P.C., 31 January 1836, Proceeding Nos. 36–40." This archival file corresponds to p. 8 in Burnes et al., in the chapter titled "On the Persian Faction in Cabool." Burnes authored this report and he indicated four thousand Qizilbash families then resided in Kabul. The Qizilbash were associated with the section of the city known as Chindawul, and were divided into three main groups, the Afshars, Jawanshers, and Murad Khanis. Furthermore, "even though their military influence has declined, they now have more power because every man of rank has (them) for his secretaries and all home and foreign correspondence is in their hands which ramifies their influence in every direction." Burnes used the term secretary as a translation for mirza, and it is important to note that Macnaghten was designated as the Secretary to the Governor General of India before becoming the Envoy and Ambassador to Shuja's government during the first British occupation. In 1775–76, Timur Shah transferred the Durrani capital from Qandahar to Kabul, and there are indications that the move was undertaken to be nearer the Qizilbash community. See Barakzai, p. 152.

2. Higher-ranking mirzas reported directly to Abd al-Rahman, his sons Sardars Habibullah and Abdullah, and Diwan Naranjan Das who rose to become arguably the most important financial officer in Abd al-Rahman's government, a status he seems to have maintained during the reigns of Habibullah (ruled 1901–19) and Amanullah (ruled 1919–29). See Adamec (1991), p. 174 for more on Naranjan Das, Kakar (1979), pp. 27–30 and 33–34 for more on mirzas, and Martin, pp. 245–49 for a picture and useful description of mirzas and their professional business practices in Kabul at the beginning of the twentieth century.

3. The *Kandahar Newsletters* indicate that diwans and mirzas could act as sarishtadars. For example, in 1890 the sarishtadar of Qandahar, or the central government revenue official in that province, was replaced. Entries from April 5 and May 11 indicate Diwan Lal Chand, a Hindu from Kabul, once imprisoned but now favored by the Amir, was sent to replace the former office-holder Mirza Muhammad Hassan Khan. Shortly thereafter it was reported Lal Chand's inexperience with local practices created confusion in the Qandahar mint that led to a shortage of copper coinage in the bazaar and caused much inconvenience for ordinary consumers.

4. See ibid., entries from January 11 and February 9 for a probable testimonial in this regard. There it is reported another Hindu Diwan deputed by Abd al-Rahman to Qandahar to audit the past five years of the provincial account books, Sada Nand, claimed to have detected forged vouchers which led him to conclude significant sums had been repeatedly embezzled by the provincial Governor. After Diwan Sada Nand reported this to Abd al-Rahman the Qandahar Governor was noted as having begun to pray publicly for an end to his own existence.

5. See "Information Received by Peshawar Merchants Which Makes Them Cease

Trade With Bokhara," NAI, Foreign Secret F, June 1889, Proceeding Nos. 142–55, in which we find the person in charge of *awqaf* or religious endowments funds, Muhammad Ismail Khan, as the subject of a mirza audit. From an 1891 Kandahar Newsletter entry we learn that a deceased occupant of arguably the most influential foreign post in Abd al-Rahman's government, his Agent or Envoy with the Government of British India, also became the subject of an audit. Sarishtadars in Kabul who reviewed the accounts of Abd al-Rahman's first Envoy with the Government of India, General Amir Ahmad Khan, reported a deficit of Rs. 1,30,000 that they suggested be realized from his surviving relatives. These relatives included the General's son, Colonel Nur Ahmad Khan, then the Commander of the Qandahar Artillery, and the General's grandson and then current Envoy, Colonel Aziz (Wali) Ahmad Khan.

6. See Kakar (1979), p. 237.

7. Such as the Peshawri Sethi family may have been for the administrative divisions encompassing the timber-rich Jaji forest in the Paktia province of eastern Afghanistan in the late-nineteenth and early-twentieth century. See below Chapter 6.

8. A number of aspects and features of Hindki account books and bookkeepers are not clear. Points of uncertainty include whether such accounting skills could be transferred between firms of bankers, and if firms maintained unique forms of books requiring different types of maintenance and literacy, and to what extent the actual handling and deciphering of those texts might have fallen under the purview of a select few or minority within the general banking community.

9. See Braudel (1973), pp. 352–54.

10. Jenkyns, p. 11. In the pukhta system 50 *dinars* equaled 1 shahi, 2 shahis equaled 1 sanar, 2 sanars equaled 1 abbasi, 3 abbasis equaled 1 Kabuli rupee. In the kham scheme of computation 10 dinars equaled 1 *paisa*, 5 paisas equaled 1 shahi, 10 shahis equaled 1 rupee, 20 rupees equaled 1 toman. One toman equaled 16 rupees 8 shahis pukhta. The distinction between kham and pukhta rupees was also evident during the first British occupation of Kabul when Trevor reorganized the Durrani state fiscal registers in Kabul (see above Chapter 3). The imaginary, invisible kham rupee book money required a parallel intangible system of weights and measures. The system of weight used by ordinary consumers in retail settings, in at least Jalalabad and Laghman, worked with 1 *charak* equal to 16 *khurds*, 4 charaks equal to 1 *seer* or *dhari*, 8 seers equal to 1 *maund*, 10 maunds equal to 1 *kharwar*. One ordinary Kabuli seer equaled 7 seers 13.5 *chittacks* British Indian standard weight, and therefore one ordinary Kabuli kharwar equaled 15 maunds 27 seers and 8 chittacks British Indian standard weight. In the official *tabrizi* state weight scheme 2.5 chittacks equaled 1 maund and 100 maunds equaled one kharwar. One official Kabuli maund equaled 4 seers and 14.5 chittacks British Indian standard weight, and a tabrizi kharwar equaled 12 maunds, 10 seers, and 10 chittacks British Indian standard weight.

11. Braudel (1973), pp. 352–54, where it is also noted that before being reincarnated into real money to balance a particular account, book money itself arose in transforma-

tion from an "earlier" existence as real money. See later in this chapter for reference to agents of Peshawar firms in Kabul being summoned home regardless of whether any book debts were settled.

12. For comparative purposes, see Fleischer for a well-documented and thoughtful consideration of an Ottoman bureaucrat's career.

13. S. M. Khan, vol. II, pp. 63–64.

14. Ibid. Abd al-Rahman's characterization of the state account books before his reforms does not seem to match Trevor's characterization of the same set of documents during the first British occupation of Kabul. See above Chapter 3.

15. For example, during Sher Ali's reign (1863–66 and 1868–79), the Kabul merchant Dada Sher arranged for twenty-our camel loads of indigo he purchased in Multan to be sent to Bukhara. Of those loads, six were turned over to the Kabul agents of an Indian trader based in Tashkurgan (likely Mian Ilahi Paracha of Nowshera), six were sold to merchants in Kabul, and twelve were dispatched to Bukhara through firms with agents stationed at Tashkurgan. Receipts were issued for the latter two transactions. A larger case brought this episode to the panchayat's notice. Abd al-Rahman used the panchayat's ruling in this regard to not only invalidate the original receipts, but to justify similar sums being extracted a second time from the parties holding them: "The Amir has also sent orders to the Naib Kotwal to realize the price of the six loads of indigo which were made over to the Kabul merchants. Although they hold receipts for the same, the money will be realized from them. The merchants to whom the Amir has addressed a letter (the Tashkurgan agents of the Bukhara firm/s) . . . will also be made to pay His Highness's demand. Such is the state of trade in Afghanistan." See "Information Received by Peshawar Merchants Which Makes Them Cease Trade with Bokhara," NAI, Foreign Secret F, June 1889, Proceeding Nos. 142–55.

16. *Kandahar Newsletters* (1886–87), p. 99, from the entry dated 14 January 1887. The same report also indicates public notices were posted in Qandahar, but armed sentries prohibited people from reading them, and that "neighbours of accused persons and prisoners, such as Muhammad Alam Khan, the late Kotwal of Kandahar, Mulla Majid, (a) merchant, and others, are forced to purchase their (the accused's and imprisoned's) lands, though they (the neighbors) explain their inability to pay for them." While the first situation speaks for itself rather well, the second situation deserves notice as an example of the kind of collateral damage regularly inflicted on those associated with someone who underwent a state audit.

17. *Kandahar Newsletters* (1891–92), p. 32, from the entry of 6 July 1891. The indebted ghi seller in this scene was named Afzal. Whether an avid tea drinker or not Afzal had a critical eye on the revenue to be made from the consumption of that commodity. In his correspondence Afzal suggested that Abd al-Rahman monopolize the trade in tea, sugar and matches in Qandahar. Afzal either implicitly or explicitly suggested himself as the monopolizing agent. Abd al-Rahman likely stationed spies in tea houses. See S. M.

Khan, vol. II., pp. 202–4, for more Abd al-Rahman's advocacy of a strong intelligence service.

18. S. M. Khan, vol. II., p. 62.

19. Ibid., pp. 62–63.

20. Ibid., pp. 76–77.

21. *Kandahar Newsletters* (1888–89–90), p. 89, corresponding to the entry from 11 January 1889. See later in this chapter for more on Jita's role as Abd al-Rahman's sole commercial brokerage agent in Qandahar. The dastur al-amals mentioned are analogous to the *nezam namas* issued during Amanullah's reign in Kabul (1919–29), for which see Nawid, p. 66, Appendix B, and *passim*. See Kakar (1979), pp. 307–8, for notice of a number of other similar Durrani state regulatory and instructional texts.

22. *Kandahar Newsletters* (1888–89–90), p. 107, corresponding to the 11 May 1889 entry. Abd al-Rahman appointed Diwan Sada Nand as the Qandahar Pension Fund sarishtadar to execute these orders. See later in this chapter for more on how Abd al-Rahman's innovative state texts altered the routing of nomadic carriers known as kochis, Lohanis, and pawendas.

23. *Kandahar Newsletters* (1891–92), p. 29, corresponding to the entry from 22 June 1891.

24. S. M. Khan, vol. II, pp. 46–47.

25. State trading monopolies established by Abd al-Rahman before the one on fruit in 1892 (see later in this chapter) include that on almonds in 1885 (see above Chapter 4 for more on the badami or Durrani state official in charge of the almond monopoly [and more] in Peshawar), asafetida in 1890 (monopoly rights leased to Nur Muhammad [see later this chapter in the context of fruit monopoly] who used Fazl Kadir Sethi and Ralla Ram as brokers in Peshawar), and pistachio nuts in 1891 (leased to Omar Khan [Abd al-Rahman's son] who used Shankar Das and Bhagwan Das as brokers in Peshawar). After fruit, commodities Abd al-Rahman monopolized the trade of included, but were not limited to, alcoholic spirits, candles, carpets, gunpowder, opium, timber, salt, skins and furs of certain animals (including karkul, postins, wools), soap, and sugar. See Kakar (1979), pp. 207–8.

26. Indian merchant capital is here glossed as the moveable and immoveable resources controlled by Shikarpuri Hindus, Peshawri Sikhs, and various Muslim communities whose fiscal operations extended broadly within and between South and Central Asia, and throughout many local economic sectors and networks therein, but who were culturally and historically associated with certain localities in India. I employ the "Indian merchants" label here broadly to include individuals with either small and scattered commercial means, or substantial and diverse financial portfolios, as well as collectivities of many and various types of individuals' resources including the merchant firms and houses formed within the larger social categories such as Shikarpuris or Peshawris. See above Chapter 4 for more on the presence of Indian bankers (identified both as

"Shikarpuri Hindus" and "Peshawri bankers") at the time of Abd al-Rahman's accession, and how he moved to displace that community with his own agents over time. See above Chapter 1 for more on the identity of Indian merchants in Afghanistan.

27. See later in this chapter for Abd al-Rahman's displacement of brokers from Peshawar. See below Chapter 6 for the transit tax regime Abd al-Rahman instituted that led to Indian traders circumventing Afghanistan in their commercial dealings with Central Asia.

28. Noelle is the most thorough published source on the two reigns of Dost Muhammad (1826–39 and 1842–63). However, the political history orientation of this work results in little information being provided about commercial brokerage or revenue farming in the fruit-producing districts addressed here. Gregorian, pp. 105–17, covers the period from 1855 until the British appointment of Abd al-Rahman and creation of Afghanistan as a "unique client state" in 1880. This section of Gregorian's very useful though somewhat teleological political history does not shed light on the economic conditions of eastern Afghanistan during those years. Arguably the most useful published source for economic data collected between the Anglo-Afghan wars is Davies. See Appendix XVI therein for a useful statement by Nawab Foujdar Khan on the commercial activities of nomad traders who plied their trade between Central and South Asia using the Gomal Pass route.

29. For a condensed list of published sources on the second Anglo-Afghan war, see Adamec (1996), pp. 325–26. For additional information on the second Anglo Afghan war, see ibid., pp. 198–208 and 253–56, and Adamec (1991), pp. 33–34, and L. Dupree, pp. 403–13.

30. See "Establishment by the Amir of a Monopoly of the Sale of all Fruit Exported from Afghanistan to British India," NAI, Foreign Secret F, May 1893, Proceeding Nos. 425–54, and "Monopoly for the Sale of Fruit, etc., Exported from Afghanistan and Levy of Tolls thereon by the Amir of Kabul," NWFPA, Peshawar Commissioner's Office Files, Serial No. 1522C, Bundle No. 60. These are the two primary sets of files relied on for information about Abd al-Rahman's fruit monopoly. Each is quite extensive and they overlap in many respects. However, certain distinctions are worth mentioning. The latter file was seen in Peshawar, and it has a local feel with comments and marginalia directed at immediate practical considerations. There is more data and description in the fruit file from Peshawar, but the whole file is very large, handwritten, and not well organized. The former file was seen in Delhi, and it has a more distant tone and structure about it. The Afghan fruit monopoly file in Delhi is also thick, but it is more organized, typed, and contains a generalized summary of events and issues contextualized by broader (pan-Indian and greater Imperial) political and legal concerns.

31. Ibid. (referring to both fruit citations). In the original Persian document "brokerage and weighmen's fees" is rendered *arth wa dharat*. "Broker" is there represented as *arth furosh* and not the more common dalal. Literally, arth means brokerage dues and

furosh means seller. However, in some instances arth is associated with export duty, which is more commonly termed *arat*. *Arati* connotes commission fees. Peshawar came under British control in 1849 (see Dani, p. 134).

32. Abd al-Rahman issued the *sanad*, translated here as a deed of partnership, that inaugurated the monopoly.

33. Ibid. Persian terms with no clear translation have been left in the original language. In all of this terminology it is important to consider that many of the items referred to receive different labels in the many different linguistic communities involved in the marketing of eastern Afghan fruit. The Appendix provides Persian and Pashto translations for most of the commodities and other commercial terms rendered in English in the text.

34. The security deposit rates charged the kochis were Kabuli Rs. 12 per camel load of seedless pomegranates, pistachio nuts and buz ganj or pistachio tree flowers, Rs. 11 per camel load of boxed grapes (sometimes equated with grape baskets known as *khuttis*), and Rs. 6 per camel load on all other recently monopolized commodities. The original intent of the monopoly was to close the Gomal Pass and all other routes except the Khaibar to the fruit trade. However, that aspect of the original plan was revoked and provisions made to tax the fruit trade through the Gomal and the Indian market most associated with it, Dera Ismail Khan. See "Establishment by the Amir of a Monopoly of the Sale of all Fruit Exported from Afghanistan to British India," NAI, Foreign Secret F, May 1893, Proceeding Nos. 425–54. A similar injunction on the kochi carriage of fruit through Kohat was also rescinded, see "Monopoly for the Sale of Fruit, etc., Exported from Afghanistan and Levy of Tolls thereon by the Amir of Kabul," NWFPA, Commissioner's Office, Peshawar, Serial No. 1522C, Bundle No. 60.

35. The countersigned receipts associated with the monopoly drew the fruit carrying kochis to the attention of the Peshawar qafilabashi who was the Durrani state official responsible for the transmission of state property, especially that purchased with subsidy money, from Peshawar to Kabul. The qafilabashi and the fruit monopolist, and other Afghan state officials stationed in Peshawar and elsewhere in India, communicated regularly with one another.

36. "Monopoly for the Sale of Fruit, etc., Exported from Afghanistan and Levy of Tolls thereon by the Amir of Kabul," NWFPA, Peshawar Commissioner's Office Files, Serial No. 1522C, Bundle No. 60. Common terms for brokers and weighmen are dalals and *dharwais*, respectively.

37. "Establishment by the Amir of a Monopoly of the Sale of all Fruit Exported from Afghanistan to British India," NAI, Foreign Secret F, May 1893, Proceeding Nos. 425–4.

38. Ibid.

39. Abd al-Rahman wrote to Chaudri Sujan Singh, Radha, Mohan Lal, Nainu Singh, Viru Mal, Shankar Singh, Laud Lall, Ganga Bishen, Teja Singh, Jawala Singh, Jiwan

Singh, Jiwan Mal, Kishen Singh, Mitha Mal, Birbal Singh, Dali Mal, Kharku Singh, Kaku Singh, Nar Singh, Ishar Das, Mathra Das, Harji Singh, Mishyari Chand, Ishar Singh, Buta Singh, Panna Singh, Nand Lal, Nihal Chand, Narain Das, and Ishar Das. Ibid.

40. During the late-nineteenth-century period of routinized Anglo-Afghan relations in Peshawar, brawls and resulting court cases were not uncommon between Durrani officials and their entourages, on the one hand, and groups of ordinary Afghan merchants and their local supports and business associates in the city, on the other. These seem to have been precipitated most often by Durrani officials coming to know about then trying to seize fruit argued to have been illegally exported, or the taking as hostage or prisoner those committing such alleged crimes. Ibid. and "Monopoly for the Sale of Fruit, etc., Exported from Afghanistan and Levy of Tolls thereon by the Amir of Kabul," NWFPA, Peshawar Commissioner's Office Files, Serial No. 1522C, Bundle No. 60.

41. One British official commented as follows about Abd al-Rahman and the fruit monopoly. "He has, I believe, at heart the interests of Afghan trade (but) they are largely subordinated to the interests of his own pocket, and his idea of how to serve trade interests are utterly warped by a conviction that whatever profits are made by the people of Hindustan, out of trade in the produce of Afghanistan, are unjust and a loss to his people." Ibid.

42. Ibid. See above Introduction for more on similarities and distinctions between kochis, Lohanis, and pawendas.

43. The British political and economic relationship to Afghanistan during the period after the second Anglo-Afghan war was routinized around the cash subsidy granted to Abd al-Rahman. See earlier in this chapter and above Chapter 4.

44. In the logic of the "Great Game," Abd al-Rahman's appointment was one step toward Kabul becoming the certain center of a defined territory between the British colonial empire in South Asia and that of the Russians in Central Asia. Arguably the main step toward Afghanistan's assumption of statehood status, however tenuous the claim, was the marking of its boundaries, and that activity is epitomized by the Durand line of 1893 which was supposed to represent a 'permanent' boundary between Afghanistan and British India. The Durand line reflects a decided shift among colonial policy makers away from the commercial considerations that structured the first Anglo-Afghan war (see above Chapter 2), to an overwhelmingly political orientation to the region fifty years later.

45. See Ferdinand (1962 and 1969), and Rubin (2000), for more on the kochis' role in money lending and property acquisition on local repayment defaults in the Hazarajat in central Afghanistan.

46. "Establishment by the Amir of a Monopoly of the Sale of all Fruit Exported from Afghanistan to British India," NAI, Foreign Secret F, May 1893, Proceeding Nos. 425–4.

47. "Establishment by the Amir of a Monopoly of the Sale of all Fruit Exported from Afghanistan to British India," NAI, Foreign Secret F, May 1893, Proceeding Nos. 425–4, and "Monopoly for the Sale of Fruit, etc., Exported from Afghanistan and Levy of Tolls thereon by the Amir of Kabul," NWFPA, Peshawar Commissioner's Office, Bundle No. 60, Serial No. 1522C.

48. "Levy of Tolls by the Amir's Kafilabashi in Peshawar," Punjab Government, Foreign Frontier, June 1897, Proceeding Nos. 164–69, Part A. This file was consulted at the NWFPA.

49. "Establishment by the Amir of a Monopoly of the Sale of all Fruit Exported from Afghanistan to British India," NAI, Foreign Secret F, May 1893, Proceeding Nos. 425–54, and "Monopoly for the Sale of Fruit, etc., Exported from Afghanistan and Levy of Tolls thereon by the Amir of Kabul," NWFPA, Peshawar Commissioner's Office, Bundle No. 60, Serial No. 1522C.

50. Ibid.

51. "Monopoly for the Sale of Fruit, etc., Exported from Afghanistan and Levy of Tolls thereon by the Amir of Kabul," NWFPA, Peshawar Commissioner's Office, Bundle No. 60, Serial No. 1522C. Arat and the security deposits associated with the fruit trade were distinct forms of new text-based Durrani state exactions imposed on the nomad traders.

52. Although a limited supply of this important commodity was domestically available from mines in Afghan Turkistan, the majority of the salt used in Afghanistan was imported from India.

53. "Monopoly for the Sale of Fruit, etc., Exported from Afghanistan and Levy of Tolls thereon by the Amir of Kabul," NWFPA, Peshawar Commissioner's Office, Bundle No. 60, Serial No. 1522C.

54. Jamrud was and remains a toll post and small fort at the eastern opening of the Khaibar where the pass meets the Peshawar valley. The valley was then entirely subject to colonial administration and remains under Pakistani jurisdiction.

55. To rent additional camels for the transport of Durrani state property the qafilabashi relied on a number of "tahsil thekadars," who functioned as brokers in Peshawar's animal labor market and received an anna or one sixteenth of a rupee on each camel they provided. See "Levy of Tolls by the Amir's Kafilabashi in Peshawar," Punjab Government, Foreign Frontier, June 1897, Proceeding Nos. 164–9, Part A. This file was consulted at the NWFPA.

56. Nomads could and often did receive their qafilabashi passes, and other forms of Durrani state paperwork, directly from the qafilabashi and his monshi at Jamrud.

57. "Question of Levying usual Khaibar Tolls on a Consignment of 100 Cases of Loaf Sugar, Weighing 6½ Tons, Imported Into Afghanistan by the Amir," NWFPA, List of Foreign and Frontier Files, 1880–1900, including a List of Files Transferred from the TARC, 1896-A, Serial No. 271, File No. 27. This file corresponds to Punjab Government, Foreign Frontier Department, February 1896, Proceeding Nos. 31–36, Part A.

58. Ibid.

59. Ibid.

60. Ibid. See above Chapter 4 for more on the Durrani state commercial agent stationed in Karachi.

61. See above Chapter 4 for more on Abd al-Rahman's badami or almond agent in Peshawar. It appears arguments proffered by Durrani and some British officials that the enormous amounts of sugar being imported were being used for legitimate purposes of state ultimately prevailed. The successful reasoning described the circumstances that initiated and validated the Durrani state's dependence on Indian sugar. These included the distribution of huge amounts of various sweets at *durbar* or court during "public" holidays such as *naw ruz* or New Year's and other celebrations including the Islamic calendar holidays or *eids*, its nearly unlimited availability to accompany the tea that was continually consumed by those attending regular court sessions, its use during life course rituals for local notables such as weddings and births when Abd al-Rahman distributed bountiful helpings of sweetmeats to the family/families in question, and the huge supplies of sugar-laden drinks and edibles presented directly to domestic and foreign state guests during their stays in Kabul. There were additional reasons for the British decision to allow the sugar consignments to continue to pass tax-free through the Khaibar. These included their reluctance to review and reevaluate the Jamrud darogha's bookkeeping practices and inhibitions about the appearance of revoking precedent because of how much sugar had already been conveyed to Kabul without paying Khaibar tolls. Furthermore, representatives of an influential business family based in Peshawar that also operated in Kabul and Afghanistan, the Sethis, who were trusted by both British and Durrani officials (see below Chapter 6), claimed that Abd al-Rahman rescinded his plans to monopolize the sugar trade in his realm.

62. "Proposed Withdrawal of Certain of the Agencies of His Highness the Amir at Peshawar," NWFPA, Foreign Frontier Ex. D. D. 1880–1900, Serial No. 1409, Bundle 14. This file corresponds to Punjab Government, Foreign Department Frontier, June 1896, Proceeding Nos. 94–111, Part A.

63. See Yapp, p. 381, where he refers to "the jolt (which the occupation) gave to the whole economy by the import of bullion and the creation of new demands."

64. "Resources and Expenditure of Afghanistan, 1841," NAI, Foreign S.C., 25 October 1842, Proceeding Nos. 32–35. For more on Durrani coins see Dames, King, and Singh, pp. 365–74. The Durrani minting techniques described here can be usefully compared to similar practices in Mughal India and Safavid Iran. For the Mughal era see Allami's *Ain-i Akbari*, vol. I, pp. 16–39 (ains 4–12, including drawings of various mint workmen). For coinage and minting in Safavid Iran see Minorsky's *Tadhkirat al-Muluk*, pp. 58–65 (of the English translation of the original Persian), and the commentary on that portion of text on pp. 126–35.

65. S. M. Khan, vol. II, p. 28. See ibid., pp. 21–31, for Abd al-Rahman's comments

on European machinery in general, and pp. 15–19 for his opinion on the employment of foreigners in Kabul, some of whom accompanied the imported machines and instructed local officials in their use. A Mr. McDermot, formerly employed at the Government Mint in Calcutta, instructed Kabuli workmen in the new minting processes, and Abd al-Rahman took pride that local personnel were soon able to function without McDermot's superintendence. Abd al-Rahman, likely through some kind of an interlocutor, states: "Not only do my workmen coin the rupees, but they also make the dyes and stamps; and since the first set of tools and dies was brought from England we have never had to buy fresh ones, everything is made in Kabul itself." See ibid., p. 32.

66. Kakar (1979), p. 217, indicates the new European minting machinery to have been capable of producing between 40,000 and 120,000 coins a day. Kakar also quotes a figure of 10,000,000 coins produced during the first year of the machinery's placement in Kabul, which would put daily production at about 27,400. Rupee production levels were uneven and determined by the availability of silver that Abd al-Rahman went to extreme lengths to acquire.

67. According to Kakar (1979), p. 216, the copper *paisa* was the primary subunit of a Kabuli rupee against which secondary subunits were valued. He indicates 1 Kabuli rupee was composed of either 60 paisas, 12 copper *shahis*, 3 silver *abbasis*, or 6 silver *sanars*, and that 20 rupees made one *toman*. Kakar also states a Kabuli rupee had the value of 2 *qirans*. Qirans and *tangas* were the silver currencies preponderant in Persia and Bukhara. Other silver currencies circulating in late-nineteenth-century Afghanistan include Chinese *yamus* and Tabrizi *tomans*. Bukharan *tilla* and the Belgian *ducats*, also called Venetians by the British and *bujagli* or *budki* by locals, were two of the gold currencies circulating in Afghanistan during Abd al-Rahman's reign. In addition to the British Indian rupee that was known locally as a kaldar rupee, and the Russian ruble called *surs*. See ibid., p. 236, for another breakdown of Durrani currency and its equivalents. (The change from Company to British Indian rupee came in 1857 when the crown assumed direct oversight of the British East India Company.) Gregorian, p. 401, notes the British Indian rupee was composed of 16 *annas* with each anna being equal to 12 *pice*. Gregorian, p. 402, divides the Kabuli rupee as follows for the nineteenth century: 10 *dinars* to 1 paisa; 5 paisas to 1 copper shahi; 2 shahis to 1 silver sannar or sadinar or misqali; 2 sannar to 1 abbasi or tanga; 1.5 abbasi to 1 kran (qiran); 2 krans to 1 rupee; 2/5 rupees to 1 nim *sanad*; 5 rupees to one sanad; 20 rupees to 1 toman. Adding to the detail is Gray, p. 294. Gray served as Abd al-Rahman's personal surgeon and noted 12 annas composed a rupee and that there was no such coin as an anna in circulation. This odd claim may result from his unconscious resort to exchange rate evaluation, in other words, Gray may have considered 12 annas as the value of a Kabuli rupee in relation to a British Indian rupee, but not have informed his readers of such. He says ½ a rupee formed a qiran, and an anna was composed of five copper coins called paisa. He also indicated 60 or more paisa formed a rupee, the exact rate being determined by moneychangers in the bazaar.

Gray claims the machine-minted rupee to be "scarcely artistic as old: it is Europeanized, and is said to be worth an anna less." Ibid. Gray's final comment on the new machine-minted Kabul rupee is instructive, and will remind readers of Rawlinson's experience in Qandahar: "The Amir is introducing the new rupee into circulation by paying the soldiers of his army with that coin." Ibid.

68. See above Chapter 4. The amount of the subsidy was regularized in 1882 and remained constant at 1 lakh per month until 1893 when it was increased to 18 lakhs per year. On Abd al-Rahman's death, the British declared the subsidy and many other facets of Anglo-Afghan relations null and having been personal to that ruler.

69. Although I conclude this particular accumulated subsidy disbursement went directly to the mint for re-coining, a good deal if not most of these colonial cash grants went to purchase European and Indian commodities through commercial agents and brokers appointed by Abd al-Rahman who were stationed in various Indian cities. See above Chapter 4. Nevertheless, in the case considered here and in many other instances, substantial sums of British rupees were conveyed from Peshawar to Kabul through the Khaibar pass under the direction of the Durrani state-appointed superintendent of caravans. This official, known locally as the qafilabashi, was stationed in Peshawar and was in charge of transporting government property from India to Afghanistan. See later in this chapter for more on the Peshawar qafilabashi.

70. Kakar (1979), p. 217.

71. De facto emphasizes Abd al-Rahman's ability to impose these claims in market settings controlled by neither the British nor the Russians.

72. See Kakar (1979), pp. 215–20. The ban on cash remittances abroad was lifted in 1883 after which Abd al-Rahman imposed a 3 percent duty on such transactions. But this rate also changed, as did the mechanism of its realization, probably unevenly across regions. In this section of his book, Kakar also discusses how ongoing currency debasement led to domestic inflation during Abd al-Rahman's reign.

73. Ibid., p. 205.

74. *Kandahar Newsletters* (1889), pp. 88–89.

75. Ibid. From the Mirza title, it appears the Qandahar Police Chief may not have been relying on physical coercion as much as accountant-based or bookkeeping tactics to mulct the local merchant.

76. *Kandahar Newsletters* (1889), p. 106.

77. *Kandahar Newsletters* (1891), p. 1.

78. Ibid., p. 25. This quote from the British Agent in Qandahar comes from the June 8, 1891, entry.

79. Ibid, p. 3. Abd al-Rahman's collection and confiscation of British Indian or kaldar rupees continued after the opening of the new machine mint in Kabul in 1890 and the closing of the Qandahar mint early in 1891. The Kandahar Newsletter entry from June 8, 1891, also included the following: "A *Tahsildar* has been appointed to collect all

the 'Kaldar' rupees procurable in Kandahar. He is to send his subordinates to the gates of the city and to the bazaar to search for and bring him all 'Kaldar' rupees, as they can find in the possession of the people. Kandahari and Kabuli rupees are to be given to the people in exchange. The 'Kaldar' rupees thus collected are to be sent to Kabul to be re-coined. This puts the people to great inconvenience."

80. S. M. Khan, vol. I, pp. 202–63. The mirzas were the state-appointed accountants, bookkeepers, and collectors who wielded such great power through their reviews and manipulations of various sets of financial records. See earlier in this chapter for more on mirzas.

81. Stoler and Cooper, p. 20.

82. See Kakar (1979), pp. 220–21, for money transfer facilities provided by the state in the form of drafts known as *barats*. See S. M. Khan, vol. II, p. 76, for merchant loans, and ibid., p. 208, for hundis issued by Abd al-Rahman.

83. See ibid., p. 76, for Abd al-Rahman's remonstrance against Indians for this reason.

Chapter 6

1. Interview with Nissar Ahmed Sethi and Manzur Ahmed Sethi, Peshawar, May 15, 1995. The family's move from Bhera to Chamkani probably occurred in the 1820s or 1830s. While in Bhera the Sethis dealt primarily in the export of indigo to Central Asia. Bhera is located near Sargodha and was founded by Sher Shah Suri. Bhera became a center of local governance during the Mughal period and is said to have been plundered by the Durranis. Apparently, Bhera was then re-populated by the Sikhs and thrived under early British rule until waning with the development of canal colonies in the Punjab. The site is now deserted. The preceding information on Bhera comes from a tourist guidebook for Pakistan consulted in Lahore in the spring of 1995 that remains regrettably uncited in my notes.

2. Muhammad Ismail Sethi, interviewed on April 2, 1995, refers to Vladivostok, while other family members cite only Shanghai as the family business branch that organized the export of a variety of Chinese teas to Central Asia.

3. Interviews with Nissar Ahmed Sethi and Manzur Ahmed Sethi, Peshawar, May 15, 1995, and Yunus Sethi, Islamabad, April 12, 1995. Jaji is a *woleswali* or sub-province of Paktia. The Afghan timber was apparently sold to the British who used it, among other ways, in their construction of railroads in India. The Sethis indicate the Jaji forest-leasing privilege was removed from them by Nadir Shah (ruled in Afghanistan from 1929 to 1933), whose reentry into Afghanistan from India the family claims to have funded.

4. Nissar Ahmed Sethi and Manzur Ahmed Sethi (ibid.) indicate their family funded the construction of the Islamiyya College mosque and the renovation of the Mahabat Khan mosque in addition to contributing in some form to mosques near the Reti gate,

Shaheen Bazaar, Namak Mandi, and Sarbani street. They also indicate financial involvement in the madrassa Jettan Yakatut and the Mia Guja bridge across the Barra river.

5. Interview with Yunus Sethi, Islamabad, April 12, 1995.

6. Interview with Muhammad Ismail Sethi, April 2, 1995. See above Chapter 1 for
more on Markovits's model of the Shikarpuri merchant network (see also Markovits,
chs. 3 and 5).

7. In the 1990s, at least, most Sethi family members, as well as the general populace
in Peshawar, dated the end of the firm to the Soviet Revolution of 1917. One prominent
exception to that understanding is Yunus Sethi (interviewed in Islamabad on April 12,
1995) who indicates the family business survived in some form until 1930 when the focus
of activity shifted to exporting furs to England and Germany from Delhi. According to
Yunus, the demise of the family firm came at the beginning of World War II when a ship
carrying some of their furs was sunk on the way to Germany.

8. Interview with Muhammad Ismail Sethi, April 2, 1995. The Sethis had agents in
Bukhara, Samarqand and Tashkent, and this correspondence would have likely occurred
after 1860. The Sethi family member mentioned by Muhammad Ismail who was then in
correspondence with the Viceroy of India may in fact have been Karam Elahi who wrote
to the Viceroy 1914. See later in this chapter.

9. See Kakar (1971), Appendix VII for the text of this agreement, and S. M. Khan,
vol. II, pp. 243–58 for Abd al-Rahman's reasons for wanting a Durrani representative in
London, which never occurred.

10. "Restrictions on the Kabul Agent's Intercourse with His Friends by the Amir,
and the Execution of Taj Muhammad Khan and Others," NAI, Foreign Secret-F K.W.,
February 1885, Proceeding Nos. 346–52. See Kakar (1971), p. 212 for a list of the British
Agents in Kabul during Abd al-Rahman's reign.

11. Ibid. The British Agent was then Sardar Muhammad Afzal Khan and he was visited at his residence in the Murad Khani neighborhood of Kabul (in the chindawul or
Qizilbash section of the city) by his uncle Taj Muhammad Khan and the tutor of his
brothers, Mullah Muhammad Shah. This contact was reported to Abd al-Rahman by a
new "policeman," Jafar Ali. Abd al-Rahman ordered these two men removed from their
homes during the night of 28 January 1885 and confined to an underground cell or *tab-
khana* in the palace of the former Durrani Amir Sher Ali. On February 3, Taj Muhammad
Khan, Mullah Muhammad Shah, and a cousin of the British Agent, Rustam Ali, were
each cut with swords into three pieces. Their remains were placed in a public square or
maidan with a sentry stationed nearby to inform passers by who inquired that the body
parts belonged to spies of the British Agent. In this case and many others Abd al-Rahman
relied on the local kotwal or magistrate and his deputy the naib kotwal to execute his
orders. See S. M. Khan, vol. II, pp. 202–63 for Abd al-Rahman extolling the virtues of his
Intelligence Department composed of spies and detectives "who thwarted the extortion-
ate practices of local chiefs and officials who were accustomed to taking bribes."

12. Ibid. The Peshawar merchant was Mian Ahmad Gul Raur, and his agents, Muhammad Bakhsh Anryal and Muhammad Bakhsh Lakhesar, were from Rawalpindi.

13. "1. Question of Russian Customs Supervision in Central Asia and of the Measures Adopted in Regard to It and 2. The British Agent at Kabul Instructed to ask the Amir to Relax His Heavy Transit Duties," NAI, Foreign Frontier A, December 1885, Proceeding Nos. 3–8.

14. "Proposed Organisation of an Improved News Agency on the Russo-Persian-Afghan Frontier," NAI, Foreign Secret F, March 1886, Proceeding Nos. 303–13.

15. MacGregor was then the Quarter-Master General and is perhaps best known to contemporary scholars as the compiler of the military and political reference handbook on Central Asia, part II of which concerns Afghanistan (see MacGregor).

16. "Proposed Organisation of an Improved News Agency on the Russo-Persian-Afghan Frontier," NAI, Foreign Secret F, March 1886, Proceeding Nos. 303–13.

17. Ibid. Of these seventy-seven, eight resided in Kabul, seventeen in Tashkurgan, thirty-nine in Bukhara, three in Katta Kurgan, two in Karshi, three in Kolab, one in Charjui, one in Yarkand, and four in Ourganj or Khiva. The "tribal" affiliations of these seventy-seven possible recruits were broken down as follows: sixty-seven Paracha, one Lakesar, four Sethi (Mir Ahmad, Ghulam Jelani, and Mokam Din in Khiva, and Rahim Bakhsh in Bukhara), one Matha, one Zargar, one Bhati, one Cabdol. A different breakdown of these seventy-seven possible recruits has forty-four labeled natives of Nowshera, five from Attock, fifteen from Peshawar, nine from Bhera (see earlier in this chapter), and four from Makhad.

18. "Report Compiled by Haji Karam Elahi Sethi of Peshawar Containing an Account of His Visit to Europe and Other Countries," NAI, Foreign General B, March 1914, Proceeding No. 166.

19. Ibid., where we also find the following useful characterizations, first about Bukhara: "As a habit all Bukharis are given more or less to trade which is chiefly comprised in skin, cotton, silk and tea. The first two articles are of local produce, while the last ones wholly or solely depend on China. The business is carried on interest system." The quote in the text is noticeable as evidence that Indian traders were then extending their provisioning of cash and extension of credit into the lower layers and outer reaches of the regional economy centered on Bukhara. This statement also indicates Chinese tea filled the niche resulting in large measure from Abd al-Rahman's transit trade policies that curtailed the flow of Indian tea to Central Asia (see later in this chapter).

20. Ibid. The pawenda nomadic carriers were known for transporting silver-based Kabul rupees and other coins, such gold tillas from Bukhara, to Dera Ismail Khan. In Dera Ismail Khan the Kabul rupee was known as the *Nandrami*, a word having Hindu connotations. See *Gazetteer of the Dera Ismail Khan District, 1883–1884*, p. 149.

21. "Refusal of Permission to Khan Bahadur Haji Karam Elahi Sethi & Messrs. Sher

Ahmed and Iqbal Ahmad of Peshawar, to Import Russian Ruble Notes into Afghanistan," NAI, Foreign and Political, Frontier B, October 1920, Proceeding Nos. 165–66.

22. Ibid.

23. For the increasing consumption of tea in Qajar Iran see Matthee, and for the same in England see Mintz. In both locations the consumption of tea was preferably accompanied by sugar as a condiment. See above Chapter 4 for more on the import of sugar into Afghanistan.

24. "Commercial Relations Existing Between India and Afghanistan and Central Asia," and "Representation Made to the Amir by the Tea Planters of Northern India Regarding the Tea Trade with Central Asian and Afghanistan," NAI, Foreign Secret F, November 1890, Proceeding Nos. 114–29.

25. Ibid. Rs. 6,84,000 is one possible estimate of the potential annual revenue for the Durrani state deriving from tea transit taxes. This figure is arrived at by taking Rs. 114 as the mean between 106 and 120, then multiplying by 6,000, representing the number of camels estimated to have been involved in the tea trade organized by the single consortium under discussion.

26. "Customs and Other Dues Levied in Afghanistan," NAI, Foreign Secret F, May 1893, Proceeding Nos. 287–91. It is important to appreciate that many other categories of commodities in addition to tea were subject to these taxes while moving through Afghanistan. Besides "Indian and Chinese teas," the commodities listed as moving from India to Central Asia in this document are: "candles; raw cotton; manufactured cotton piece goods including European chintz, long cloth, muslin, turkey red, European thread, and Indian piece goods including plain and gold edged lungis, country cloth, and Indian thread; the dyeing materials indigo, tumeric, saffron; earthenware and porcelain; manufactured leather shoes; metals and manufactures of metals including brass, copper, and iron; kerosene oil; salt; manufactured silk kimkhab; spices; refined and unrefined sugar; manufactured woolens including Abra, Kashmiri embroidered cloth, and khalil khani shawls."

27. Regarding these additional fees, the qafilabashi fee is addressed in Chapter 5, and state brokerage is addressed above in Chapter 3 and later in this chapter.

28. S. M. Khan, vol. I, pp. 200–201, and vol. II, pp. 64–65.

29. "Customs and Other Dues Levied in Afghanistan," NAI Foreign Secret F, May 1893, Proceeding Nos. 287–91.

30. "Memorandum of Information Available in the Foreign Department on the Government, Revenue, Population, and Territorial Divisions of Afghanistan," NAI, Foreign Secret (Supplementary), January 1880, Proceeding Nos. 536–44.

31. Ibid.

32. "Proposal to Ask Amir of Afghanistan to Concede Certain Points in Regard to the Trade Carried on With Afghanistan," NAI, Foreign Frontier B, November 1888, Proceeding No. 25.

33. As the tea planters' petition was funneled up and down the colonial bureaucratic

ladder, commentary about the case was attached. Some of that fascinating marginalia has survived the censors' and weeders' cuts. The following excerpts reveal a noticeable British reluctance to complicate Great Game politics with economic realities and address Abd al-Rahman about his commercial conduct: "when advising him to reduce his trade duties (Abd al-Rahman replied) our representation was an interference with his internal affairs (and) he refused point blank to reduce the duties," "I would not put any pressure on (Abd al-Rahman) or write in an aggrieved tone," "I would on no account complicate matters by criticising his financial policy," "we had rather not move in the matter," "it will be convenient to wait a few weeks to see what (Abd al-Rahman's) temper will be like once he has settled down again in Kabul," "the time, I think, has not yet come for administering a lecture on free trade," "we cannot touch the question," "the present would be a particularly unfavorable time for anything of the sort." See "Commercial Relations Existing Between India and Afghanistan and Central Asia," and "Representation Made to the Amir by the Tea Planters of Northern India Regarding the Tea Trade with Central Asian and Afghanistan," NAI, Foreign Secret F, November 1890, Proceeding Nos. 114–29. The British voiced disapproval of Abd al-Rahman's transit trade policies primarily to his Envoy with the Government of India. See "Restrictions Placed by Amir on Trade Passing Through Afghanistan," NAI, Foreign Frontier A, April 1888, Proceeding Nos. 126–32, and above Chapter 4 for more on Durrani state commercial agents in India, including the Envoy. Abd al-Rahman's opinion on free trade can be found in S. M. Khan, vol. II, p. 209: "Though I am not ignorant of the advantages of free trade, yet it is not at present the time for us to adopt the policy of free trade; we are obliged to place certain restrictions on the foreign goods we import."

34. "Restrictions Placed by Amir on Trade Passing Through Afghanistan," NAI, Foreign Frontier A, April 1888, Proceeding Nos. 126–32.

35. Ibid.

36. Ibid.

37. "Customs and Other Dues Levied in Afghanistan," NAI, Foreign Secret F, May 1893, Proceeding Nos. 287–91. In addition to fruit and currencies, which are also addressed above in Chapter 1, the commodities listed as moving to the southeast in this document are animals (horses and mares), silk (raw, and manufactured varieties such as Gulbadan Kanarwez, Jamakarrawa, Satari, Postins and Shashgula, Bistgula, Nim Astin, Astindar, Kot Guldar, Jackets and Bibiana, and plain and worked rugs), wool (manufactured Kabuli Puttoo cloth, and Shinjab and Khazz furs), and drugs and dyes such as opium and asafetida, respectively.

38. "Restrictions Placed by Amir on Trade Passing Through Afghanistan," NAI, Foreign Frontier A, April 1888, Proceeding Nos. 126–32.

39. Ibid.

40. "Transit Duties on Indian Goods Passing Through Afghanistan," NAI Foreign Secret F, June 1887, Proceeding Nos. 181–85, where it is also reported Abd al-Rahman or-

dered Jan Muhammad Khan to "(m)ake a memo of the goods forwarded by the Peshawar merchants to Bokhara through Afghanistan. As they received the money through Moscow and Bombay, they should be called upon to pay duty on it calculated on the value of the goods originally sent through Afghanistan during the last years." The author of the Kabul Newsletter of February 18, 1887, enclosed in this file then comments "[t]he transit dues paid by them from Dakka to Tashkurgan amount to 18 or 20 lakhs of rupees per annum. If they had to pay dues on the cash as well for the last seven years, their shops would be ruined."

41. Ibid. "Mian Fazl-i-Kadir, Mir Ahmad, Muhammad Amin, Mian Ilahi Bakhsh, Ahmad Gul, Mian Abdul Majid, Rahim Bakhsh, Mian Muhammad ud-din, Sadr ud-din, Mian Pir Bakhsh, Shukrullah, Mian Ghulam Muhammad, and Ataullah" were the Peshawar merchants to whom Abd al-Rahman wrote on December 20, 1887.

42. Ibid.

43. Monshi Ahmad Jan is referred to as the "head of the Accounts Office" in the extract from the Kabul Newsletter dated 4 March 1887 enclosed in the file "Transit Duties on Indian Goods Passing Through Afghanistan," NAI, Foreign Secret F, June 1887, Proceeding Nos. 181–85. Abd al-Rahman apparently threatened to double transit dues at or around this time. At least one British official called such a proposal "humorous" and felt that even were it not instituted "the Peshawar trade (would be left) to die a lingering death instead of killing it with a 'short, sharp, shock.'" Ibid.

44. "Information Received by Peshawar Merchants Which Makes Them Cease Trade With Bokhara," NAI, Foreign Secret F, June 1889, Proceeding Nos. 142–55. Abd al-Rahman relied on a diverse and growing class of accountants, secretaries, and clerks, known locally as diwans, sarishtadars and mirzas, to execute his commercial policies and practices. See above Chapter 5 for more on these revenue functionaries and their management of Durrani state texts and account books.

45. Ibid. Haji Asad Khan may have then held the influential post of Naib Kotwal or deputy magistrate in Kabul. The Kabul agents' representation of their two superiors in Peshawar varies from the three people identified in the targeted Peshawri firm. Among the four people identified in those two groupings, only one person, Abdur Rashid, was not among the thirteen Peshawar merchants to whom Abd al-Rahman wrote in December 1887. See earlier in this chapter. In reviewing all of these names the inconsistent application of the title or rank of *Mian* to Muhammad Amin and Fazl Kadir stands out, but the implications of the title in this context are not clear.

46. Ibid.

47. Ibid.

48. Ibid., quoting the Newsletter written by the Monshi to the British Agency in Kabul, Sayyid Diwan Muhammad, dated May 1, 1889.

49. Ibid., citing the Kabul Newsletter of May 8. Muhammad Amin and Mir Ahmad are here identified as firms in their own right.

50. Kakar (1979), pp. 34–35, describes how Abd al-Rahman replaced the Indians on the panchayat with Afghans, thus 'nationalizing an international court.' The panchayat was clearly contrived and manipulated by Abd al-Rahman, and Kakar, ibid., indicates the panchayat "did not influence [Abd al-Rahman's] commercial policy." See above Chapter 1 for more on Abd al-Rahman's panchayat.

51. Ibid. The author of the Newsletter indicated his belief that even if the case was not proved through standard mercantile proceedings, that is, through the panchayat, Abd al-Rahman would nevertheless "seize their firm and take all their property consisting of goods and cash, and they would not say anything." The Durrani state was here estimated to gain "50 lakhs of rupees [if] the case be proved against them."

52. Ibid., quoting the May 15, 1887, Kabul Newsletter.

53. Ibid.

54. The Peshawar Confidential Diary excerpt is quoted in "1. Introduction of New Octroi Duty in Central Asia by Russia, 2. Necessity for the Appointment of a British Consul at Bokhara, 3. Condition of Trade between India and Afghanistan, 4. Depression of British trade in Khorasan," NAI, Foreign Secret F, April 1895, Proceeding Nos. 81–94. See above Chapters 3 and 5 for more on book debt.

Conclusion

1. NAI, Foreign Secret F, April 1895, Proceeding Nos. 81–94.

2. Braudel (1979).

3. Today, Afghanistan's state budget is approximately 90 percent subsidized by external capital. This leaves the state virtually dependent on that capital and significantly effected by the competing agendas behind its provisioning. See later in this chapter.

4. See for example http://www.usaid.gov/press/factsheets/2003/fs031214_1.html .

5. http://www.bergerafghanistan.com/ and http://www.louisberger.com/ .

6. On October 7, 2002, a new Afghan state paper currency set, printed in Germany and Britain, was introduced in Kabul and gradually but incompletely phased there and in other markets over the next few weeks. On January 2, 2003, its value was dramatically reconfigured in relation to the U.S. dollar, on the order of one thousand degrees of paper strength, moving from 4726.30 on January 1, 2003, to 42.7850 the next day (see http://www.oanda.com for currency conversion statistics). The Afghan state's budget for the solar year 1384 (2005) was based on $333 million in domestic revenue and $3,178 million in external donor assistance. This means that the Afghan government relies on donations for nearly 90 percent of its revenue, and gathers slightly more than 10 percent of its resources from domestic sources. The Donor Assistance Data base, run by the Synergy International Systems (http://www.synisys.com) Technology Firm that is based as least partially in Vienna, Virginia, in the suburbs of Washington, D.C., is the bureaucratic space where patrons and clients can exchange fiscal information and track

resource flows. According to the company's fact sheet, "(t)he Donor Assistance Database (DAD) is an Aid Management and Coordination system for use in national reconstruction environments that strengthens the effectiveness and transparency of international assistance. DAD is a powerful, Web-based information collection, tracking, analysis, and planning tool for use by national governments and the broader assistance community, including bilateral donors, international organizations, and NGOs." The DAD does not appear to be accessible to the general public, but one link to it is through the United Nations Development Programme's Afghanistan Web site at http://www.undp.org.af/. Similar to the impact of the British subsidy for Abd al-Rahman and Afghanistan, the sources, intentions, means of transmitting, and handling external funding have significant domestic implications for the current regime and state-society relations in the country now and in the future.

7. For a view of the hawala system from the vantage point of a diaspora hawaladar, see S. M. Hanifi (2006), wherein citations to additional hawala literature can be found.

8. See Allen (2004) and Goodhand (2000 and 2005) for considerations of Afghanistan's opium economy. Local memories of the economic hardships caused by the failure of the Helmand Valley Project, a U.S.-funded (privately through the Morrison-Knudsen Corporation first, then by the United States Agency for International Development) project designed for Afghanistan's "development and modernization" in the Cold War era may contribute to today's resistance to internationally sponsored *cum* Afghan state "alternative livelihood" initiatives and projects in the region. For more on the first phases of what appears historically as an ongoing Helmand Valley development project, see Calluther and Michel, and 1954 USG document "Obtaining Financial Aid for a Development Plan."

9. See Yapp, Part III.

10. See, for example, http://www.aisa.org.af/Media/mag-vol-01/Benefits.html.

11. See Louis Dupree's (1989) comment about the ethnography of Afghanistan in the *Encylopaedia Iranica* to the effect that everything said about "Afghan peoples and cultures" since Elphinstone comprises mere footnotes to the foundational colonial appraisal of the country.

12. See Ardner for some brief insights about "remote areas" that belie orientalist renditions of remoteness that connote social homogeneity and historical stasis.

Sources and Notes for
Maps and Figures

———◆·◆———

Maps

Map I.1. Interregional Satellite Map, 2008, page 4. Image courtesy of Qais Jabar Hanifi, created using ESRI software. See http://www.esri.com/. To understand the major markets of Afghanistan in their own right and in relation to one another and to external market stimuli, one must utilize an interregional perspective encompassing land and sea routes, specifically a combined Silk Road and Indian Ocean commercial network frame of reference. Awareness of long-distance trade and migration patterns and other transnational phenomena necessarily involves intellectual migrations through Middle East, South Asia, and Central Asia regional studies literatures.

Map I.2. Kabul, Peshawar, and Qandahar Satellite View, 2008, page 5. Image courtesy of Qais Jabar Hanifi, created using ESRI software. See http://www.esri.com/. The markets of our concern are identified here. Market relations between Kabul, Peshawar, and Qandahar have been constructed by humans but are determined in the first and final instance by geography.

Maps I.3, I.4, and I.5. Proto-Afghanistan 1844, 1846, and 1851, pages 14, 16, and 17. Images courtesy of David Rumsey. See http://www.davidrumsey.com. These three maps, and other maps like them (see http://www.gutenberg-e.org/hanifi/detail/slideshow. html), succinctly demonstrate how Afghanistan is at first unmapped, then emerges faintly in the vicinity of Kabul, Qandahar, and Peshawar. After the first Anglo-Afghan war, the colonial category Afghanistan "competes" with Kabul and Qandahar, while Peshawar becomes firmly ensconced in British India with the creation of the North West Frontier Province in 1849. Afghanistan eventually triumphs over Kabul and Qandahar, with the former favored and viewed as central, and the latter marginalized in cartographic and, as the narrative of this book demonstrates, economic terms. These maps are of European and North American provenance, and I am grateful to David Rumsey for their use. The boundary-based and border-focused literature of Afghanistan and surrounding areas in the Middle East, South Asia, and Central Asia is not fully engaged in this book. A good entrée to these issues and areas is Hopkins (2007). The issues surrounding maps and mapping of national categories are not engaged here, one reason being that Afghanistan's "historic lag time" renders "nationalism" largely a twentieth-century phenomenon for Afghanistan. Nationalism in twentieth-century Afghanistan is usefully considered by both Gregorian and Schinasi, while the growing literature on national historic cartography was in many ways mapped on to contemporary academic discourse through the work of Winichakul.

Figures

Figure 1.1. Grape Drying Hut in Vineyard, 2004, page 40. Image courtesy of the Afghanistan Research and Evaluation Unit (originally published in Lister et al., p. 4). See http://www.areu.org.af/. Grape-drying huts are often found in or near vineyards.

Figure 1.2. Peshawar Market, 1930s, page 40. Image courtesy of Omar Khan. See http://www.harappa.com/. This Peshawar scene from the 1930s captures the export dimension of this local economy.

Figure 2.1. Full Accounting of Sayyid Muhin Shah's Fourth British-Sponsored Commercial Experiment in Central Asia, 1835, page 59. From "Results of Muhim Shah's Commercial Speculation," NAI, Foreign P.C., August 17, 1835, Proceeding nos. 70–73.

Figure 2.2. Afghan Nomads and Commerce, 1978, page 73. Image courtesy of Luke Powell. See http://www.lukepowell.com/. Kochis, Lohanis, and Pawendas are the communities most associated with transportation of commodities to, between, and beyond Kabul, Peshawar, and Qandahar during the nineteenth century. See the Introduction for attention to cultural and historical distinctions between these communities that perform vital commercial services for the region. The Ghilzai group shown here has halted in the Helmand province that gravitates primarily toward Qandahar's commercial orbit.

Figure 4.1. Kabul Subsidy Receipt, 1908, page 100. Copyright 2008 by author. The subsidy was arguably the key element in Anglo-Durrani relations throughout the nineteenth and well into the twentieth century. Although this particular subsidy receipt comes from 1908, it represents an important component in the structure of relations between the Durrani state and British India during the 1800s.

Figure 4.2. Abd al-Rahman Document for John P. Guthrie, 1898, page 112. Copyright 2008 by author. There are a few points worth noting before providing the translation of this document. First, the subject of this text is John P. Guthrie, whose name is inconsistently expressed throughout the document. Second, the "engine" referenced is the mash-in khana or Durrani state workshop complex in Kabul, and "tartuqi" carries a number of connotations including "wheeled" and "heavy." Furthermore, "Jadid al-Islam" means a convert to Islam, and in this case Muhammad Salim was likely born a Hindu or a Sikh. Finally, it is important to draw attention to Abd al-Rahman's own handwritten signature, appended to which is the acronym of an English title.

Translation: "It is known to my dear friend, the Honorable Mr. Merk Sahib, Commissioner of Peshawar, that the respected Mr. John P. Kotrie has returned from London and might now be in Peshawar. Since your friend desires him [Kotrie] to come to Kabul for the oversight of the engine, we have sent the trustworthy Muhammad Salim Khan, jadid al-Islam, to Peshawar to accompany the above-named [Kotrie] and [together] come to Kabul. I ask my kind friend that the herein named Mr. John P. Gotrie who has some wheeled or heavy equipment with him and wants to bring them to me, accompanied by the above-named Muhammad Salim Khan who has come from and [is] returning to Kabul, to issue them letters of transit [rahdari] and cause your friend not to worry and that they [Salim and Kotrie] will not be delayed.

"Lastly, with God's mercy, all is well. Written on Wednesday, 28 Ramadan al-Mubarak 1314 Hijri corresponding to 3 March 1897. Sealed and signed, Amir Abd al-Rahman, Zia al-Millat wa Din, G. C. S. I. G. C. B."

Figure 4.3. Mashin Khana Aerial Photograph, c. 1928, page 116. Image courtesy of May Schinasi (originally published in Schinasi, facing page 137).

Figure 4.4. Mashin Khana Interior Illustration, 1893, page 116. It is unclear whether this image is from *The Graphic* or *The London Illustrated News*. Image is from May 1893. Copyright 2008 by author. This image of the mashin khana is notable for referencing the use of steam power, which was incorporated into older production processes involving ropes and pulleys. The original caption also compares the industries in Kabul with that of India, and it is important to note that most of Afghanistan's "industrial modernity" was modeled on European processes and techniques as filtered through British India. In that sense India was Afghanistan's window and doorway to the world, and the Europeans employed by Abd al-Rahman such as those portrayed in the image were the key actors in this transfer of modern technology, much of which was geared toward the production of military hardware and supplies. See Figure 4.2 for a state document dealing with the movements of one of those European technocratic confidantes of Abd al-Rahman.

Figure 5.1. Landowners and Laborers in Kabul, 1878, page 128. Image courtesy of the National Army Museum, London. See http://www.national-army-museum.ac.uk/. This image is from the John Burke collection that comprises the first series of photographs relevant to the market region and period of our concern that were taken in the context of the second Anglo-Afghan war. For more from the Burke Collection see O. Khan.

Figure 5.2. Public Execution, 1913, page 129. Image is from Le Petit Journal, 1913, page 380. Copyright 2008 by author. This form of public execution by cannon may have been used prior to Abd al-Rahman's reign in Kabul, but it became more common there during his reign. Staged killing for public display continued episodically through the twentieth century and remains a periodic practice for competitors for state power in Kabul in the twenty-first century.

Bibliography

Abd Allah. 1969 (1576–77). *Tarikh-i Daudi.* S. Abdur Rashid (ed.). Aligarh: Aligarh Muslim University.

Adamec, Ludwig W. 1996. *Dictionary of Afghan Wars, Revolutions, and Insurgencies.* Lanham, Maryland: The Scarecrow Press, Inc.

———. 1991. *Historical Dictionary of Afghanistan.* Metuchen, New Jersey: The Scarecrow Press, Inc.

Akhtar, M. Saleem. 1990. *Sind under the Mughuls: An Introduction to, Translation of and Commentary on the Mazhar-i Shahjahani of Yusuf Mirak (1044/1634).* Islamabad: National Institute of Historical and Cultural Research.

Akin, David, and Joel Robbins (eds.). 1999. *Money and Modernity: State and Local Currencies in Melanesia.* Pittsburgh: University of Pittsburgh Press.

Alam, Muzaffar. 1994. "Trade, State Policy and Regional Change: Aspects of Mughal-Uzbek Commercial Relations, c. 1550–1750." *Journal of the Economic and Social History of the Orient* 37 (3): 202–27.

———. 1986 [1993]. *The Crisis of Empire in Mughal North India.* Karachi: Oxford University Press.

Ali, Shahamat. 1847. *The Sikhs and Afghans, in Connexion with the India and Persia, Immediately before and after the Death of Ranjeet Singh; from the journal of an expedition to Kabul, through the Panjab and the Khaibar Pass.* London: John Murray.

Allami, Abul Fazl. 1989 [c. 1598–99]. *The A'in-i Akbari.* H. Blochman (trans.). Delhi: Low Price Publications.

Allan, Nigel, J. R. 2004. "Opium Production in Afghanistan and Pakistan." In Michael K. Steinberg (ed.), *Dangerous Harvest: Drug Plants and the Transformation of Indigenous Landscapes.* Cary, North Carolina: Oxford University Press.

Allen, I. N. 1843. *Diary of a March through Sinde and Affghanistan with Troops under the Command of General Sir William Nott, K. C. B., & C.* London: J. Hatchard and Son.

Ansari, Bayazid. c. 1560. *Khair ul-Bayan.* London: British Museum, Pakhto MS (microfilm).

Appadurai, Arjun. 1992 [1986]. "Introduction: Commodities and the Politics of Value." In Arjun Appadurai (ed.), *The Social Life of Things: Commodities in Cultural Perspective*. Cambridge: Cambridge University Press.

Ardener, Edwin. 1989. "Remote Areas: Some Theoretical Considerations." In Malcolm Chapman (ed.), *The Voice of Prophecy and Other Essays*. New York: Blackwell.

Arlinghaus, Joseph T. 1988. *The Transformation of Afghan Tribal Society: Tribal Expansion, Mughal Imperialism and the Roshaniyya Insurrection, 1450–1600*. Ann Arbor: University Microfilms International. (PhD dissertation, Duke University)

Astarabadi, Muhammad Mehdi Khan. 1875 [1765–66]. *Tarikh-i Jahangusha-ye Nadiri*. Bombay: Matba-i Haidari.

Babur, Mirza Zahiruddin Muhammad. 1993 [Persian translation of Turki text c. 1757–58]. *Baburnama: Three Parts*. W. M. Thackson Jr. (trans. and ed.). Cambridge, Massachusetts: Harvard University, Department of Near Eastern Languages and Civilizations.

Balikci, Asen. 1981. "Pastoralism and Class Differentiation among the Lakenkhel." *Journal of Asian and African Studies* 16 (1–2): 150–57.

Balland, Daniel. 1991. "Nomadism and Politics: The Case of Afghan Nomads in the Subcontinent." *Studies in History* (n.s.) 7 (2): 205–29.

Barani, Ziya ud-Din. 1974 [c. 1320]. *Tarikh-i Firoz Shahi*. Lahore: Sind Sagar Academy.

Barfield, Thomas J. 1993. *The Nomadic Alternative*. Englewood Cliffs, New Jersey: Prentice-Hall, Inc.

Barth, Fredrik. 1969. "Introduction." In Fredrik Barth (ed.), *Ethnic Groups and Boundaries: The Social Organization of Cultural Difference*. Boston: Little, Brown and Company.

———. 1964. "Ethnic Processes on the Pathan-Baluch Boundary." In *Indo-Iranica: Melanges Presentes a Georg Morgenstierne*. Wiesbaden: O. Harrassowitz.

———. 1961. *Nomads of South Persia: The Basseri Tribe of the Khamseh Confederacy*. Boston: Little, Brown and Company.

Bayly, C. A. 1996. *Empire and Information: Intelligence Gathering and Social Communication in India, 1780–1870*. Cambridge: Cambridge University Press.

———. 1989. *Imperial Meridian: The British Empire and the World, 1780–1830*. London: Longman.

———. 1988 [1983]. *Rulers, Townsmen and Bazaars: North Indian Society in the Age of British Expansion, 1770–1870*. Cambridge: Cambridge University Press.

Beck, Lois. 1986. *The Qashqa`i of Iran*. New Haven: Yale University Press.

Beley, Mathieu, and Barnett Rubin. 2004. "The Benefits and Drawbacks of doing Business in Afghanistan." *Afghanistan Investment and Support Agency Media Magazine* I. http://www.aisa.org.af/Media/mag-vol-01/Benefits.html.

Bell, Marjorie Jewett. 1948. *An American Engineer in Afghanistan: From the Letters and Notes of A. C. Jewett*. Minneapolis: The University of Minnesota Press.

Bentley, G. Carter. 1987. "Ethnicity as Practice." *Comparative Studies in Society and History* 29 (1): 24–55.

Bernier, Francois. 1891. [French original]. *Travels in the Mogul Empire, A. D. 1656–1668.* Archibal Constable (trans.). Karachi: Indus Publications.

al-Beruni, Abu Rayhan. 1964 [c. 1020]. *Alberuni's India.* Eduard Sachau (trans. and ed.). London: S. Chand.

Bose, Sugata. 2006. *A Hundred Horizons: The Indian Ocean in the Age of Global Empire.* Cambridge, Massachusetts: Harvard University Press.

Bosworth, Clifford Edmund. 1984. "The Coming of Islam to Afghanistan." In Yohanan Friedmann (ed.), *Islam in Asia: Volume 1 South Asia.* Boulder: Westview Press.

———. 1977. *The Later Ghaznavids, Splendour and Decay: The Dynasty in Afghanistan and Northern India, 1040–1186.* New York: Columbia University Press.

———. 1963. *The Ghaznavids: Their Empire in Afghanistan and Eastern Iran, 994–1040.* Edinburgh: University Press.

Boulnois, Luce. 2004. *Silk Road: Monks, Warriors & Merchants on the Silk Road.* Hong Kong: Odyssey.

Boxberger, Linda. 2002. *On the Edge of Empire: Hadhramawt, Emigration, and the Indian Ocean, 1880s–1930s.* Albany: State University of New York Press.

Braudel, Fernand. 1979. *Civilization and Capitalism, 15th–18th Century.* 3 Vols. (1, Structures of Everyday Life, 2, The Wheels of Commerce, 3, The Perspective of the World). New York: Harper and Row.

———. 1973 [1967]. *Capitalism and Material Life, 1400–1800.* New York: Harper and Row.

Broadman, Harry G. 2007. *Africa's Silk Road: China and India's New Economic Frontier.* Washington, D.C.: The World Bank.

Burnes, Alexander. 1992 [1834]. *Travels into Bokhara; Being the Account of a Journey from India to Cabool, Tartary, and Persia; Also a Narrative of a Voyage on the Indus.* 3 vols. New Delhi: J. Jetley for Asian Educational Services.

Burnes, Alexander, R. Leech, P. B. Lord, and J. Wood (eds.). 1839. *Reports and Papers, Political, Geographical, and Commercial.* Calcutta: G. H. Huttmann, Bengal Military Orphan Press.

Caroe, Olaf. 1992 [1958]. *The Pathans: 550 B. C.–A. D. 1957.* Karachi: Oxford University Press.

Chakrabarti, Dilip K. 1990. *The External Trade of the Indus Civilization.* New Delhi: Munshiram Manoharlal Publishers.

Chandra, Satish. 1987. *The Indian Ocean: Explorations in History, Commerce, and Politics.* New Delhi: Sage Publications.

Chaudhuri, K. N. 1993. "The Unity and Disunity of Indian Ocean History from the Rise of Islam to 1750: The Outline of a Theory and Historical Discourse." *Journal of World History* 4 (1): 1–22.

———. 1985. *Trade and Civilisation in the Indian Ocean: An Economic History from the Rise of Islam to 1750.* Cambridgeshire: Cambridge University Press.

Christian, David. 2000. "Silk Roads or Steppe Roads? The Silk Roads in World History." *Journal of World History* 2 (1): 1–26.

Cohn, Bernard S. 1996. *Colonialism and Its Forms of Knowledge: The British in India.* Princeton: Princeton University Press.

———. 1987. *An Anthropologist among the Historians and Other Essays.* Delhi: Oxford University Press.

Conolly, Arthur. 1838. *Journey to the North of India, Overland from England, through Russia, Persia, and Affghaunistaun.* 2 vols. London: Richard Bentley.

Cullather, Nick. 2002. "Damming Afghanistan: Modernization in a Buffer State." *The Journal of American History* 89 (2): 512–37.

Curtin, Philip D. 1996 [1984]. *Cross-Cultural Trade in World History.* Cambridge: Cambridge University Press.

Dale, Stephen Frederic. 1994. *Indian Merchants and Eurasian Trade, 1600–1750.* Cambridge: Cambridge University Press.

Dames, M. Longworth. 1888. "The Coins of the Durranis." *Numismatic Chronicle* VIII: 325–63.

Dani, Ahmad Hasan. 1995. *Peshawar: Historic City of the Frontier.* Lahore: Sang-e-Meel Publications.

Darweza, Akhund (Abdul Karim Nangrahari). c. 1580. *Makhzan-i Afghani.* Pashto MS. Oxford: Bodelian Library #2350.

Das Gupta, Ashin. 1979. *Indian Merchants and the Decline of Surat: c. 1700–1750.* Wiesbaden: Steiner.

Das Gupta, Ashin, and Uma Dasgupta. 2001. *The World of the Indian Ocean Merchant, 1500–1800: Collected Essays of Ashin Das Gupta.* New Delhi: Oxford University Press.

Davies, R. H. 1862. *Report on the Trade and Resources of the Countries on the North-Western Boundary of British India.* Lahore: Government Press.

Dictionary of National Biography. 1885–1901. 66 vols. Leslie Stephen (ed.). London: Smith, Elder, & Co. (entries for Henry Vansittart, Sir William Jones, Mountstuart Elphinstone, Alexander Burnes, Claude Wade, Henry George Raverty)

Dorn, Bernhard. 1829–36. *History of the Afghans.* London: Susil Gupta.

Duarte, Adrian. 1976 [n.d.]. *A History of British Relations with Sind, 1613–1843.* Karachi: National Book Foundation.

Dupree, Louis. 1994 [1973]. *Afghanistan.* New Delhi: Rama Publishers.

———. 1989. "Afghanistan iv: Ethnography." *Encyclopaedia Iranica,* Vol. I, pp. 495–501.

Dupree, Nancy Hatch. 1990. "Chehel Sutun, Kabul." *Encyclopaedia Iranica,* Vol. V, pp. 115–16.

———. 1977 [1970]. *An Historical Guide to Afghanistan.* Kabul: Afghan Air Authority and Afghan Tourist Organization.

Eaton, Richard M. 2006. "The Rise and Fall of Military Slavery in the Deccan, 1450–1650." In Indrani Chatterjee and Richard M. Eaton (eds.), *Slavery & South Asian History*. Bloomington: Indiana University Press.

Edwards, David B. 1996. *Heroes of the Age: Moral Fault Lines on the Afghan Frontier*. Berkeley: University of California Press.

Eisenstein, Elizabeth L. 1983. *The Printing Revolution in Early Modern Europe*. Cambridge: Cambridge University Press.

Elphinstone, Mountstuart. 1992 [1815]. *An Account of the Kingdom of Caubul, and Its Dependencies in Persia, Tartary, and India*. 2 vols. Karachi: Indus Publications.

Emerson, John, and Willem Floor. 1987. "Rahdars and Their Tolls in Safavid and Afsharid Iran." *Journal of the Economic and Social History of the Orient* 30 (3): 318–27.

Faiz Muhammad Katib. 1913–15. *Seraj al-Tawarikh*. 3 vols. Kabul: Matb'a-i Hurufi-ye dar al-Sultana-ye Kabul.

Fattah, Hala. 1997. *The Politics of Regional Trade in Iraq, Arabia, and the Gulf, 1745–1900*. Albany: State University of New York Press.

Ferdinand, Klaus. 1969. "Nomadism in Afghanistan: With an Appendix on Milk Products." In Laszlo Foldes (ed.). *Viehwirtschaft und Hirtenkultur: Ethnographische Studien*. Budapest: Akademiai Kiado.

———. 1962. "Nomad Expansion and Commerce in Central Afghanistan." *Folk* 4: 122–59.

Fleischer, Cornell H. 1986. *Bureaucrat and Intellectual in the Ottoman Empire: The Historian Mustafa Ali (1541–1600)*. Princeton: Princeton University Press.

Franck, Peter G. 1960. *Afghanistan between East and West: The Economics of Competitive Coexistence*. Washington, D.C.: National Planning Association.

Frederiksen, Birthe, and Ida Nicolaisen. 1996. *Caravans and Trade in Afghanistan: The Changing Life of the Nomadic Hazarbuz*. London: Thames and Hudson.

Frye, Maxwell J. 1974. *The Afghan Economy: Money, Finance, and the Critical Constraints to Economic Development*. Leiden: E. J. Brill.

Furdoonjee, Nowrozjee. "Report on the Weights, Measures, and Coins of Cabool and Bokhara." In Burnes et al.

Gankovsky, Yu. V. 1982 [1981]. "The Durrani Empire." In *Afghanistan Past and Present*. Moscow: U.S.S.R. Academy of Sciences.

Gankovsky, Yu. V. (ed.). 1985 [1982]. *A History of Afghanistan*. Moscow: Progress Publishers.

Gazetteer of Afghanistan, Vol. 6: Kabul and Southeastern Afghanistan. 1985 [1914]. Ludwig W. Adamec (ed.). Graz, Austria: Akademische Druck-u. Verlagsanstalt.

Gazetteer of the Dera Ismail Khan District, 1883–84. 1989 [1884]. Punjab Government (ed.). Lahore: Sang-e-Meel Publications.

Gazetteer of the Zhob District. 1907. Punjab Government (ed.). Bombay: Bombay Education Society Press.

Geertz, Clifford. 1973. "The Integrative Revolution: Primordial Sentiments and Civil Politics in New States." In Clifford Geertz (ed.), *The Interpretation of Cultures.* New York: Basic Books.

Gommans, Jos J. L. 1995. *The Rise of the Indo-Afghan Empire, c. 1710–1780.* Leiden: E. J. Brill.

Goodhand, Jonathan. 2005. "Frontiers and Wars: The Opium Economy in Afghanistan." *Journal of Agrarian Change* 5(2): 191–216.

———. 2000. "From Holy War to Opium War: A Case Study in Badakhshan." *Disasters* 24(2): 87–102.

Goody, Jack. 1996. *The East in the West.* Cambridge: Cambridge University Press.

———. 1988 [1986]. *The Logic of Writing and the Organization of Society.* Cambridge: Cambridge University Press.

Gray, John Alfred. 1987 [1895]. *At the Court of the Amir: A Narrative.* London: Darf Publishers, Ltd.

Gregorian, Vartan. 1969. *The Emergence of Modern Afghanistan: The Politics of Reform and Modernization, 1880–1946.* Stanford: Stanford University Press.

Habib, Irfan. 1986 [1982]. *An Atlas of the Mughal Empire: Political and Economic Maps with Detailed Notes, Bibliography, and Index.* Delhi: Oxford University Press.

Habibi, A. H. 1971. "Khaljis are Afghan Tarak or Turk." *Afghanistan* 24 (2–3): 76–87.

Haig, Wolseley (ed.). 1928. *The Cambridge History of India, v. 3, Turks and Afghans.* New York: Macmillan Co.

Hamilton, Angus. 1906. *Afghanistan.* London: William Heinemann.

Hanifi, M. Jamil. 2004. "Editing the Past: Colonial Production of Hegemony through the 'Loya Jerga' in Afghanistan." *Iranian Studies* 37 (2): 295–322.

———. 2000. "Anthropology and the Representations of Recent Migrations from Afghanistan." In Elzbieta M. Gozdziak and Dianna J. Shandy (eds.), *Rethinking Refuge and Displacement: Selected Papers on Refugees and Immigrants, Vol. VIII.* Arlington: American Anthropological Association.

Hanifi, Shah Mahmoud. 2008. "Jalalabad." *Encyclopaedia Iranica* Vol. XIV, Fascicle 4, pp. 400–403.

———. 2006. "Material and Social Remittances to Afghanistan." In C. Wescott and J. Brinkerhoff (eds.), *Converting Migration Drains into Gains: Harnessing the Resources of Overseas Professionals.* Manila: The Asian Development Bank.

———. 2004. "Sulayman Khel." *The Encyclopedia of Islam (new edition).* Supplement Fasc. 11–12, p. 763.

Harlan, Josiah. 1862. *On the Fruits of Kabul and Vicinity, with a View to the Introduction of the Grapevine of that Region in the Central Climate of the United States.* U.S. Congress. Senate. *Report of the Commissioner of Patents for the Year 1861, Agriculture.* 37th Cong., 2nd sess., 1862. S. Exec. Doc. 39. Serial Set 1122, Session Vol. 5. Readex. Archive of Americana. U.S. Congressional Serial Set. Record Number: 106F11B5654A18C8.

————. 1854. *On the Importation of Camels: Agricultural Report. Report of the Commissioner of Patents for the Year 1853, Agriculture*. 33rd Cong., 1st sess., 1854. S. Exec. Doc. 27, pt. 2. Serial Set 697, Session Vol. 7. Readex. Archive of Americana. U.S. Congressional Serial Set. Record Number: 1079B144DC2CD460.

Hart, Lockyer, Willis Atkinson, and Charles James Haghe. 1843. *Character and Costumes of Afghanistan*. London: H. Graves & Co.

Haziya, Muhammad Kabir. n.d. *Afsanah-i Shahan*. London: British Museum MS Add. 24,409.

Hill, Julie. 2006. *The Silk Road Revisited: Markets, Merchants and Minarets*. Bloomington: AuthorHouse.

Ho, Engseng. 2006. *The Graves of Tarim: Genealogy and Mobility across the Indian Ocean*. Berkeley: University of California Press.

Hopkins, B. D. 2008. *The Making of Modern Afghanistan*. New York: Palgrave Macmillan.

————. 2007. The Bounds of Identity: The Goldsmid Mission and the Delineation of the Perso-Afghan Border in the Nineteenth Century. *Journal of Global History* 2 (2): 233–54.

Hough, W. 1841. *A Narrative of the March and Operations of the Army of the Indus, in the Expedition to Affghanistan in the Years 1838–1839*. London: Wm. H. Allen and Co.

al-Hussaini, Mahmud ibn Ibrahim. 1974 [c. 1773]. *Tarikh-i Ahmad Shahi*. 2 vols. D. Saidmuradov (ed.). Moscow. U.S.S.R. Academy of Sciences.

Irons, William. 1979. "Political Stratification among Pastoral Nomads." In *Pastoral Production and Society*.

Iqbal, Afzal. 1976 [1975]. *Circumstances Leading to the First Afghan War*. Lahore: Research Society of Pakistan, University of the Punjab.

Jenkyns, W. 1879. *Report on the District of Jalalabad, Chiefly in Regard to Revenue*. Calcutta: Foreign Department Press.

Jones, Sir William and Henry Vansittart. 1979 [1790]. "On Descent of the Afghans from the Jews." *Asiatic Researchers Comprising History and Antiquities, the Arts, Sciences, and Literature of Asia*, Vol. 2, pp. 54–61.

Juzjani, Minhah Siraj. 1970. *Tabakat-I-Nasiri: A General History of the Muhammadan Dynasties of Asia, Including Hindustan; from A.H. 194 (810 A.D.) to A.H. 658 (1260 A.D.) and the Irruption of the Infidel Mughals into Islam*. H. G. Raverty (ed. and trans.). New Delhi: Oriental Books and Munshiram Manoharlal.

Kakar, M. Hasan K. 1979. *Government and Society in Afghanistan: The Reign of Amir 'Abd Al-Rahman Khan*. Austin: University of Texas Press.

————. 1971. *Afghanistan: A Study in International Political Developments, 1880–1896*. Lahore: Punjab Education Press.

Kandahar Newsletters, 1880–1905. 1990. 10 vols. Directorate of Archives Department (ed.). Quetta: Government of Baluchistan (Pakistan).

Kasaba, Resat. 1988. *The Ottoman Empire and the World Economy: The Nineteenth Century.* Albany: State University of New York Press.

Kaye, John William. 1851. *History of the War in Afghanistan.* 2 vols. London: Richard Bentley.

Khan, Hussain. 1994 [1987]. *Sher Shah Sur "Ustad-I-Badshahan Humayun"* alias Sher Shah Suri. Lahore: Ferozsons.

Khan, Omar. 2002. *From Kashmir to Kabul: The Photographs of John Burke and William Baker, 1860–1900.* Munich: Prestel.

Khan, Sultan Mahomed. 1980 [1900]. *The Life of Abdur Rahman, Amir of Afghanistan, G.C.B., G.C.S.I.* 2 vols. Karachi: Oxford University Press.

Khazanov, Anatoly. 1986 [1983]. *Nomads and the Outside World.* Julia Crookenden (trans.). Cambridge: Cambridge University Press.

Khoury, Philip S., and Joseph Kostiner (eds.). 1990. *Tribes and State Formation in the Middle East.* Berkeley: University of California Press.

King, L. White. 1896. "History and Coinage of the Barakzai Dynasty of Afghanistan." *Numismatic Chronicle* XVI: 277–347.

Kumar, Sunil. 2006. "Service, Status, and Military Slavery in the Delhi Sultanate: Thirteenth and Fourteenth Centuries." In Indrani Chatterjee and Richard M. Eaton (eds.), *Slavery & South Asian History.* Bloomington: Indiana University Press.

Kurin, Richard. 2002. "The Silk Road—The Making of a Global Cultural Economy." *AnthroNotes* 23 (1).

Lal, Kishori Saran. 1967. *History of the Khaljis, A.D. 1290–1320.* Bombay: Asia Publishing House.

Lal, Mohan. 1978 [1846]. *Life of the Amir Dost Muhammed Khan of Kabul.* 2 vols. Karachi: Oxford University Press.

———. 1977 [1846]. *Travel in the Punjab, Afganistan and Turkistan to Balk, Bokhara and Herat and a Visit to Great Britain and Germany.* Calcutta: K. P. Bagchi.

Levi, Scott Cameron. 2002. *The Indian Diaspora in Central Asia and Its Trade, 1550–1900.* Leiden: Brill.

Lindholm, Charles. 1980. "Images of Pathan: The Usefulness of Colonial Ethnography." *Archives Europeanes Sociologique* 21: 350–61.

Lister, Sarah, and Tom Brown with Zainiddin Karaev. 2004. *Understanding Markets in Afghanistan: A Case Study in the Raisin Market.* Afghanistan Research and Evaluation Unit.

Lockhart, L. 1993 [1938]. *Nadir Shah: A Critical Study Based Mainly upon Contemporary Sources.* Jalandhar, India: Asian Publishers.

———. 1958. *The Fall of the Safavi Dynasty and the Afghan Occupation of Persia.* Cambridge: Cambridge University Press.

Macintyre, Ben. 2004. *The Man Who Would Be King: The First American in Afghanistan.* New York: Farrar Straus, and Giroux.

MacGregor, C. M. 1995 [1871]. *Central Asia, Part II: A Contribution toward the Better Knowledge of the Topography, Ethnology, Resources, and History of Afghanistan.* Petersfield, U.K.: Barbican Publishing Company Limited.

MacKenzie, D. N. 1964. "The Xayr ul-bayan." In Morgenstierne 1964.

Markovits, Claude. 2000. *The Global World of Indian Merchants, 1750–1947: Traders of Sind from Bukhara to Panama.* Cambridge: Cambridge University Press.

Martin, Frank A. 1907. *Under the Absolute Amir.* London: Harper and Brothers.

Masson, Charles. 1997 [1842]. *Narrative of Various Journeys in Balochistan, Afghanistan and the Panjab, Including a Residence in Those Countries from 1826 to 1838.* 3 vols. New Delhi: Munshiram Manoharlal.

Matthee, Rudi. 1996. "From Coffee to Tea: Shifting Patterns of Consumption in Qajar Iran." *Journal of World History* 7 (2): 199–230.

McChesney, R. D. 1999. *Kabul under Seige: Fayz Muhammad's Account of the 1929 Uprising.* Princeton: Markus Weiner Publishers.

———. 1991. *Waqf in Central Asia: Four Hundred Years in the History of a Muslim Shrine, 1440–1889.* Princeton: Princeton University Press.

McPherson, Kenneth. 1993. *The Indian Ocean: A History of People and the Sea.* Delhi: Oxford University Press.

Michel, Aloys Arthur. 1939. *The Kabul, Kunduz, and Helmand Valleys and the National Economy of Afghanistan.* Washington, D.C.: National Academy of Sciences.

Minorsky, V. (ed. and trans.). 1980 [1943]. *Tadhkirat Al-Muluk: A Manual of Safavid Administration, Circa 1137/1725.* Cambridge: Trustees of the E. J. Gibb Memorial, c/o Spicer and Pegler.

———. 1940. "The Turkish Dialect of the Khalaj." *Bulletin of the School of Oriental and African Studies* 10 (1): 419–37.

———. 1937. *Hudud al-Alam, "The regions of the world"; A Persian Geography, 372 A.H.–982 A.D.* London: Luzac & Co.

Mintz, Sidney. 1986 [1985]. *Sweetness and Power: The Place of Sugar in Modern History.* New York: Penguin Books.

Morgenstierne, Georg. 1964. *Indo-Iranica: Melanges Presentes a Georg Mongenstierne a L'occasion de son soixante-dixieme anniversaire.* Wiesbaden: Otto Harrassowitz.

———. 1960. "Khushal Khan—National Poet of the Afghans." *Journal of the Royal Central Asian Society* 47: 49–57.

———. 1939. "Notes on an Old Pashto Manuscript Containing the Khair ul-Bayan of Bayazid Ansari." *New Indian Antiquary* 2 (8): 566–74.

Mushtaqi, Abd (al-Rizq) Allah. n.d. [1581]. *Waqiat-i Mushataqi.* Lucknow: Moti Mahal Library.

Nawid, Senzil K. 1999. *Religious Response to Social Change in Afghanistan, 1919–1929: King Aman-Allah and the Afghan Ulama.* Costa Mesa, California: Mazda Publishers.

Nebenzahl, Kenneth. 2004. *Mapping the Silk Road and Beyond: 2,000 Years of Exploring the East*. London: Phaidon.

Nelson, Cynthia (ed.). 1973. *The Desert and the Sown*. Berkeley: Institute of International Studies, University of California.

Newell, Richard S. 1972. *The Politics of Afghanistan*. Ithaca: Cornell University Press.

Niazi, Ghulam Sarwar Khan. 1990. *The Life and Works of Sultan Alauddin Khalji*. Lahore: Seraj Munir.

Nimat Allah. 1612. *Tarikh-i Khan Jahani and abridgment Makhzan-i Afghan*. Rampur: Rampur State Library Mss #374 and #381.

Noelle, Christine. 1997. *State and Tribe in Nineteenth-Century Afghanistan: The Reign of Amir Dost Muhammad Khan (1826–1863)*. Richmond, Surrey: Curzon Press.

Norris, J. A. 1967. *The First Afghan War, 1838–1942*. Cambridge: Cambridge University Press.

Pastoral Production and Society: Proceedings of the International Meeting on Nomadic Pastoralism. 1979. L'Equipe Ecologie et Anthropologie des Sociétés Pastorales (ed.). Cambridge: Cambridge University Press.

Pedersen, Gorm, and Ida Nicolaisen. 1994. *Afghan Nomads in Transition: A Century of Change Among the Zala Khān Khēl*. London: Thames and Hudson.

Pottinger, Henry. 1976 [1816]. *Travels in Beloochistan and Sinde*. Karachi: Indus Publications.

Poullada, Leon B. 1973. *Reform and Rebellion in Afghanistan, 1919–1929: King Amanullah's Failure to Modernize a Tribal Society*. Ithaca: Cornell University Press.

Priestly, Henry (trans.). 1981 [1871]. *Afghanistan and Its Inhabitants: Translated from the "Hayat-i Afghan" of Muhammad Hayat Khan*. Lahore: Sang-e-Meel.

Qandahari, Ali Muhammad. c. 1660. *Hal Namah*. Persian MS (final recension of Bayazid Ansari's Autobiography) Aligarh: Aligarh Muslim University, Maulana Azad Library, Subhanullah Collection, No. 920/37.

Qanungo, Kalika Ranjan. 1965. *Sher Shah and His Times: An Old Story Retold by the Author after Decades from a Fresh Standpoint*. Bombay: Orient Longmans.

Rahim, M. A. 1961. *Afghans in India, A.D. 1545–1631, with Special Reference to their Relations with the Mughals*. Karachi: Pakistan Publishing House.

Raverty, H. G. 1987 [1855]. *A Grammar of the Puk'hto, Pus'hto, or Language of the Afghans*. New Delhi: UBS Publishers.

———. 1982a [1860]. *A Dictionary of the Pukhto, Pushto, or, Language of the Afghans: With Remarks on the Originality of the Language and Its Affinity to the Semitic and Other Oriental Tongues, Etc. Etc.* Karachi: Indus Publications.

———. 1982b [1878]. *Notes on Afghanistan and Parts of Balulchistan*, 2 vols. Quetta: Nissa Traders.

———. 1981 [1867]. *Selections from the Poetry of the Afghans: From the Sixteenth to the Nineteenth Century, Literally Translated from the Original Pushto; with Notices of the*

Different Authors, and Remarks on the Mystic Doctrine and Poetry of the Sufis. Pesha-war: De Chapzai.

———. 1978 [1880]. *Selections from Pushto Poetry.* Lahore: al-Biruni.

Richards, John. 1993. *The Mughal Empire.* New York: Cambridge University Press.

Robinson, J. A. 1980 [1934]. *Notes on the Nomad Tribes of Eastern Afghanistan.* Quetta: Nisa Traders.

Rubin, Barnett. 2006. *Statement to the United States Congress, "Afghanistan: Is the Aid Getting Through?"* Hearing before the Subcommittee on Oversight and Investiga-tions of the Committee on International Relations, House of Representatives 109th Congress, Second Session, March 9, 2006.

———. 2000. "The Political Economy of War and Peace in Afghanistan." *World Devel-opment* 28 (10): 1789–1803.

———. 1996 [1995]. *The Fragmentation of Afghanistan: State Formation and Collapse in the International System.* Lahore: Vanguard Books.

———. 1995. *The Search for Peace in Afghanistan: From Buffer State to Failed State.* New Haven: Yale University Press.

Sahlins, Marshall. 1994. "Cosmologies of Capitalism: The Trans-Pacific Sector of the 'World System.'" In Nicholas B. Dirks, Geoff Eley, and Sherry B. Ortner (eds.), *Cul-ture/Power/History: A Reader in Contemporary Social Theory.* Princeton: Princeton University Press.

Saikal, Amin. 2004. *Modern Afghanistan: A History of Struggle and Survival.* London and New York: I. B. Tauris.

Salzman, Philip Carl. 1980. "Introduction: Processes of Sedentarization as Adaptation and Response." In Philip Carl Salzman (ed.), *When Nomads Settle: Processes of Seden-tarization as Adaptation and Response.* New York: J. F. Bergin Publishers.

Sarwani, Abbas. 1964 [1579]. *Tuhfah-i Akbar Shahi or Tarikh-i Sher Shahi.* S. M. Imam aI-Din (trans.). Dacca: University of Dacca.

Schinasi, May. 1979. *Afghanistan at the Beginning of the Twentieth Century: Nationalism and Journalism in Afghanistan: A Study of Seraj Ul-Akhbar (1911–1918).* Naples: Isti-tuto universitario orientale.

Singh, Ganda. 1981 [1959]. *Ahmad Shah Durrani: Father of Modern Afghanistan.* Lahore: Tariq Publications.

Stoler, Ann Laura, and Fredrick Cooper. 1997. "Between Metropole and Colony: Re-thinking a Research Agenda." In Fredrick Cooper and Ann Laura Stoler (eds.), *Ten-sions of Empire: Colonial Cultures in a Bourgeois World.* Berkeley: University of Cali-fornia Press.

Subrahmanyam, Sanjay. 1995. "Of Imarat and Tijarat: Asian Merchants and State Power in the Western Indian Ocean, 1400 to 1750." *Comparative Studies in Society and His-tory* 37 (4): 750–80.

———. 1992. "Iranians Abroad: Intra-Asian Elite Migration and Early Modern State Formation." *Journal of Asian Studies* 51 (2): 340–63.

———. 1990. *Merchants, Markets and the State in Early Modern India.* Delhi: Oxford University Press.

Subrahmanyam, Sanjay, and C. A. Bayly. 1990. "Portfolio Capitalists and the Political Economy of Early Modern India." In Sanjay Subrahmanyam (ed.), *Merchants, Markets and the State in Early Modern India.* Delhi: Oxford University Press.

Tapper, Richard. 1990. "Anthropologists, Historians, and Tribespeople on Tribe and State Formation in the Middle East." In Philip S. Khoury and Joseph Kostiner (eds.).

———. 1983. "Introduction." In Richard Tapper (ed.), *The Conflict of Tribe and State in Iran and Afghanistan.* London: Croom Helm Ltd.

Thornton, Ernest, and Annie Thornton. 1910. *Leaves from an Afghan Scrapbook: The Experiences of an English Official and his Wife in Kabul.* London: John Murray.

Tilly, Charles. 1992 [1990]. *Coercion, Capital, and European States, A. D. 990–1992.* Cambridge, Massachusetts: Blackwell.

Trautmann, Thomas R. 1998. "The Lives of Sir William Jones." In Alexander Murray (ed.), *Sir William Jones 1746–1794: A Commemoration.* Oxford: Oxford University Press.

———. 1995. "Indian Time, European Time." In Diane Owen Hughes and Thomas R. Trautmann (eds.), *Time: Histories and Ethnologies.* Ann Arbor: University of Michigan Press.

United States 83rd Congress, 2d session. 1954. *Obtaining Financial Aid for a Development Plan: The Export-Import Bank of Washington Loan to Afghanistan.* Washington, D.C.: U.S. Government Printing Press.

al-Utbi, Muhammad b. Abd al-Jabbar. 1955 [c. 1056]. *Tarikh-i Yamini.* Tehran: Muhammad Ali Fardin.

Varahamihira. 1987 [c. 550]. *Brhat Samita.* N. C. Iyer (trans.). Delhi: Sri Sataguru Publications.

Vigne, G. T. 1986 [1840]. *A Personal Narrative of a Visit to Ghuzni, Kabul, and Afghanistan.* New Delhi: Gian Publishing House.

Wallerstein, Immanuel. 1976 [1974]. *The Modern World-System I: Capitalist Agriculture and the Origins of the European World-Economy in the Sixteenth Century.* New York: Academic Press.

Warburton, R. 1880. *Report on the District of Lughman, Chiefly in Regard to Revenue.* Simla: Government Central Branch Press.

Waqiat-i Shah Shuja. 1954. Herati, Muhammad Husain (ed. [parts I and II from Shuja, part III from Herati]. Kabul: Afghan Historical Society.

Whitfield, Susan. 2004a. *Aurel Stein on the Silk Road.* Chicago: Serindia Publications.

———. 2004b. *The Silk Road: Trade, Travel, War and Faith.* London: British Library.

———. 1999. *Life along the Silk Road.* Berkeley: University of California Press.

Winichakul, Thongchai. 1994. *Siam Mapped: A History of the Geo-Body of a Nation*. Honolulu: University of Hawaii Press.

———. 1996. "Maps and the Formation of the Geobody of Siam." In Stein Tønnesson and Hans Antlöv (eds.), *Asian Forms of the Nation*. Richmond, Surrey: Curzon.

Wolf, Eric. 1982. *Europe and the People without History*. Berkeley: University of California Press.

Wolpert, Stanley. 1993 [1977]. *A New History of India*. New York: Oxford University Press.

Wood, John. 1872. *A Journey to the Source of the River Oxus*. Alexander Wood (ed.). London: John Murray.

Yang, Anand A. 1998. *Bazaar India: Markets, Society, and the Colonial State in Gangetic Bihar*. Berkeley: University of California Press.

Web Sites

http://afghanistandl.nyu.edu/
http://www.aisa.org.af/Media/mag-vol-01/Benefits.html
http://www.alamahabibi.com/
http://www.bergerafghanistan.com/
http://www.louisberger.com/
http://www.oanda.com/
http://www.synisys.com/
http://www.undp.org.af/
http://www.usaid.gov/press/factsheets/2003/fs031214_1.html

Index

Index

Remoteness, 174
Retail prices, 123
Revenue farming, 9, 42, 48, 64, 81, 85–86, 88–94, 123, 131–32, 136, 138, 148
Revenue, officials, 121, 148
Robbins, Joel, 31, 168
Roh, 21
Romanticism, 174
Roshaniyya, 20
Rupee: British Indian/Company, 79–80, 82–83, 146; Cabool/Kabul, 145–46; Kaldar, 148; Kham, 124; Pukhta, 124; Qandahar, 79–80
Russia: Abd al-Rahman, 11; Arthur Conolly, 52; gold currency 77–78; goods, 58–59; The Great Game, 54, 99, 102, 154, 157, 169; hundis, 43; Mithenkote, 63–67, 69, 76; Multani merchants, 42–44; Mushka Khan, 76; rubles 156–57; Sayyid Muhin Shah, 57, 59; scholars, 48

Sahlins, Marshall, 31
Sahukar, 154. *See also* Sarraf
Salary/ies, 108
Saleh, Haji, 105
Salt, 36, 140
Samarqand, 11, 37
Sanctions, 89, 110–11, 154
Sandukdar, 161
Sardar, 52
Sarishtadar, 121–22, 125–26, 148
Sarraf, 154. *See also* Sahukar
Sayyid/s, 51
Secret Asiatic Agents, 153, 155. *See also* Sethi, Haji Karam Elahi
Security deposits, 56, 132, 135–36, 138–41
Sedentarization, 45
Seistan, 52
Serai, 119, 153
Seraj al-Tawarikh, 8
Sethi, Haji Karam Elahi, 155–56
Sethis, 34, 153–57, 160, 165. *See also* Russia, rubles
Shagird/s, 115
Shahpur, 156
Shakur, Mulla, 84–85

Shanghai, 153
Sharia, 164
Shia, 8, 121
Shignan, 100
Shikarpur: Alexander Burnes's account, 44, 70–71; British Agent, 71; British intelligence, 43; carriage service, 70–71, 75; experimental period, 50; Hindus, 24; Khattri Hindus, 44–45; Lohanis and Sarwar Khan, 67, 71, 75; market, 9, 44, 63, 70–71; money market/banking center, 43, 50, 63; panchayat, 47; quarter, 41; revenue base, 97; trade, 46, 50
Shikarpuri/s: bankers, 43, 46–50, 78, 103–6, 124; brokers, 88, 94, 105, 124–25, 137, 154, 160; extortion, 103; financiers, 88, 103; Hindki, 47–50; 124, 151; Kabul, 43–44, 47, 103, 106; Kabul quarter, 41; Khattri Hindus, 24, 43–44, 47–48, 50, 88; Lohanis, 67, 71, 75; merchants, 43, 47–48, 67, 104–5; prominence, 9, 24, 43–44, 50; subsidy, 103–5
Shor Bazaar, 153
Sikh, 8, 69, 73–74, 135, 153; Qandahar, 73; territory, 42, 60, 63, 69, 73; rupees, 42, 44
Silk, 42–43, 60, 66, 132, 159
Silk Road, 3–5, 9
Silver, 12, 36, 42, 66, 146–48, 150; bullion and coins, 11, 13, 24, 42, 53, 78, 119, 146–47, 150, 161, 168
Simla, 106, 111, 119
Sind, 11, 42–43, 51, 53, 57, 63, 106
Singh, Maharaja Ranjit, 73
Sirhind, 97
Slaves, 19, 51–52
South Asia, 3, 6, 37; bills of exchange, 81, brokers, 87–88, 90, 130; commercial experiments, 55; fruit monopoly, 136–37; markets, 7, 63; migration, 139; Sethis, 153–54; subsidy transactions, 112; trade, 24, 43–44, 88, 130, 151
South East Asia, 3
Soviet Revolution, 156
St. John, Colonel, 101
State: Afghan/Durrani, 3, 6, 11, 22, 85, 88,